Auditor Independence

Corporate Social Responsibility Series

Series Editors:
Professor Güler Aras, Yildiz Technical University, Istanbul, Turkey
Professor David Crowther, De Montfort University, Leicester, UK

Presenting applied research from an academic perspective on all aspects of corporate social responsibility, this global interdisciplinary series includes books for all those with an interest in ethics and governance, corporate behaviour and citizenship, regulation, protest, globalization, responsible marketing, social reporting and sustainability.

Recent titles in this series:

Towards Ecological Taxation
David Russell
ISBN: 978-0-566-08979-4

Human Dignity and Managerial Responsibility
Edited by Ana Maria Davila Gomez and David Crowther
ISBN: 978-1-4094-2311-9

Managing Responsibly
Edited by Jane Buckingham and Venkataraman Nilakant
ISBN: 978-1-4094-2745-2

Social and Environmental Reporting
Riham R. Rizk
ISBN: 978-0-566-08997-8

Territories of Social Responsibility
Patricia Ashley and David Crowther
ISBM: 978-1-4094-4852-5

Regulating Multinationals in Developing Countries
Edwin Mujih
ISBN: 978-1-4094-4463-3

Auditor Independence

Auditing, Corporate Governance and Market Confidence

ISMAIL ADELOPO

Routledge
Taylor & Francis Group
LONDON AND NEW YORK

First published in paperback 2024

First published 2012 by Gower Publishing

Published 2016 by Routledge
4 Park Square, Milton Park, Abingdon, Oxon OX14 4RN

and by Routledge
605 Third Avenue, New York, NY 10158

Routledge is an imprint of the Taylor & Francis Group, an informa business

Publisher's Note
The publisher has gone to great lengths to ensure the quality of this reprint but points out that some imperfections in the original copies may be apparent.

Gower Applied Business Research
Our programme provides leaders, practitioners, scholars and researchers with thought provoking, cutting edge books that combine conceptual insights, interdisciplinary rigour and practical relevance in key areas of business and management.

British Library Cataloguing in Publication Data
Adelopo, Ismail.
Auditor independence : auditing, corporate governance and market confidence. -- (Corporate social responsibility series)
1. Auditor-client relationships. 2. Corporate governance.
3. Corporations--Investor relations.
I. Title II. Series
657.4'5-dc23

Library of Congress Cataloging-in-Publication Data
Adelopo, Ismail.
Auditor independence : auditing, corporate governance and market confidence / by Ismail Adelopo.
p. cm.
Includes bibliographical references and index.
ISBN 978-1-4094-3470-2 (hardback) -- ISBN 978-1-4094-3471-9 (ebook)
1. Auditing. 2. Professional employees. 3. Corporate governance--Moral and ethical aspects. I. Title.
HF5667.A34 2012
657'.45--dc23

2012022803

ISBN: 978-1-03-292533-2 (pbk)
ISBN: 978-1-4094-3470-2 (hbk)
ISBN: 978-1-315-56830-0 (ebk)

DOI: 10.4324/9781315568300

Contents

List of Figures

List of Tables

1

Corporate Misbehaviour and Corporate Governance

As the modern firm or corporation we know today evolved, the information gap created by the separation of corporate ownership from management produced the demand for both internal and external forms of control and monitoring (Weir et al., 2002; Walsh and Seward, 1990). This has been achieved internally through the Board of directors and externally through the report of the external auditors. Auditors' reports certify the accounts of stewardship prepared by the management for the shareholders. Agency Theory applied to corporate behaviour has been unequivocal about the array of conflicts of interest that tend to manifest themselves where ownership is separated from management (Berle and Means, 1932). These conflicts affect diversification decisions, investment decisions, remuneration decisions and management behaviour during takeover and anti-takeover situations (Denis et al., 2002). The objective function in these scenarios has been said to be how to minimize agency cost and consequently maximize the return to residual claimants (Jensen and Meckling, 1976).

However, recent times have seen huge and perhaps unprecedented waves of corporate misbehaviour. These have adversely affected confidence in the market system, and key players in the market have had to respond quickly and with an approach indicating competence and a broad understanding of the causes, as well as an apt appreciation of the solutions to the problems arising. The restoration of confidence in the market system, following the adverse consequences of corporate failures and financial crises is critical.

A cursory glance at Corporate Governance guidelines produced in the wake of these events, especially the corporate failures of ENRON and other colossal organizations, suggests a significant anticipated role for Audit Committees. Although Audit Committees have been in existence, at least in the UK, since the 1970s, they have not been nearly as prominent (Collier, 1993) and have not enjoyed as much legitimacy as is the case now (Rezaee, 2009). According to the Cadbury Report (1992), Audit Committees should be important governance mechanisms that protect the interests of the shareholders, ensure transparent reporting and improve audit quality. Despite this confidence, there are doubts expressed by some academics about the ability of an Audit Committee to perform these anticipated roles (Menon and Williams, 1994; Sommer, 1991; Spira, 2003). There are no definite and authoritative assertions regarding their effectiveness, either from academic perspectives or from the professionals' or regulators' viewpoints. This book examines auditor independence in the context of Corporate Governance by focusing on the role of the Audit Committee in UK listed companies. It provides an important missing link in the discussions regarding the auditing profession and its role in financial crises and, of course, how it might recover from the negative image created as a result of the profession's complicity in failures of Corporate Governance.

On the theme of the Audit Committee and its activity, it is imperative to consider precisely how the Audit Committee relates to the external auditors and how its activities may affect auditors' independence. There have also been suggestions that the Audit Committee should act as a buffer between the auditors and the executive directors and thereby enhance their independence (Cadbury, 1992; Smith, 2003). This has become even more important since the remuneration, appointment, and the selection of the type and scope of services bought from the external auditors, previously decided by the management, have come within the remit of the Audit Committee. Later in the book the relationship between the Audit Committee and the external auditor with respect to the level of economic bonding between the external auditor and their audit clients and the impact of the Audit Committee upon this will be examined.

The book also contributes to the debate on the joint provision of audit and non-audit services by auditors to their audit clients and the impact of Audit Committees on these. The arguments in support of joint provision suggest that there may be economies of scope and knowledge spillover from one service to the other. On the other hand, an alternate view suggests that the joint provision of audit and non-audit services by auditors to their audit clients may threaten auditor independence. This is because auditors may end up auditing their own work, or become too familiar with their clients' systems to the extent of being involved in their management, and the level of economic bonding may become so high as to compromise independence. However, the debate is broader than this. In chapter five of the book, the author reports the result of an empirical study on the nature of interactions between Audit Committees and

Auditor Independence. Consequently, the book provides a basis for readers to appreciate the type of relationship that currently exists between the Audit Committee as a tool of Corporate Governance and auditor independence. This involves a review of developments in the roles and responsibilities of the Audit Committee as a Corporate Governance mechanism. The book also empirically examines the determinants of the committee's activity and diligence, analyzes the impact of an effective Audit Committee on auditor independence and finally evaluates the relationship between audit and non-audit fees.

Although the objective of the author is to make this book accessible and helpful to users across the spectrum, it is likely that, as a result of a number of limitations, the requirements of some readers may not be met. This is not due to laxity on the part of the author, but is for reasons with which the audience are likely to identify. Corporate Governance and auditor independence are sensitive issues which companies are very reluctant to disclose information about. Companies may view some information, that some readers of this book consider to be quite unthreatening, as confidential. Such differences in perception bear on many issues, including for instance the structure of Board meetings, and communication and power structures within the Board. From the auditors' perspective, the sensitivity might extend to issues such as the frequency of their meetings with members of the Audit Committee, their assessments of the impact of the Audit Committees on internal control, audit services and risk management within the organization. The topic itself imposes a number of limitations on its investigation, essentially because of the sensitivity of the issues involved. The internal administration and working of an organization may provide it with competitive advantage and to discuss issues on these or related themes freely in an interview or through questionnaires requires significant caution so as not to compromise an organization's existence and performance. The sensitivity attached to Corporate Governance and performance impeded access that would have enabled the author to conduct a qualitative study, such as interviews with Board-level personnel in the organizations or through using a focus group approach. The author's efforts at the beginning of his research, and through to the end to gather evidence through qualitative means in order to bolster the findings reported in the study (Curran and Blackburn, 2001), was largely unsuccessful, mainly due to lack of access (Saunders et al., 2007; Bryman and Bell, 2007).

The use of secondary data provided an opportunity to search for a more genuine and intrinsic relationship between the variables. This afforded the author the benefits of a greater focus on analyzing the available data more closely in a way that would enhance the achievement of his objectives. However, selecting the right combination of variables to proxy for unobservable phenomena is always a problem in empirical quantitative research. For example, others may question the choice of the proxy to measure committee activity and diligence; equally, the measure of economic bonding between the client and the auditor may also be criticized. It is therefore important to mention up front that these measures are the best available observable proxies of the variables. In most quantitative investigations, the effects and methods of handling measurement error in the dependent variables have been well documented (Maddala, 2001). Lastly, the constraint of resources in terms of time cannot be overemphasized. It is extremely difficult to set a time line for a study such as this; however, finishing the book within a reasonable time was also crucial. The speed and nature of changes in the corporate environment can make a modest effort stale and inconsequential, as new events and situations emerge. The effect of globalization on the spread of corporate practices and, of course, corporate misbehaviours and the contagious effects of these, is truly phenomenal. This globality at times plays an unhelpful role in relation to giving meaning to and interpreting events and situations. It provides a veritable ground on which to perpetuate irony and exaggerate implications. Some issues disguised as new problems are found on closer examination to be inherently the same problems as have already been seen, in somewhat different form. Despite the fluid nature of problems and the environment that perpetuates them, coupled with the lack of will and at times understanding on the part of those confronting them, the author has been able to shine important lights on a number of very pervasive issues that might be regarded as 'wicked problems'.

The author's study leading to this book started in April 2005, when the global economy was just settling down from news of the successive collapses of various corporate giants. This chain of events started first with the high-profile collapse of ENRON in December 2001 and this was quickly followed in June 2002 by WorldCom and then others. Further, the debate surrounding harmonization of accounting standards which had been going on for some time came to a seemingly significant climax in June 2000. This is because, on this date, the Commission of the European Communities issued a communiqué to the Council and European Parliament to the effect that all listed companies would be required to prepare their consolidated accounts in line with an International Accounting Standard (IAS) from 2005 onwards (Elliot and Elliot, 2005). These events may have been responsible for the tendency to present a global response to the global corporate crises of the early twenty-first century, starting in 2001. This was the result of the sense of there being a well and truly global economy and the fact that harmonization and integration of accounting and auditing practices were, by then, at the top of the agenda for most accountancy professionals and their professional bodies. However, by 2007, it was the UK mortgage giant, Northern Rock, that led the second wave of twenty-first century corporate mishaps. Northern Rock's problems were traced back to the subprime mortgage market in the US. The rumbles continued and by 2008 the effects had become clear and the full impact of the 'Credit Crunch' had emerged. A number of high-profile corporations were either bailed out by their national governments, collapsed or bought out by other companies. These events constituted a significant threat to the study in a number of ways. For instance, the changing landscapes surrounding corporate activity during the periods of the study have necessitated changes in the methodology, the focus and scope of the analyses as well as in the interpretation of the results from the study.

The Structure of the Book

Each chapter contributes particular insights to the wider issues addressed in the whole book. In the following chapter, the author provides a broad but detailed background for the subsequent analysis. This includes a thorough review of the definition of Corporate Governance, an analysis of the Corporate Governance mechanism and historical context for the development of the discourse on this subject.

In Chapter 3, the author provides important information on the evolution and impact of regulation on the auditing profession and Corporate Governance in the UK. Professional guidance on ethics and professionalisms is examined, along with the attitude of professional accounting and auditing associations. The implications of these for investment safety and market confidence in the UK are analyzed in a detailed review of relevant literature. In Chapter 4, the author discusses the role of theory in amplifying corporate phenomena and understanding interactions within and between organizations. Theories shape meanings and help analyses of concepts and their implications (Riahi-Belkaoui, 2000). Different authors and commentators have used a number of theoretical frameworks to study the nature of the governance relationship that subsists in the corporate environment. This chapter discusses the various theories that have shaped the meanings of Corporate Governance and that are used in the book to achieve its objectives. The focus is on the suitability and relevance of the theories, rather than their deployment in the literature. This is to ensure that the real essence of the theories is captured and the value they have added or could potentially provide for our understanding of Corporate Governance and its interactions with the auditing profession are adequately accounted for and appreciated in the discourse on these subjects. Chapter 5 presents the author's empirical analyses on Audit Committees and auditor independence and reports the findings. It draws out the specific implications of the findings in the context of the particular discourse in this book and their general applicability to broader issues within which the discourse in the book is situated. In the final chapter, the author discusses policy challenges and makes recommendations regarding these and some pathways for future research.

2

Defining Corporate Governance – The Background

Introduction

The objective of this chapter is to provide a background to issues addressed in the book by examining the definitions of Corporate Governance and its internal and external control mechanisms, and then to give a historical perspective on the development of Corporate Governance in the UK. The discussions in this chapter enable the author to provide a broader perspective of the various debates around Corporate Governance and auditor independence and they set the stage for further discussion relating to the theoretical underpinnings of those debates.

Corporate Governance: Towards a Definition

The logical point from which to start the discussion on Corporate Governance is to present an understanding of the antecedents of the corporation. This can be traced as far back as the Middle Ages (between the fifth and fifteenth centuries), the period of the Renaissance (between the late fifteenth century and early eighteenth century) and the Great Industrial Revolution (in the late eighteenth century and early nineteenth century). Modern firms are historically a product of a small quasi-governmental arrangement often chartered by the 'Crown' to undertake a specific trading purpose. In other words, the modern firm evolved from a financing arrangement, whereby a group of people with similar interests 'acting as one body', embarked on a substantial trade expedition that could not be sponsored by a single individual due to the huge capital investment required. Some of these trade missions included the Dutch East India Company, the British East Indian Company and the Hudson's Bay Company (Morck, 2006).

However, part of that process of evolution, precisely the period between the thirteenth to the later part of the nineteenth century, witnessed landmark developments that continue to have significant impacts on our perceptions and understandings about and the operation of the modern corporation. For instance, we can trace the modern stock market back to the resistance against the attempt by the shareholders to liquidate the Dutch East India Company, based on the argument that its formation was for a limited time and purpose, and, since it had achieved its set objectives, it had outlived its usefulness and should therefore liquidate. The appointed 'Board of governors' resisted this move and successfully challenged it in court. Those investors who were keen on selling their shares in the company had the right to do so. This thus became the antecedent of the modern day stock market that facilitates the sales and purchase of shares. Furthermore, the ability of shareholders to sell their holdings in the company rather than liquidating it ensured perpetuity for the firm. This is because, not only were the shareholders able to sell their holdings in the enterprise, there were many more people interested in contributing to new trade expeditions who thus bought into these corporations and indeed into many other forms of trade and business endeavour. Some of these commercial endeavours were unsuccessful, for example the South Sea Company, speculation in whose stocks caused the famous Bubble in 1720 (Crowther and Martinez, 2007). However, the sponsors and shareholders in these companies became liable to the extent of the total losses. This was seen to be unfair and this perception may have contributed to the series of events that eventually gave rise to the Limited Liability Act of 1855 which provided that shareholders in such companies should be liable for the debts of the company only to the extent of their initial investments (Hickson and Turner, 2005).

However, while these important developments were unfolding, it was becoming ever more important to understand the structure and operation of the firm. It was therefore not surprising that Berle and Means's (1932) study enjoyed huge acceptance. Their work provided substantial insight into the interactions within organizations. They suggested that there is a separation between the owners of businesses and their management and that this separation requires that there should be a formal contract and bond between the two parties. Their explanations further suggested that this separation is, in part, due to the expansion in corporations' size and, as businesses become bigger, owners are less likely to be involved in the day-to-day running of the 'new' organization. Their observations should have drawn attention to the issues of governance in organizations, but Corporate Governance escaped the spotlight until the studies by Jensen and Meckling (1976) and Fama (1980) on the possibility of conflicts of interest between the shareholders and management representing the Principals and the Agents respectively that launched discussions on Corporate Governance. Even then, the term was rarely mentioned or used in analyses. It was not until 1983 that it featured as the title of a paper in Perspectives on Management (Earl, 1983). In 1984, the term appeared as the title of a report to the American Law Institute and in the same year as a book title in the UK with the caption 'Corporate Governance – Practices, Procedures and Powers in British Companies and Their Boards of Directors' by R .I. Tricker.

However, discussions of Corporate Governance have now gained in popularity due to the increase in high-profile corporate collapses, which have brought it into the spotlight. In other words, the conflicts of interests in organizations, management recklessness and greed, corporate dishonesty and ethical breakdowns, weak internal control and poor risk assessments are some of the factors that may have caused corporate failures and have been the herald of Corporate Governance discourse. Despite the recent fluent and widespread use of the term, it has no generally accepted definition (Razaee, 2009), due, perhaps, to the fact that the term cuts across disciplines. It is widely used both professionally and in its academic sense. It is now a commonly used term in management, law and behavioural sciences, similar to its fluent use in Humanities. It lends itself well to the private and business world, just as it is relevant to issues regarding public affairs and the business of governments. Other terms used with Corporate Governance include 'transparent reporting', 'corporate accountability' and 'corporate honesty' among many others. However, just as it is with many other concepts (for example, accounting efficiency, effectiveness, communication) and especially with a term that is capable of many uses and applications, it is increasingly difficult to present a generally accepted definition of Corporate Governance. It means different things to different people depending on discipline and context. The following quotation captures how difficult it is to agree a meaning and scope of the concept:

> *Some commentators take too narrow a view, and say it (Corporate Governance) is the fancy term for the way in which directors and auditors handle their responsibilities towards shareholders. Others use the expression as if it were synonymous with shareholder democracy. Corporate governance is a topic recently conceived, as yet ill-defined, and consequently blurred at the edges … Corporate Governance as a subject, as an objective, or as a regime to be followed for the good*

> *of shareholders, employees, customers, bankers and indeed for the reputation and standing of our nation and its economy.*
>
> *(Maw et al., 1994: 1)*

This quotation illustrates the extent of the differences that exist in perceptions of Corporate Governance. It also illustrates the diversity of its applications. For instance, it argues that Corporate Governance transcends the limited scope of just firm applicability to include perceptions of Corporate Governance at a national or country level. It also shows that the term is relatively new and therefore not very well understood.

However, previous authors, academic and professionals have pointed in some directions in an attempt to provide a robust definition of the term. According to Cadbury (1992), Corporate Governance refers to a whole system of controls, financial and otherwise, which ensure that management of a firm direct its affairs in the right way and towards the right direction. The Cadbury Committee's definition focused on the ways in which organizations are controlled and managed to achieve their main objectives. It also suggested that 'Corporate Governance is concerned with holding the balance between economic and social goals and between individual and communal goals'. The Corporate Governance framework is there to encourage the efficient use of resources and equally to require accountability for the stewardship of those resources. The aim is to align as nearly as possible the interests of individuals, corporations and society (Global Corporate Governance Forum, World Bank, 2000). This definition is distinctive as it asserts the multi-faceted role of businesses. It implies that businesses are not just vehicles for the achievement of the shareholders' wealth maximization objectives, but rather they are an integral part of the community with its own share of societal duties and responsibilities. Therefore, managements have a duty of care to society as well as to their shareholders. Although the definition is detailed, it failed to recognize the importance of Corporate Governance's role at the macro-level of society. A comprehensive view of Corporate Governance that underscores its importance on its micro as well as its macro impact is required. This is even more the case in situations where good Corporate Governance can attract foreign direct investment into the economy.

Monks and Minow (1995) defined Corporate Governance in terms of interactions between various players in the corporate environment and the processes used in achieving consensus in the allocation of corporate resources and in the determination of corporate direction to ensure improved performance. Since organizations' resources are limited and have alternative uses, their allocation deserves considerable attention in order to optimize returns from such usage. This definition seems to link Corporate Governance with the strategic position of organizations and perhaps sees Corporate Governance as the preserve of strategic-level management. It defines Corporate Governance in the light of the firm alone rather than in terms of the various stakeholders and definitely not in the realization of the interdependence between the firm and its environment especially the society in which it operates.

However, Yadong's (2004: 2) definition addressed the concerns of stakeholders. It sees Corporate Governance 'as the relationship between the corporation and the stakeholders that determines and controls the strategic direction and performance of the corporation. It is the system by which corporations are directed and controlled'. He further suggested that 'this structure specifies the distribution of rights and responsibilities among various corporate participants including Board members, executives, shareholders and other stakeholders; it spells out the rules and procedures for making decisions on corporate affairs'. It '… also provides the structure through which the company sets objectives, the strategy for attaining those objectives and the guidelines for monitoring performance.' This comprehensive definition has important implications not just for the nature of interaction between corporate structures but also for interactions between the individuals within the structures. In other words, what sort of relationships exist between the Board and the shareholders on one hand, but also how the relationship between individual members of the management is regulated and how this impacts upon their interactions with members of other structures. What rules, rights and obligations each structure faces, and what affects each individual member in the structure all seem to have become the subject of Corporate Governance. However, it is important to understand Yadong's (2004) definition in the context of governance issues that confront multi-national enterprises (MNEs). Such issues include interdependence between the parent and subsidiary companies, the problems with resource allocation and monitoring for performance. One possible criticism of this definition is in its inability to specify the potential roles of stakeholders in the governance system. Although it mentioned the setting of rules and procedures for making decisions on corporate affairs, it is not explicit on the involvement of the stakeholders in governance and modalities for the allocation of corporate resources. Furthermore, the definition is silent on the roles of regulation and regulatory authority in Corporate Governance. Achieving effective Corporate Governance may be impossible in a weak or inefficient regulatory environment (La Porta et al., 2002).

The Organisation for Economic Cooperation and Development's (OECD) (1999) approach to defining Corporate Governance is principle based. It provides five principle bases to Corporate Governance assessments that focus on: (1) the right of shareholders and key ownership functions; (2) the equitable treatment of shareholders; (3) the role of stakeholders in Corporate Governance; (4) disclosure and transparency; and (5) the responsibilities of the Board. It also produces a regular report on governance in member countries. The OECD five principles are the benchmark against which significant improvements and developments are used to assess individual member countries. This approach by the OECD favours macro-economic perceptions of Corporate Governance issues. It essentially sees Corporate Governance beyond the purviews of just the firm but also includes its impacts on the national economy and the likely implications of its adoption or rejection for economic growth. This macro-perception seems to be lacking in previous definitions of Corporate Governance. Unlike Yadong (2004), the OECD's definition appreciates the importance of a regulatory and legal framework that can guarantee shareholders' rights and that can ensure equitable treatment of shareholders whether they are in the minority or majority.

Corporate Governance and Shareholders' Returns

So far, the definitions mentioned above more or less represent the stakeholders' perceptions of the corporation and Corporate Governance. However, there are alternative views of the organization and certainly of Corporate Governance. For example, Shleifer and Vishny (1997) give a definition, which sees Corporate Governance as the way in which suppliers of finance to corporations assure adequate returns on their investments. This is similar to the definition suggested by Mathiesen (2002) who defined Corporate Governance as a field in economics that examines the use of incentives to motivate and secure management performance and efficiency in the organization. This could be with contracts and organizational designs and legislations. Tipuric et al. (2007) also sees Corporate Governance from the perspective of enhancing shareholders' wealth by suggesting that Corporate Governance comprises of a system of effective monitoring by the supplier of crucial inputs to ensure handsome returns on their investments in corporations.

One common theme in these definitions is the central position of the shareholder and the overriding objective of shareholders' wealth optimization. The relevant question here is how to manage the organization to achieve shareholders' objective of profit maximization. Although the debate (that is, about what constitutes and what should constitute the main objectives of the corporation) is enduring and inconclusive, these definitions suggest that the primary objective of the firm is to produce sufficient return to investors, to persuade them to continue to hold their investment in the organization. Otherwise, shareholders will look for alternatives that can provide the expected rate of return from the level of investment. In other words, shareholders may 'flex' their power in the face of poor performance by switching their investment to a higher return firm (Cuthbertson and Nitzsche, 2004) and may even instigate a corporate takeover either to bring about change in control or as a threat to realize better performance.

Corporate Governance and Business Culture

Keasey and Wright (1993) defined Corporate Governance to include the entire paraphernalia of an organization's culture, ethos, beliefs, shared values, systems and structures that support the successful achievement of corporate objectives. These abstract phenomena play a powerful role in piloting organizational success. They tend to provide enormous depth from which organizations are able to draw strengths and provide a strong basis on which to build competitive advantage (Johnson and Scholes, 2002).

However, organizations have norms and build culture over time as part of their strategic stance, so this also affects upon their perceptions and outlook on issues. Keasey and Wright's (1993) suggestion that an organization's posture on Corporate Governance depends to a great extent on its culture, ethos, beliefs and so on is not implying that Corporate Governance precedes culture but that each organization's culture and strategic behaviours are dynamic and change in relation to the changing needs and expediencies of society. Organizations need to portray good Corporate Governance postures as these may project a positive image and may impact upon corporate performance (Davidson III et al., 2004).

It may also be possible to use good Corporate Governance behaviour as a corporate risk management tool. To the extent that good corporate cultures and ethos are ingrained in an organization and its functionaries, it is likely that corporate dishonesty, underhand activity, reputational damage, fines and penalties may be avoided. This definition may also imply that there is an inherent business benefit in being good and that society and other stakeholders may be keen to reward organizations that act properly as well as sanctioning improper behaviours by organizations and their functionaries (Moir, 2001). It may be far too costly for organizations to be indifferent to public perceptions of their reputation and their attitude to Corporate Governance.

Management's attitude and perceptions of governance will probably be reflected in the role of Corporate Governance in an organization's strategic planning process, in the considerations of other stakeholders' interests, the extent of transparency and accountability, utilization of resources and their disclosures and the extent of communication with shareholders, so that all these factors will be affected by the governance environment. It may then be possible to judge an organization's Corporate Governance stance from a consideration of its culture, ethos, beliefs and strategy. It may be intuitive to expect that organizations with a strong and aggressive management culture with domineering executives may pose a threat to good Corporate Governance practices. However, it may be that firms that embrace Corporate Governance best practices have a culture that places great emphasis on reputation and corporate honesty (Agrawal and Mandelker, 1990).

Corporate Governance and Power

Another way of describing Corporate Governance is to examine the repository of power in an organization. Corporate Governance in many ways touches on the interplay of power, influence and authority in the organization. Where does power reside in the organization and who controls the use of organizational wealth to achieve set objectives and to determine the distribution of resources in the organization? The ability to influence organizational decisions, chart its direction in the short and long term, coordinate the mobilization and application of its funds, determine the nature, scope and method of its interactions within and with other organizations all signify the repository of organizational power and authority. This will ultimately have a significant bearing on an organization's structure and governance (Pfeffer, 1981; Tjosvold, 1989). For instance, studies have suggested that 'director duality', a situation where the role of the chief executive and the chair of the Board are combined, is capable of compromising Corporate Governance best practice because it may make the chief executive very powerful and dominant to the disadvantage of other stakeholders in the corporation (Collier and Gregory, 1999). This may facilitate management override of internal controls and increase corporate risk exposures (Donaldson and Davis, 1991).

Most recently, in March 2008, the management of Marks and Spencer (M&S) announced the decision to combine the role of the chief executive and chairman in Stuart Rose until 2011 (Davey and Laurance, 2008). This caused a number of protest votes by some shareholders on the grounds that it would make the CEO too powerful and may compromise internal control and also because it is not a good Corporate Governance practice or signal. Management, on the other hand, argued that such a structure was necessary to enable the CEO to have sufficient authority to initiate any necessary strategic changes, especially in the current economic climate and the company struggling with challenging circumstances such as falling profits, falling like for like sales and stiff competition from other high street stores which could afford to sell at lower margins. This, coupled with the Credit Crunch, meant that shoppers were looking for bargains and lower prices. In addition, it was suggested that it was difficult to find a successor for the CEO and a way to retain him within the company was to combine the two positions. This aptly underscores the likely arguments on the balance of power in the organization, that is, between projecting a good corporate image or the achievement of core shareholders' objectives. The reaction from institutional investors to this development was that of outrage and disbelief. This is reflected in the newspaper headline, which reads 'M&S under fire: how the city turned against Stuart Rose' (Davey and Laurance, 2008). Some of the major shareholders including Legal & General, M&S's second-largest shareholder, issued a statement voicing their displeasure at such a decision. Legal & General described it as 'unwelcome', they also added that it raised serious Corporate Governance concerns (Davey and Laurance, 2008). However, at the end of the day, management had their way; the roles of the CEO and chairmanship of the Board of directors were combined in one person. This scenario summarizes an attitude of institutional investors to governance in their investee companies, in that their power to effect changes in their investee companies is limited . Institutional investors now hold managements to account more than ever before, although, management still continue to get their way.

Still on the theme of Corporate Governance and power, while it may not be contestable that equity holders own the business, what is contestable is the amount of real influence or power they possess or can exert on the organization. The transformation of businesses from small sole proprietorships to gigantic corporations with numerous shareholders exacerbates owners' difficulties in generating consensus on governance and this seems to have practically eroded equity's power. This may be due to the problem of 'free riding' as no single individual shareholder will be willing to take the initiative and bear the costs of intervening. Such an attitude may be premised on the expectation that other shareholders will intervene but nobody eventually does (Berle and Means, 1932; Fama and Jensen, 1983). Monk (2001), while commenting on the subject of shareholders' power and the dispersed nature of corporate ownership, reiterated that:

> *... the tendency during this period (in the twentieth century) has been the dilution of the controlling blocks of shares to the present situation of institutional and widely dispersed ownership – ownership without power.*
>
> *(cited in Mallin, 2004: 12)*

The significance of this assertion is in highlighting the fact that dispersed share ownership weakens shareholders' power. Theoretically, shareholders are the owners of the business and should be the repository of corporate power and authority, meaning that they should be able to determine the extent, scope and nature of Corporate Governance practices in their organization. This is, however, different from the reality of shareholders' involvement, influence or what is specifically referred to as shareholder activism. The likely causes and consequences of equity's inability and reluctance to intervene in management have been documented in researches (Black, 1990; Coffee, 1991; Charkman, 1994).

Although the dispersal of share ownership may have weakened individual shareholders' power as they hold a very minute fraction of the total shares in the company, the rise in institutional investors might be seen as a solution. Institutional investors manage individual shareholders' funds as well as pension funds on their behalf and this might be expected to enhance shareholders' powers to monitor and intervene in governance through substantial and collective holdings (Cadbury, 1992). This should give shareholders more 'voice' in organizations and where their expectations are not met shareholders should have the ability to 'exit' the firm through their fund managers, but Pound (1988) showed that this may not be the case. He presented three hypotheses which indicated the nature of the relationship that may exist between a company and its institutional investors and which may affect their behaviour towards them. These are the 'efficient monitoring hypothesis', the 'conflict of interest hypothesis' and the 'strategic alignment hypothesis'.

Under the 'efficient monitoring hypothesis', he suggested that institutional investors are more likely to intervene because they are efficient at doing so compared to small or individual shareholders. He argued that the marginal benefits of such intervention are greater than their marginal cost. On the other hand, the 'conflict of interest hypothesis' suggests that institutional investors will be reluctant to intervene to curb management discretion due to current or potential business relationships they have with the firm, fearing that intervention may strain these relationships, so they avoid the conflict of interest, and lastly the 'strategic alignment hypothesis' refers to the situation where, rather than intervene to curb management discretion, institutional investors may consider it beneficial to actually promote areas of mutual benefits and negotiate cooperation and agreement on those issues rather than stir up disagreements with management.

Discussions about shareholder activism are very broad and present many interesting areas of debate. Essentially, while it may be persuasive to suggest that shareholders need to be more active, especially with the waves of corporate misbehaviour stirred up by management, to mitigate management excesses, the likely attitude to intervention has been discussed along two main lines, the active and the passive shareholder tendencies. Both of these attitudes may be affected by how the shareholders or their representatives perceive and are prepared to use their powers.

Cadbury (1992) confirms the high expectations of the willingness of institutional investors to intervene when it states that:

> *... because of their collective stake, we look forward to the institutional shareholders in particular, with the backing of the Institutional Shareholders' Committee, to use their influence as owners to ensure that the companies in which they have invested comply with the code*

thereby invoking shareholders' active tendencies. This has also been implied by studies such as Shleifer and Vishny (1986), Jarrel and Poulsen (1987) and Brickley et al. (1988). On the other hand, Sykes (1994b) suggested that it is possible for institutional investors to act as 'absentee owners', referring to a situation where they consider their intervention decisions strictly on a cost–benefit basis.

Further, on the theme of the impact of power in the definition of Corporate Governance, Kalbers and Fogarty (1993) considered the contribution of power in the discourse of Audit Committee effectiveness. They referred to the typology of power provided by French and Raven (1959), which encompasses legitimate, sanctuary, information, expert, referent and will powers. They inferred these types of power on Corporate Governance structures such as the Audit Committee. For instance, Kalbers and Forgarty (1993) suggested that the Audit Committee have 'legitimate' power, since they derive their authority from the shareholders through the Board of directors. The Committee is also deemed to have a 'sanctuary' power since it is able through its activities to bestow reward and punish erring officers of the corporation. It has informational power, because members have knowledge of important pieces of information which others not in their position cannot access. This confers 'informational' power on the Committee. Furthermore, the Committee will often comprise individuals who are experts and who have the potential to influence others, since they possess both 'expert' and 'referent' power. Lastly, as part of its oversight function, the Committee has to approve some reports and thus this requires the use of its 'will' power. The importance of power in organizations has also been amplified by earlier studies such as Berle (1931) and Dodd (1932).

Discussion and Summary on Definitions of Corporate Governance

In summary, it is difficult to pin down a definition of Corporate Governance. Current attempts at a definition have been based on two major paradigms. Firstly, a framework which sees Corporate Governance as an economic construct that should benefit only the firm and its shareholders, in line with Milton Freidman's (1957) assertion that the major objective of the firm is to maximize the shareholder's wealth. The other perspective sees Corporate Governance in terms of its benefits to the firm and its stakeholders and this suits the stakeholder model of corporations (Freeman, 1984).

Authors and researchers who believe that shareholders' value maximization is the ultimate aim of the firm tend to see Corporate Governance strictly from the purview of return on investment and the 'bottom line' arguments as opposed to the idea of a 'triple bottom line' of economic, social and environmental considerations (Elkington, 2004). Investments in Corporate Governance mechanisms seem to be based on cost–benefit analyses (Moerland, 1995). Therefore, all procedures, policies and structures that will enhance the efficient and effective utilization of corporate resources and protect the interests of the shareholders will qualify as a central theme of Corporate Governance. This attitude represents the Contractarian hypotheses (Bradley et al., 1999)

On the other hand, the 'fairness' or 'equity' arguments which are also implicit in the stakeholder approach to Corporate Governance contend that corporations need to deal with all its stakeholders with equity and fairness. However, the problem is finding the best formula or mechanism to allocate resources to all stakeholders that will be seen to be fair and equitable by all. Stakeholder theorists would probably suggest stakeholders 'mapping' as a way of indentifying the interplay of power and influence of stakeholders and by extension a tool for addressing stakeholders' interests (Mitchell et al., 1997; Ullmann, 1985). In addition, Jensen (2001) offered a solution to this problem, by suggesting that a kind of 'pareto optimality' point (the 'best that could be achieved without disadvantaging at least one group' (Gawthrop, 1970: 32) can be reached by firms through maximizing shareholders' returns and without leaving any stakeholder unattended. It may be assumed that proponents of the stakeholder perspective of Corporate Governance expect a higher moral level from businesses. Often they envisage a broader level of objectives for business that encompass efficient utilization of corporate resources and protection of the interests of all stakeholders of the enterprise (Van der Laan Smith et al., 2005). This is the Communitarian view of the firm (Bradley et al., 1999). Therefore, in arriving at a definition of Corporate Governance, it is essential to recognize these two sharp divides and forge a feasible and acceptable common ground on a suitable definition that addresses the concerns of the these two main paradigms.

Although there is no universally accepted definition of Corporate Governance (Solomon and Solomon, 1999), for the purpose of this book, two working definitions of Corporate Governance will be used in formulating an integrated definition that will serve as the frame of reference throughout the book. Firstly, Cadbury's (1992) definition stated earlier in the chapter and, secondly, the definition suggested recently by Rezaee (2009).

> *... the process affected by a set of legislative, regulatory, legal market mechanisms, listing standards, best practices and efforts of all Corporate Governance participants, including the company's directors, officers, auditors, legal counsel and financial advisors, which creates a system of checks and balances with the goal of creating and enhancing enduring and sustainable shareholder value, while protecting the interest of other stakeholders.*
>
> *(Rezaee, 2009: 30)*

From these two definitions and others that have been reviewed earlier, this study suggests an *integrated definition of Corporate Governance* which is represented diagrammatically in Figure 2.1 as:

> *The process and system through which an organization achieves reasonable balance in its allocation of resources between all its stakeholders.*

This study thus sees Corporate Governance as embodying two essential dimensions, which are the *process* Corporate Governance dimension and the *system* Corporate Governance dimension.

This study views Corporate Governance as a process in three main ways:

- An evolutionary process: since Corporate Governance practices develop over time.
- A controlling process: since it allows the determination of corporate objectives and strategies for their achievement which entail a series of controlling activities.
- A communicating process: since Corporate Governance involves interaction between people within and outside the organization.

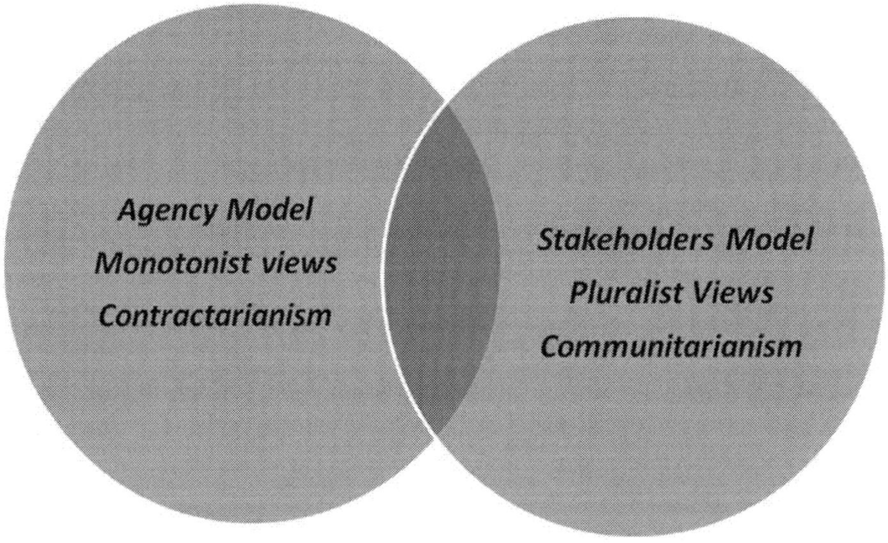

Figure 2.1 Domains of definitions of Corporate Governance

The study considers Corporate Governance to be a system in three ways:

- An economic system: that enhances firms' performance and creates value.
- A social system: that facilitates social interactions that appreciate the link between business and the society in which business operates.
- An ethical system: that ensures that firms operate in a fashion that is consistent with corporate ethical values and expectations.

Corporate Governance also centres on the allocation of resources. However, their allocations need to reflect stakeholders' power and influence. Thus, the real essence of Corporate Governance is achieving reasonable balance in the allocation of organization resources among all stakeholders. Table 2.1 shows these dimensions in a grid.

Table 2.1 Dimensions of Corporate Governance definition

The Corporate Governance Process: Evolutionary Control Communication	The Corporate Governance System: Economic Social Ethical
The Resource: Efficiency in allocation Effectiveness in utilization	The Stakeholders: Balance resource allocation with measure of power and influence And consideration of corporate goals

Justifications for Corporate Governance in Organizations

Until now, we have focused on identifying various definitions of the Corporate Governance, in order to decide on the most suitable working definition for the purpose of this book. Here, the author examines the business justifications for Corporate Governance in organizations. The following questions are asked:

- Is there a business case for adopting Corporate Governance?

- What are the other benefits an organization stands to gain by instituting Corporate Governance best practice?

These questions very much relate to the important debate concerning the main purpose and objectives of an organization, which followed on from the last section on the Contractarian vs. the Communitarian arguments. The Contractarian sees the firm as consisting of a complex structure of contracts among various constituents in the organization, each bonded by the terms of the contract that applies. However, there is the realization that the contracts are probably never going to be perfect and that there are costs incurred in writing and maintaining the contract that affect the firm has cost structures (Coase, 1936). The main objective of the organization in this sense can be inferred to be how to perfect or at least reduce the imperfection in the contracts and consequently the costs associated with writing and maintaining those contracts (Williamson, 1984). On the other hand, the Communitarians see the enterprise as an integral component of the community and suggest that the main purpose of the enterprise is for the benefit of all the stakeholders (Bradley et al., 1999).

These views are also basic to the debate between a monotonic and pluralist outlook of the corporation, which is essentially the debate between the shareholder and stakeholder focus of the firm. The earliest modern discourse on these issues dates back to the works by Berle (1931) and Dodd (1932).The monotonists follow the argument that the sole remit of the firm is profit maximization and therefore so long as Corporate Governance enhances shareholders' wealth maximization objectives then there is a justification for its adoption in organizations. However, if the cost of control is greater than the benefit of control, according to these shareholder-centred arguments, Corporate Governance adds no further value. On the other hand, the pluralist will probably still look at the benefits not just to the shareholders but also to other stakeholders (the employees, the bondholders and society as a whole). Thus good governance practice may enhance corporate monitoring and reduce conflicts of interest between the Principal and Agent (Eichenseher and Shields, 1985; Pincus et al., 1989). Though findings are inconclusive, Agrawal and Mandelker (1990) argued that organizations with good governance experience better performance. Davidson III et al. (2004) found positive market reactions to the appointment of independent directors on the Board as reflected in the stock price rise.

Equally, in line with Signalling Theory (Spence, 1973), organizations may adopt good governance mechanisms for appearance and to signal best practice to the market (Menon and Williams, 1994). This is not to suggest that Corporate Governance does not have its own intrinsic benefit for the organization, rather it is to indicate that it is also beneficial to project the right image and to indicate compliance with good Corporate Governance requirements where these are required by statute or imposed by corporate imperatives. Corporate isomorphism or mimicry (DiMaggio and Powell, 1983; Nelson and Winter, 1982) may also be a reason for adopting Corporate Governance. This implies that organizations imitate each other in doing well.

It could be argued that the ultimate reason why corporations embrace Corporate Governance is the business argument. This suggests that Corporate Governance impacts upon firm performance (Baysinger and Butler, 1985) and reduces firm risk exposures both internally (as employees may have imbibed good corporate behaviours, so the firm will avoid underhand practices and reduce the risk of employees' misbehaviour, dishonesty and so on) and externally as companies may avoid sanctions for not complying with regulations. They may also enjoy reductions in cost of capital (Gebhardt et al., 2001; Sengupta, 1998), since lenders may judge the risk profile of complying firms as lower than otherwise (Jensen and Meckling, 1976), and such firms will enjoy a good reputation and image for adhering to corporate best behaviours which may impact upon performance either by way of increases in share prices or patronage in the market (Ayuso and Argandona, 2007).

The Control Mechanisms

Subsisting conflicts of interest between owners and management provide incentives for investment in forms of controls to reduce information asymmetry (Fama and Jensen, 1976). The presence of control mechanisms should constrain management and bind them to pursue the profit maximization objective of the shareholders, an objective considered as primary focus of the firm among classical economists (Friedman, 1957). Equally, such control mechanisms should also enhance reporting quality as organizations become more transparent and accountable and thereby improve the market's confidence in the information provided by the firm (Jensen and Meckling, 1976). Although the primary beneficiaries of investment in control mechanisms are the shareholders (Fama and Jensen, 1976), it has been shown that other stakeholders in the corporate environment such as bondholders and even the management benefit from such diversion of resources into control mechanisms (Fama, 1980). This is due to a number of reasons.

Firstly, because investment in good corporate control mechanisms signals good practice and the managerial labour market may react to such decisions positively, this may improve each individual manager's market worth in terms of compensation, remuneration and future opportunities (Fama, 1980). Coughlan and Schmidt (1985) documented a positive relationship between a firm's poor performance and the likelihood of top management turnover.

Secondly, investments in control mechanisms may also provide some form of job security for management as the cost of fraud or negative press due to poor governance may adversely affect their human capital worth (Shivdasani, 1993), while good Corporate Governance practice improves their marketability and enhances their human capital, social worth and future opportunities. This may translate into appointments to serve on other Boards and enhance their reputation. Gilson (1989) found that top executives resigning from firms that experienced financial distress hold one-third fewer appointments on the Board in other firms in their future careers. Kaplan and Reishus (1990) found differences in the number of subsequent Board appointments of managers who have served on a dividend reducing Board compared to a non-dividend reducing Board. They found that top management in dividend reducing Boards have 50 per cent fewer subsequent appointments serving on other Boards compared to their counterparts from non-dividend reducing Boards. These findings suggest that serving on the Board of an underperforming firm has negative repercussions and that directors suffer reputational losses as a result.

Control mechanisms are either internal or external (Walsh and Seward, 1990). Internal control mechanisms include the roles of institutional investors, the Board of directors and its sub-Board committees (which include the audit, remuneration and nomination committees), Managerial Ownership (otherwise called insider ownership) structure and firm capital structure. On the other hand, the external control mechanisms include legislative and regulatory frameworks such as the capital market regulations, the external auditor, market for corporate control and the managerial labour market.

The discussion of control mechanisms is important in the context of a broader understanding of Corporate Governance and in being able to understand the position of the Audit Committee and the external auditors in the overall Corporate Governance picture.

External Control Mechanisms

THE REGULATORY FRAMEWORK FOR CORPORATE GOVERNANCE IN THE UK

The UK has one of the most developed and advanced capital markets in the world. The Corporate Governance regulatory framework in the UK has its roots in a series of high-profile 'ad-hoc' committee reports, some of which were responses to corporate failures internally in the UK (for example, Polly Peck, Maxwell and BCCI) or a reaction to similar failures in other parts of the globe. The Cadbury Report of 1992 on the financial aspects of Corporate Governance provided the fundamental background to Corporate Governance codes in the UK, followed by the Greenbury Report (1995), the Hampel Report (1998), the Higgs Report (2003) and the Smith Report (2003), while in 2003 the London Stock Exchange adopted the Combined Code as part of its listing requirements.

Empirical studies have examined the impact of various Corporate Governance reports on Corporate Governance developments in the UK. Clarke (1998) reported on the impact of three UK Corporate Governance committees – the Cadbury Report (1992), the Greenbury Report (1995) and the Hampel Report (1998) – on the role and importance of non-executive directors. He concluded that the roles of non-executive directors have grown in importance over the years, and that 'independent non-executive directors will have increasing influence upon company direction'. His conclusion came as a result of a survey conducted by MORI on 'The Role of the Non-Executive Directors' on behalf of GHN Executive Coaching. Goddard and Masters (2000) suggested that adherence to the Cadbury Committee recommendations on Audit Committees had had no effect whatsoever on audit fees as at 1995. Dahya et al. (2002) examined the relationship between CEO turnover and firm performance before and after the Cadbury Report and reported a stronger post-Cadbury Code negative relationship between CEO turnover and firm performance with the adoption of the Code. Collier and Gregory (1996) reported significant increases in the formation of Audit Committees post-Cadbury Report than in any other period in the UK.

MARKET FOR CORPORATE CONTROL (M&A) IN THE UK

Another important external control mechanism is the market for corporate control. In some situations of underperformance, coupled with conflicts of interest between shareholder and management, one option available to the shareholders is to support a takeover bid (Kennedy and Limmack, 1996; Sudarsanam et al., 1996). Such a move could be seen as disciplinary on the management for continuous poor performance or non-compliance with the shareholders' profit maximization objective. Although the market for corporate control in the UK and US is comparable in terms of their sophistication, there seem to be more instances of hostile takeovers in the US than in the UK (Armour and Skeel, 2007). However, hostile takeovers are rare in Continental Europe perhaps due to the shareholding structure, which favours concentrated ownership and because the numbers of listed companies on most of these exchanges are small in contrast to the situation in the UK and the US where shareholdings are widely dispersed with many listed companies on the exchanges (Franks and Mayer, 1996). The debate surrounding the potency of takeovers' disciplinary role in UK Corporate Governance has been inconclusive. Some studies indicate that UK takeovers play some disciplinary role for a number of reasons (Parkinson and Dobbins, 1993; Kennedy and Limmack, 1996; Dickerson et al., 1998; Nuttall, 1999).

Firstly, shareholders enjoy abnormal returns after the takeover bid which may also indicate improvements in performance, and because there is a correlation between successful takeovers and CEO turnovers. Others (Franks and Mayer, 1996; Sudarsanam et al., 1996) have argued that takeovers in the UK market do not play a managerial disciplinary role. They suggest that a takeover bid is not the same as an actual takeover. For example, a protest bid instigated to communicate a grievance and not necessarily to change managerial leadership and an actual takeover will have more far-reaching effects on the firm and its stakeholders than a mere bid. Secondly, the cost of prosecuting a takeover or a bid is usually high and so the net benefit to the bidding organization needs to be greater than its associated cost before the bid can make economic sense. The discussions on the disciplining role of the market for corporate control can be appreciated in the context of shareholders activisms and in signalling shareholders' preferences to the management.

The Managerial Labour Market

The managerial labour market under Corporate Governance examines the relationship between Corporate Governance structure and employment, retention, dismissal and remuneration of managerial-level labour. The importance of management in corporations was underscored by Berle and

Means (1932) as well as by Agency Theory first suggested by Coase in 1937 and subsequently by other academics. Jensen and Meckling (1976) suggested that management have a stake in good firm performance and also share in the losses associated with poor performance. Their share of the loss may have both short- and long-term effects. In the short term because of the immediate effect on earnings if these are related to performance and in the long term because of the effect on their future streams of income through working as an executive or through other Board appointments in other organizations.

The main thrust of Corporate Governance provision in this respect is how to ensure an alignment of interests between principals and agents (Jensen and Meckling, 1976). This is to forestall the emergence of hyper-powerful executives who may be able to extract abnormal rents from the firm, but also to ensure adequate incentives to improve performance. This, in essence, is the balancing act between 'the carrot and the stick' so that the principal does not have the case of 'strong management–weak owners' and at the same time the principal does not end up distracting the executives from their main preoccupation of managing the firm (Roe, 2002; Bebchuck and Fried, 2004; Renneboog and Trojanowski, 2005). Earlier, the author referred to studies that confirmed a positive relationship between poor performance and executive turnover (Fama, 1983; Coughlan and Schmidt, 1985) and also noted that directors serving on Boards of poorly performing firms experience reductions in the number of subsequent similar appointments (Gilson, 1989; Kaplan and Rieshus, 1990) which indicate that the managerial labour market and market for corporate control have some disciplinary effect on management.

Internal Control Mechanisms

INSTITUTIONAL INVESTORS

One crucial internal control mechanism is the firm's ownership structure. Ownership concentration is defined by the number of large-block shareholders as well as by the proportion of shares they own. In the UK, while individual equity ownership has fallen from 54 per cent in 1963 to less than 18 per cent in 1993 and 14 per cent in 2002, institutional ownership has been on the increase, rising to approximately 62 per cent in 1993 (Short and Keasey, 1999). This rise has been attributed to the growth in pension and insurance funds which have enjoyed increases in value as a result of the rise in private retirement savings from private pension schemes and long-term insurance policies. For instance, equity ownership by insurance companies increased from 10 per cent in 1963 to 20 per cent by 2002. Similarly, equity ownership by pension fund companies increased from 6 per cent in 1963 to 16 per cent in 2002. Interestingly there have also been increases in overseas shareholdings in UK listed companies. This jumped from 7 per cent in 1963 to a staggering 32 per cent in 2002; most of the increases arose from increases in the holdings of institutional investors (Mallin, 2004). UK institutional investors hold their interests in the equity of companies on behalf of individuals so that these individuals have an indirect ownership of equity in these companies.

However, given the size and nature of institutions' share ownership it would be expected that institutional investors will play more of an active role in Corporate Governance in UK listed companies in line with the expectations of the Cadbury Report. Although the Association of British Insurers (ABI) and National Association of Pension Funds (NAPF) do urge institutional investors to query points in the accounts as well as vote against management at annual general meetings (AGMs) and against bonus schemes as these are perceived to damage pension scheme members' wealth, these protests do not seem to go far enough to effect changes in governance. At present, institutional investors as well as individual shareholders do not see themselves as more than just shareholders, owning a tradeable stock without any intrinsic value (Charkman, 1994). However, the truth is that institutional investors own shares on behalf of fund owners and are responsible to them. They probably would want them to play a more active role in the management of their fund. Block holders should take a more proactive role, a longer-term strategic review of their holding and should be able to intervene in the management of the corporation to effect the necessary control mechanisms in the optimal interest of shareholders.

Shleifer and Vishny (1986) argued that institutional shareholders, by virtue of their large stockholdings, would have incentives to monitor corporate performance since they have greater benefits through this monitoring and enjoy greater voting power that makes it easier to take corrective action when it is deemed necessary. Consistent with this 'active monitoring hypothesis' Jarrell and Poulsen (1987) and Brickley et al. (1988) documented the fact that institutional shareholders are more likely to vote against harmful amendments that reduce shareholder wealth, while Agrawal and Mandelker (1990) found a positive relationship between institutional ownership and the shareholder wealth effects of various anti-takeover charter amendments. McConnell and Servaes (1990) found a positive relationship between institutional ownership and productivity, as measured by Tobin's Q, a popular measure of firm performance in accounting and finance literature.

However, others have argued that institutional investors have limited incentives to monitor management actions. This could be because of free-riding among institutional investors making it difficult for them to take collective action (Black, 1990; Admati et al., 1994). Furthermore, institutional investors may have incentives to sell their stock in the face of poor performance rather than to initiate corrective action (Coffee, 1991) in support of the 'absentee owners'' notion (Sykes, 1994a). Karpoff et al. (1996) failed to confirm the positive effect of institutional activism on shareholder value.

Institutional ownership could therefore beneficially influence Corporate Governance and firm performance if the active monitoring hypothesis holds true or has no effect if institutional shareholders are inactive. In the UK, Faccio and Lasfer (2000) studied the impact of institutional investors in monitoring management. Their work compared the monitoring activity undertaken by pension funds owning more than 3 per cent of issued share capital in organizations to a matched sample of those having less than a 3 per cent stake and investigated their compliance with the Cadbury Code. They were unable to report any positive relationship between compliance with the Code and institutional ownership. They also failed to find any relationship between ownership concentration and firm performance.

However, as mentioned earlier, institutional investors are now playing more active roles in governance in listed companies through such organizations as the ABI and NAPF. For instance, these organizations produced guidelines on directors' remuneration and severance payments with a view to ensuring that incidences do not occur that appear to be rewarding management for poor performance.

Managerial Ownership

In addition to the two internal control mechanisms discussed above, academic literature has also identified insider ownership as part of the internal governance mechanism otherwise referred to as Managerial Ownership (Barnhart and Rosenstein, 1998). From an Agency Theoretical position, the author knows that moral hazards could lead to management shirking due to conflicts of interest with other stakeholders. One solution to this conflict of interest is to increase

Managerial Ownership (Jensen and Meckling, 1976). Increasing management share ownership in the business has the effect of increasing their risk exposure in the same way as for other residual claimants, depending on their percentage shareholding, its value and their voting rights (Hermalin and Weisbach, 1988).

As Managerial Ownership increases Management's interest coincides more closely with that of outside shareholders and hence conflicts of interest between them are moderated, reducing the agency cost of operation since shareholders now need to spend less on monitoring and control costs. While these arguments seem plausible, other studies have shown that Managerial Ownership could be counterproductive and may in fact lead to increases in agency costs (McConnell and Servaes, 1990; Short and Keasey, 1999). It has also been suggested that there is a tendency for increased Managerial Ownership to give rise to executive dominance which facilitates expropriations of corporate wealth by way of excessive pay and investment in projects that give negative net present values (NPVs) (Fama and Jensen, 1983). It also makes it easier for management to embark on empire building and self-entrenchment (Stulz, 1988).

Furthermore, there are arguments that suggest that Managerial Ownership is not only an internal control mechanism but could also enhance firm performance, although the arguments are inconclusive. Using Tobin's Q ratio as the dependent variable to proxy for firm performance and the fraction of shares owned by corporate insiders as the independent variable, both Hermalin and Weisbach (1988) and Morck et al. (1988) estimated a piece-wise linear regression on the effect of Managerial Ownership on firm performance. They found that the relationship between the two variables is not always linear. In some ranges of insider ownership (between 0–5 per cent ownership), the Q ratio was found to be positively related to insider ownership and in some other ranges (between 5–25 per cent) a negative relationship was observed and at insider ownership levels beyond 25 per cent a further positive relationship was documented. McConnell and Servaes (1990) have also shown that the Q ratio is nonlinearly related to the degree of insider ownership. These results underscore the importance of Managerial Ownership as a control mechanism. This is because it may be argued that increases in performance associated with increases in Managerial Ownership came about due to interest congruence between the two and the consequent constraining of agency costs. On the other hand, excessive increases in Managerial Ownership may become counterproductive and may facilitate managerial expropriation which may explain the inverse relationship between the two variables as reported in these studies.

In the UK, Short and Keasey (1999) confirmed the findings from the US but observed that the positive relationship between performance and insider ownership is within the range 0–13 per cent or 15 per cent depending on the definition of performance used. Further, they observed the negative relationship to be between 13 per cent and 42 per cent above which the positive relationship is documented once again.

Pfeffer (1972) documented the fact that the percentage of insider directors is higher on the Boards of declining firms. Baysinger and Butler (1985) established a relationship between the degree of financial health of a firm and the Board composition when they categorized directors into 'insider, gray and independent outsider'. Their results showed that firms with a lower proportion of insider directors achieved higher returns on investment. Also firms with above average performance were shown to have a higher percentage of outside directors than firms with lower than average performance. Judge and Zeithami (1992) found that high insider ownership and representation on the Board is associated with lower involvement in strategic decision making. The implication is that as a CEO becomes dominant it facilitates expropriation and can also lead to managerial collusion and transfer of shareholders' wealth (Fama, 1980). Dechow et al. (1996) note that fraud was more likely in a firm where inside directors had a substantial share ownership. All these results underscore the fact that although Managerial Ownership is important as it may complement other control mechanisms, there are also negative possibilities arising from such structures.

Debt Financing

Another way of constraining management from excessive perquisites is to institute additional monitoring through a firm's capital structure (Jensen and Meckling, 1976). Additional borrowing in relation to equity with attendant debt covenants imposes high expectations on management and necessarily requires a level of performance that ultimately makes consumption of perquisites impossible (Jensen, 1986). An inability to meet required credit obligations has the effect of increasing the cost of operations in the form of additional penalties for default, makes it difficult to negotiate further debt or future borrowings and may affect the human capital worth of managers in such firms (Franks et al., 2001). The threat of bankruptcy arising from payment default can lead to reputation crisis, dismissal and affect the going concern of an organization (Farinha, 2003).

Although debt may act as a control mechanism with the anticipated benefit of reducing the agency costs of operation, because management faces a tight cash flow situation given that there are debt covenants and obligations to meet, this invariably means that management need to earn sufficient income to pay both the principal borrowed and the associated interest. Jensen and Meckling (1976) indicate the possibilities of organizations incurring debt agency costs due to conflicts of interest between shareholders and debt-holders, which may appear in three forms. Firstly, the opportunity wealth loss due to the effect of debt on a firm's investment, secondly, the debt agency cost of monitoring and bonding incurred by both creditors and the firm and, lastly, the debt agency cost of bankruptcy and reorganization.

Intuitively, debt-holders will be expected to shift their debt agency cost to firms in the form of increased cost of debt which invariably increases a firm's operating costs. This implies that the effectiveness of debt financing as a control mechanism may depend on the current level of leverage in a firm, the cost of debt, the size of the organization and the firm's growth potential. The evidence is altogether inconclusive regarding the potency of debt as an effective control mechanism. While Harris and Raviv (1991), Megginson (1997), Garvey and Hanka (1999) and Safieddine and Titman (1999) all support the view that debt financing plays a controlling role in the attempt to align interests in the organization, others such as Stulz (1990) and McConnell and Servaes (1990) failed to document similar findings.

Board of Directors and Non-Executive Directors

The Board of directors is statutorily appointed by the shareholders to represent and protect their interests and represent the highest decision-making body for the firm. It is responsible for the strategic stance of the organization. It is expected to set the broad objectives, vision and mission of the organization and ensure their achievement. This is realized through providing oversight on the management. Fama and Jensen (1983) suggested that the Board of directors ratify management decisions and monitor their performance and that they also undertake decision management and decision control functions.

The Cadbury Committee Report of 1992 suggested a possible structure for the Board, indicating that the Board should consist of a substantial number of outside independent non-executive directors. The Board of directors should at least be balanced and act as a representative of the interests of the shareholders.

The Higgs Report (2003) focused on the role and importance of non-executive directors on the Board. Specifically, the Board is to operate through a number of sub-committees including the remuneration, the nomination and the Audit Committees. These committees are to comprise mainly of non-executive directors who are independent of the management. The importance of the outside non-executives is in their ability to contribute to a perfect contract between the contracting parties. Fama and Jensen (1983) argued that the outside directors have sufficient incentive to be able to perform these functions for two main reasons. First, they have the required skill and expertise and will suffer economic and reputational loss if they are found to be incompetent in these responsibilities and, secondly, because they are external to the enterprise they are expected to be dispassionate and view managerial decisions in unbiased but constructive ways.

Many changes have occurred in terms of Board composition in UK listed companies post the Cadbury Report. Dahya et al. (2002), in a study that involves a sample of 460 UK publicly quoted companies, documented the increase in non-executive directors on UK Boards suggesting that they rose from 35.3 per cent pre-Cadbury to 46 per cent post the Cadbury Report. Similar findings were documented by Song and Windram (2004) and they found that the nature and scope of the responsibilities of the non-executives and especially those serving on Audit Committees have changed significantly from oversight on just reporting to more risk management and internal control functions. Dahya et al. (2002) also reported that over 80 per cent of UK Boards have separated the role of CEO and Chairman. Faccio and Lasfer (2000) reported that the median Board size of UK companies is seven while Renneboog and Trojanwoski (2005) reported a median Board size of nine.

A number of studies have examined the impact of outside directors in providing oversight functions on the management. For instance, Weisbach (1988) indicates a positive relationship between the CEO turnover of poorly performing firms and the number of outside directors. A similar result was reported by Rosenstein and Wyatt (1990) who found a positive relationship between abnormal increases in firm value and the appointment of outside directors. Cotter et al. (1997) examined the role of outside directors in Mergers and Acquisitions (M&A) and found that they were able to enhance shareholders' wealth by resisting executive directors' blocking strategies in a takeover bid. In the UK, Vafeas and Theodorou (1998) could not report any significant relationship between firm performance and Board structure. However, both Dahya et al. (2002) and Renneboog and Trojanwoski (2005) reported on the sensitivity of CEO turnover to performance and Board characteristics that are in compliance with Cadbury recommendations. Ronneboog and Trojanwoski (2005) note the finding that larger Boards facilitate the replacement of CEOs and also that Boards with a larger percentage of outside independent directors replace underperforming CEOs more frequently. On the subject of executive dominance, they reported that combining the role of the CEO and Board chairmanship reduces the likelihood of CEO replacement, but this is because such CEOs may become too powerful and can decide their own benchmark and performance measures. Dedman (2003), as part of a wider report, documented evidence of the effect of compliance with the Cadbury Code on enhancement of Board oversight functions with respect to the manipulation of accounting figures and the discipline of top executives. She reported a negative relationship between non-routine CEO departures to both share price and accounting measures of firm performance.

History of Corporate Governance in the UK

Earlier, the book suggested that the antecedents of the modern firm could be traced to events that surrounded the organized trade expedition and the royal charter companies of the periods between the thirteenth and early nineteenth centuries and through the periods of colonialism. Subsequent events ultimately led to the evolution of the modern corporation with some of the earlier structures retained including, for instance, the stock exchange, limited liability status of the firm and its separate legal personality (Crowther and Rayman-Bacchus, 2004). Cheffins (2001) compared the development of the 'Berle and Means corporation' in the UK with the US and suggested that although the UK was the only country to have followed the US model of the firm characterized by a highly dispersed ownership and 'corporate capitalism', the achievement of this status is recent, and goes back no further than the late 1980s (Roe, 1994). Prior to this time corporations in the UK were characterized by a high proportion of family-owned public corporations tagged 'family capitalism' (Chandler, 1990 in Cheffins, 2001). Three main factors were suggested for the transformation in the corporate outlook of firms in the UK. These are the impact of company law, financial services regulations and political ideology (Cheffins, 2001).

To continue the discourse, the book now traces the major developments in the UK corporate environment that shaped the Corporate Governance structure in this country. This review is divided into three main periods: the pre-Cadbury Committee, the Cadbury Committee and post-Cadbury Committee Corporate

Governance. These are now discussed in turn. Figure 2.2 depicts the major committee reports that have had a significant impact on the development of Corporate Governance in the UK.

Figure 2.2 Development of Corporate Governance in the UK

Pre-Cadbury Committee

If we adopt the assertion made in Cheffin (2001), that the 'Berle and Means' Corporation (or indeed the 'modern firm') only became a noticeable feature of British corporate life around the mid-1980s, it may therefore be reasonable to start a review of Corporate Governance development from about this time. It is a known fact that the US led the way in corporate transformation at least in the sense of dispersed ownership of equity. Consequently it was no surprise that Berle and Means (1932) developed their seminal work on the separation of ownership from management. Equally important and timely was the work of Jensen and Meckling (1976) on Principal and Agent relations. Although these relationships had already been observed by Adam Smith (1776) in the Wealth of Nations as early as the eighteenth century in his famous quote ('The directors of companies, being managers of other people's money than their own, it cannot well be expected that they should watch over it with the same anxious vigilance with which the partners in a private copartnery frequently watch over their own'), these two impressive academic efforts have had a significant impact on the conception of how the firm operates and they have become extremely invaluable in many areas of corporate finance and Corporate Governance.

Corporate Governance in the 1970s

It is a difficult task to try to piece together the series of events that characterized Corporate Governance development in the UK in the 1970s independently of the events shaping up in the US and Europe. However, while Audit Committees had become a feature of corporate life in the US in the late 1970s, such bodies were still under intense scrutiny in the UK. Further, in the very early 1970s there were researchers in the US extolling the virtues of the Audit Committee (Auerbach, 1973; Mautz and Neumann, 1970 and 1977), and the Securities and Exchange Commission (SEC) unsuccessfully called for their establishment in listed companies in the US in 1972. Just about this time and as if in response to the move in the US, the European Economic Commission issued the 5th Directive (1972) which sought to harmonize company law practices in members states. Importantly, the Directive suggested that member states should adopt the German model of a two tier Board system in place of the unitary Board system which, of course, is dominant in the US and in the UK. This Directive was not well received in the UK and especially by company directors who considered the unitary Board system efficient and viable.

Furthermore, they also criticized the Directive because it suggested a co-determination arrangement on the supervisory Board. This refers to a situation where the supervisory Board is comprised of an equal number of representatives from the shareholders and employees of the firm. This kind of partnership arrangement between labour (employees) and capital (shareholders) was seen to be dangerous. Not only was it likely to create a power struggle in the Board room, it was also thought to have the potential to derail management focus (Schmitthoff, 1976). The UK responded to this Directive in 1977 through the report of the committee of inquiry on Industrial Democracy (1977) headed by Lord Bullock. The report of the committee favoured the employees and was almost synonymous with recommendations of the European Economic Commission 5th Directive. As was to be expected, the report was not popular with company directors and the change in government from Labour to Conservative in 1979 favoured management and the issue was relegated to the background as it was not consistent with the industrial capitalism agenda of the newly elected Thatcher government.

Whilst these events were taking place, there were also a number of corporate misbehaviours by certain company directors who had been reckless with pension funds and were behaving in ways that were inconsistent with their responsibilities as directors. There were allegations of directors overriding internal controls (Pergamon Press, 1971), improper and insider dealing (Lonrho Limited, 1976 related to acquisition deals), fraud (London and County Securities, 1976) and poor risk management (Rolls Royce, 1973). Thus in 1977, Sir Brandon Rhys-Williams sponsored a Private Members Bill in Parliament that aimed to achieve two objectives. First, he was hoping to generate and make a case for the importance of the roles of non-executive directors on the Boards of listed companies and, secondly, to call for the establishment of Audit Committees in UK companies. Unfortunately the Bill was defeated (Tricker, 2000).

The first academic research into Corporate Governance in the UK by Tricker was published in 1978. He studied the British Board structure, membership and process, and concluded that it was important first to introduce independent directorships on Boards before advocating the establishment of Audit Committees as part of the Corporate Governance structures in British companies (Tricker, 2000). This may be rationalized especially against the backdrop of the defeat of the bill proposing the establishment of Audit Committees in UK companies noted above. Another significant Corporate Governance event in the 1970s was the move towards a stakeholder perception of the company and the need for corporations to be accountable to their stakeholders. This was reflected in the UK in The Corporate Report (1975) which essentially was the output from a study sponsored by The Accounting Standards Steering Committee and which suggested that information in the financial statements should reflect the needs of all stakeholders in the corporation (Bartlett and Chandler, 1997; Berry and Waring, 1995). The historical narratives of the 1970s enumerated above acted as watersheds for a series of important Corporate Governance events that would landscape the 1980s.

Corporate Governance in the 1980s

In many respects the 1980s can be described as the decade of the 'firm' or 'market forces' (Riddell, 1993: 9). During the last years of the 1970s, there was an increasing focus on the importance of other stakeholders in the corporate environment, especially a call for more employee participation in corporations (Boyle, 1978). But this stakeholder paradigm soon withered away following the election of Margaret Thatcher in 1979 and her economic policies which were extremely pro-market in that they preferred private enterprise to state control (Tricker, 2000) and which were seen to favour shareholders and the capital markets. It was therefore not surprising that the government privatized a substantial number of previously state-owned enterprises. This encouraged private ownership of corporations in the UK and contributed in no small way to the transformation that was taking place in the UK economy. Although initially the Thatcher economic policies were slow to take effect and living standards were adversely affected, by the middle of the decade, the economy had started to pick up. Inflation and interest rates were falling. There was a substantial house price boom and people generally had a sense of being prosperous (Riddell, 1993).

The corporate transformation that was going on in the UK in the 1980s in the form of 'industrial capitalism' gave rise to a new type of industry and sector. Workers in the financial sectors began to earn huge salaries and the city gave rise to a new class of wealthy individuals who grew fat on the back of financial market deregulation (Oakland, 1998). However, there were perceived Board-level excesses: with the removal of various restraints and the dominance of the market knows best philosophy chief executives were becoming overbearing and too powerful in organizations. The view was that the ends justified the means. It was therefore possible for a dominant chief executive to expropriate a company's wealth and run the enterprise to the detriment of the shareholders. These attitudes climaxed in some high-profile cases globally, including the Guinness case, Polly Peck and the collapse of Robert Maxwell's businesses in the UK at the start of the 1990s.

It was apparent that there was an urgent need for some form of checks and balances on the excesses of corporate chief executives and Boards of directors. However, despite the growing importance of the topic of Corporate Governance at this time of directors' excess and underhand behaviour, and the growing dissatisfaction of institutional investors, academics in the UK only began to address these issues in the early 1990s after Cadbury had reported (Collier and Gregory, 1996).

The Cadbury Committee Reports and Other Reports in the 1990s

It was important that the problems arising from excessive power in directors' hands were nipped in the bud to avoid any escalation and total loss of confidence in the market system. Furthermore, the collapse of BCCI and Maxwell among others in the late 1980s and early 1990s were an ominous signal of a bad corporate culture (The Cadbury Report, 1992). Very early in the new decade, the newly formed Financial Reporting Council (FRC), the London Stock Exchange and the accountancy profession established the Committee on the Financial Aspects of Corporate Governance in May 1991. This was later to be known as the Cadbury Committee named after the chairman of that committee, Sir Adrian Cadbury. The Committee submitted its report in December 1992. Below are the main points and recommendations of the Committee's report.

THE CADBURY COMMITTEE REPORT (1992)

As part of its preface the committee chairman wrote '... it is, however, the continuing concern about standards of financial reporting and accountability, heightened by BCCI, Maxwell and the controversy over directors' pay, which has kept Corporate Governance in the public eye' (The Cadbury Report, 1992: 8). This quote summarizes the events antecedent to the Cadbury Committee. Concern was being expressed about the attitude of directors to the companies they headed. Even in periods of poor performance it was possible for directors to earn fabulous income on the backs of the shareholders. One of the phrases that was synonymous with these episodes was 'fat cat' which is still used today to describe the fact that directors earn disproportionately high sums compared to their performance or to the realities facing the enterprises they lead. Furthermore, one of the foremost sections of the report is the one that details the reasons for setting up the committee. The reports states that:

> *... its sponsors were concerned at the perceived low level of confidence both in financial reporting and in the ability of auditors to provide the safeguards which the users of company reports sought and expected.*
>
> *(The Cadbury Report, 1992: 13, section 2.1)*

Also that,

> *... the underlying factors were seen as the looseness of accounting standards, the absence of a clear framework for ensuring that directors kept under review the controls in their business and competitive pressures both on companies and on auditors which made it difficult for auditors to stand up to demanding boards.*
>
> *(The Cadbury Report, 1992: 13, section 2.1)*

Furthermore,

> *... these concerns about the working of the corporate system were heightened by some unexpected failures of major companies' and by criticisms of the lack of effective board accountability for such matters as directors' pay.*
>
> *(The Cadbury Report, 1992: 13, section 2.2)*

These quotations show clearly that the Committee was set up to address growing concerns and dissatisfaction about the spate of corporate misbehaviour and to address the dwindling confidence in the system as a result of management excess and lack of transparency in the accounting and auditing practices in the country's corporate environment. The Committee received over 200 comments and responses to its proposals contained in the report (Cadbury Report, 1992). The recommendations of the Committee covered various aspects of the corporation including the structure and composition of the main Board, structure and operations of key Board standing and ad hoc committees, the role of non-executive directors and the reporting and control mechanisms in corporate entities in the UK (Mallin, 2004). Although the report is lengthy, it also contains a code of best practice which has 19 main points across four key subjects covering:

1. the Board structure
2. non-executive directors
3. executive directors and
4. reporting and controls.

Some key recommendations of the Committee are now discussed below.

On the topic of structure and composition of the Board, the Committee recommended that the Board should meet regularly, retain full and effective control over the company and monitor the executive management. There should be a balance of power and responsibilities at the top of the company with no individual having unfettered powers of decision making. The roles of the chairman and chief executive of the organization should be vested in different individuals, but with clearly defined roles and responsibilities for each office. This is to prevent boardroom tussles and power play by achieving a balance of power and compensating controls within the Board itself. The Board should have a set of matters reserved for its attention.

On the issue of non-executive directors, the Committee recommended that they should bring an independent judgement to bear on issues of strategy, performance and resources. They should form the majority of the membership of the Board and be independent of the management. They should be appointed for a specified term without automatic reappointment.

On executive directors, the Committee recommended that directors' service contracts should not exceed three years without shareholders' approval and executive directors' pay should be subject to the recommendations of a remuneration committee made up wholly or mainly of non-executive directors. There should be full and clear disclosure of directors' total emoluments and those of the chairman and highest-paid UK director, including pension contributions and stock options. Separate figures should be given for salary and performance-related elements and the basis on which performance is measured should be explained.

On reporting and control, it recommended that the Board should establish an Audit Committee of at least three non-executive directors with written terms of reference that deal clearly with its authority and duties.

Following publication of the report in December 1992, there were various comments and criticisms of its contents and proposals. One of the most popular criticisms was the voluntary nature of the code. The provisions were presented on the basis of a comply or explain non-compliance mechanism. This meant that firms could either choose to comply with the code or where they did not comply, they should explain the reasons for such non-compliance and these should be stated in their annual report. It was thought that this disclosure would enable investors to assess the implication of non-disclosure on the level of transparency of an organization and inform investors' economic decisions. Section 2.3.7 detailed some studies that have examined the impacts of the Cadbury code on certain aspects of corporate activities.

Post-Cadbury Committee

THE GREENBURY COMMITTEE (1995)

One of the recommendations of the Cadbury Committee was that the sponsors of the Cadbury investigation should sponsor another investigation by June

1995 to review the implementation of the Cadbury Committee code and consider if there was any need to expand both the subject of the inquiry and the sponsorship so as to elicit wider support and ownership of the investigation.

> *The researchers recommend that our sponsors, convened by the Financial Reporting Council, should appoint a new Committee by the end of June 1995 to examine how far compliance with the Code has progressed, how far our other recommendations have been implemented and whether the Code needs updating in line with emerging issues. Our sponsors should also determine whether the sponsorship of the new Committee should be broadened and whether wider matters of Corporate Governance should be included in its brief. In the meantime, the present Committee will remain responsible for reviewing the implementation of its proposals and for identifying further issues which its successor body might usefully consider. These steps will establish a continuing process of governance review.*
>
> *(Cadbury Report, 1992: 17, section 3.12)*

However, it was the Confederation of British Industry (CBI) that took the initiative following public concern and the outcry over excessive directors' remuneration, and huge payments for poor performance and ridiculous severance payment packages popularly referred to variously as 'golden handshakes', 'golden parachutes', 'golden handcuffs' and so on. Equally, executive share options especially in certain privatized utility companies were becoming excessive and questionable. The CBI inaugurated the Greenbury Committee in January 1995. It was referred to as the Study Group on Directors' Remuneration with just one term of reference stated as:

> *To identify good practice in determining directors' remuneration and prepare a code of such practice for use by UK PLC.*
>
> *(Greenbury Report, 1995: 5, section 1.2)*

The Study Group which later became known as the Greenbury Committee, named after the chairman of the group, submitted a report of its findings in July 1995. The Committee also produced a Code of Best Practice which deals with the following issues:

- the establishment, membership and status of remuneration committees;

- the determination of remuneration policy for executive directors and other senior executives;
- the disclosure and approval of the details of remuneration policy; and
- the length of service contracts and the determination of compensation when these are terminated.

The Code of Best Practice is to be implemented by listed companies although both medium- and small-sized companies were also encouraged to implement the recommendations of the Committee. Public companies that do not comply with these recommendations are required to explain the reasons for non-compliance. Regarding establishment of a remuneration committee, Greenbury suggested that all public companies should have a standing remuneration committee. This committee should comprise of wholly non-executive directors with a minimum of three members with clearly defined terms of reference.

Furthermore, the Committee recommended full disclosure regarding all aspects of remuneration. It requires that such disclosure should form part of the information in the financial statements of public companies. This disclosure should include all elements of total level of remuneration, disaggregating total remuneration into all its component parts. Thus the annual bonus scheme and long-term incentive schemes including executive share options are all to be disclosed for every director in the company. Further, the measures of performance which are to be used in the determination of the reward packages and the relationship between these rewards and the long-term objectives of the firm are all to be disclosed.

On submission of its report, the Committee came in for heavy criticism in the national press and from the government. The focus of the criticism was on the complaint that the recommendations of the Committee did not go far enough in curbing excessive payouts to directors. For instance, the Labour Party claimed that the report had been watered down and its recommendations were incapable of stopping 'corporate greed' (Rodgers and Hotten, 1995). The report was rated five out of ten in meeting its objectives by Dr Cunningham, a Labour Party spokesman (Rodgers and Hotten, 1995).

In terms of its academic relevance, the Committee's report has featured in investigations into remuneration and executive payment options including studies by Canyon and Peck (1998), Tomkins and McKnight (2002), Buck et al., (2003) Konstantinos et al. (2004) among others.

THE HAMPEL COMMITTEE 1998

Both the Cadbury Committee (1992) and the Greenbury Report (1995) requested the establishment of another committee to review the implementation of their committees' recommendations. In keeping with these requests and due to the exigencies of the time in respect of the Corporate Governance situation in the country and the criticisms that trailed in the wake of the report of the Greenbury Committee, on the initiative of the chairman of the FRC, the Hampel Committee was set up in November 1995.

The Committee submitted its report to its sponsors in January 1998 against the remit which is contained on page 65 of that report. The Committee's terms of reference consisted of five main points which were:

1. Conduct a review of the Cadbury Code and its implementation to ensure that the original purpose is being achieved, proposing amendments to and deletions from the Code as necessary.

2. Keep under review the role of directors, executive and non-executive, recognizing the need for Board cohesion and the common legal responsibilities of all directors.

3. Be prepared to pursue any relevant matters arising from the report of the Study Group on Directors' Remuneration chaired by Sir Richard Greenbury.

4. Address as necessary the roles of shareholders in Corporate Governance issues.

5. Address as necessary the role of auditors in Corporate Governance issues.

6. Deal with any other relevant matters.

The Committee suggested that it consulted widely using a questionnaire which elicited over 140 submissions. It also engaged in discussions with over 200 individuals and groups. In addition, the Committee received a further 167 submissions on its preliminary report. It reported that over 252 individuals or organizations responded to its consultation. The Committee recommendations are contained on pages 16–22 of the report which states the Principles of Corporate Governance. Importantly, it made a distinction between a principle of Corporate Governance and more detailed guidelines on Corporate Governance such as the Cadbury and Greenbury Committee guidelines

The Hampel Report endorses most of the recommendations of the Cadbury and Greenbury reports. The Committee's report touched on Board structure, the separation of the roles of the chairman from the chief executive, Board balance and the role of the non-executive directors on the Board. The role of institutional investors in governance, the relationship with shareholders and the role of auditors in Corporate Governance all featured in the report. The Committee was unequivocal regarding the roles of stakeholders in organizations. It believed that stakeholders' interests should be protected but not at the expense and survival of the business. Its chairman was quoted as saying 'companies must be accountable, but they also have to be profitable' (BBC News, 1998).

THE TURNBULL REPORT (1999)

Following the Hampel Report, the Combined Code was prepared in 1998 which essentially merged the recommendations of the three previous committees viz: the Cadbury, Greenbury and Hampel Committees' reports. The Code continued to operate on the 'comply or explain' principle. In 1999, the Turnbull Committee Report was produced. The Committee had been set up by the Institute of Chartered Accountants in England and Wales to provide guidelines on the implementation of the internal control requirements of the Combined Code. The report of the Turnbull Committee focused on three main provisions of the Combined Code. These are provisions D.2, D.2.1, and D.2.2.

- D.2. states that 'the Board should maintain a sound system of internal control to safeguard shareholders' investment and company assets'.

- D.2.1 states that 'the directors should at least annually conduct a review of the effectiveness of the group's system of internal control and should report to shareholders that they have done so. The review should cover all controls, including financial, operational and compliance control and risk management'.

- D.2.2 states that 'companies which do not have an internal audit function should from time to time review the need for one'.

The report asserts the responsibility of the directors in respect of internal control and risk management. It emphasized that directors need to ascertain that appropriate internal control procedures are in place and that they are working. The nature and kind of risks facing the organization do change and directors need to be aware of these and review the procedures in place to be certain of their adequacy and relevance in view of the nature of new risks confronting the organization.

THE HIGGS COMMITTEE REPORT (2003)

The Higgs Committee reported on the role and effectiveness of non-executive directors. The remit of the Committee was set against the backdrop of current events unfolding in the corporate environment globally. Firstly there was the corporate collapse involving ENRON, the seventh biggest company in the world and also the highest-profile corporate misdemeanour in WorldCom. Secondly there were global responses to the uncertainty that seemed to confront companies in a globalized world where the impact of corporate failure in one corner of the globe was felt worldwide. For example, the US responded with the Sarbanes-Oxley Act, France unleashed the Bouton Report and in Germany it was the Cromme Code, all of which were set up with the intention of strengthening Corporate Governance in view of recent events (Higgs Report, 2003: 15).

In conducting this research and drawing up its report, the Committee sent out a consultation paper in June 2002 and received around 250 responses. Members of the Committee held meetings with people and representatives of bodies and groups of interested individuals. The reports of the Committee were based on findings from three main sources. Firstly the Committee relied on research data supplied by Hemscott Group; this was very useful in that it enabled the Committee to know the population of non-executive directors in UK listed companies. Secondly, MORI surveyed 605 executive directors, non-executive directors and chairmen of UK listed companies in August 2002 with a view to understanding current practices with respect to non-executive directors' performance, recruitment, training and effectiveness. Lastly, the Committee conducted interviews with 40 directors of FTSE 350 Boards. This was with a view to understanding the situation that facilitates an effective non-executive director's function.

In terms of its conclusions, the report supports most of the recommendations already contained in the Combined Code and made additional recommendations such as requesting listed companies to disclose in their annual reports the number of meetings of the Board and its committees as well as the attendance record of the individual directors. It endorsed the recommendation that the position of the chief executive and chairman of the Board should be separated, non-executive directors should meet as a group at least once a year without executive directors being present and annual reports should indicate that such a meeting had been held.

THE SMITH COMMITTEE REPORT (2003)

Just about the time that the Higgs Report was being released, the UK's Smith Committee Reports were also being made available in January 2003. The Smith Committee had been established in the wake of the corporate failures in the US. The concern of the Government was the possibility of such a failure happening in the UK. To find an answer to the question: CAN IT HAPPEN HERE? (referring to corporate collapses in the US), the Government requested the FRC to review the country's preparedness in preventing such a collapse in UK listed companies. In September 2002, the FRC announced the establishment of the Smith Committee with its terms of reference and membership. By January 2003 the Committee submitted its report. The summary of major points from the Committee's activity is reported below.

The Committee reported on five main areas of the Audit Committee. These are its:

- purpose;
- membership, procedure and resources;
- relationship with the Board;
- roles and responsibilities; and
- communications with shareholders.

The Committee also proposed new code provisions on the Audit Committee that should be included in the Combined Code. . It is important to reiterate that the Committee emphasized the important role of the Audit Committee in the bigger picture of Corporate Governance. The fact that while 'all directors have duty to act in the interest of the company, the Audit Committee has a particular role, acting independently from the executive, to ensure that the interest of shareholders are properly protected in relation to financial reporting and internal control' (Smith Committee, 2003: 3, para. 1.5).

THE COMBINED CODE (2003) AND (2006)AND ONWARD

Since its first edition in 1998, the Combined Code has been updated on a regular basis, usually every two years, in line with developments in the corporate environment and changes in the global Corporate Governance guidelines that are deemed necessary in the context of the UK. Listed companies are required to comply with the Code or explain non-compliance. There was a review of the Code in June 2006 for application in accounting periods beginning on or after November 2006 and the June 2008 edition for application in accounting periods beginning on or after 29 June, 2008. The main difference between the two is that the amendments to the June 2008 edition essentially present two major changes. Firstly, it removes the restriction on an individual chairing more than one FTSE 100 company. Secondly, for listed companies outside the FTSE 350, it allows the company chairman to sit on the Audit Committee where he or she was considered independent on appointment (Combined Code, 2008).

The 2010 review of the UK Corporate governance code is the most recent and most substantial because it incorporates a number of lessons learnt from the global financial crisis and how it affects the UK's financial service sector. For example, the review contains recommendations from the Turner's review (2009) which was essentially a regulatory response to the financial crisis that effectively started in 2008, and the recommendations from the Walker's review (2009) on corporate governance in UK banks and other financial industry entities. Some of the key points from Walker reports could be interpreted to suggest that:

- Unitary board and the comply and explain approach still appropriate to the UK corporate governance need
- Current deficiencies in board procedures and process are mainly behavioural rather than organizational
- Non-executives to be more questioning and challenge executive more vigorously but constructively

- Greater focus on risk management and dedicated Chief Risk Officer
- Shareholders active engagement and commitment to the Stewardship Code through institutional investors
- Remuneration issues need closer oversight by non-executive directors

THE STEWARDSHIP CODE 2010

One of the recommendations of the Walker's review was the development of a similar governance code for institutional investors and the need for institutional investors to be more actively engaged with the management in their investee companies. The Code was to be placed under the remit of the Financial Reporting Council (FRC). Following this recommendation the FRC consulted widely on its suitability to take on this responsibility and whether the code should be amended or adopted in its current form. The amended code became known as the Stewardship Code and was published for the first time in July 2010. The primary aim of the Code is to protect the interest of the shareholders through effective engagement between institutional investors and management of the companies in which they have investments. The Code is design to operate on the 'comply or explain' basis thereby allowing for flexibility and avoiding box ticking approach. UK authorized asset managers are required to report on their application of the Code.

Towards a Definition of Corporate Governance

This chapter has provided the background to what follows and reviewed the various definitions of Corporate Governance. Although the study appreciates the difficulty in having a universally accepted definition of Corporate Governance, it identifies the major ingredients of a veritable definition for the term. These include the fact that it must address the concerns of the Contractarian as well as accommodate the views of the Communitarians. Further, such definitions must appreciate the importance of a legal, regulatory and legislative framework affecting Corporate Governance. On these bases, the definitions suggested by Cadbury (1992) and Rezaee (2009) were adapted to develop an integrated definition of Corporate Governance which forms the frame of reference in this book. In the next chapter, the author explains the relevance of theory and identifies various theoretical frameworks that underpin the discourse on Corporate Governance.

3

Regulation and Auditing – Ethics and Professionalism

Introduction

Auditing and Assurance is a key aspect of the corporate market in almost all economies. The auditing profession has been traced back to the nineteenth century when it was necessary to assure on the reports rendered by tax collectors on behalf of the Crown. In the modern day market capitalism with unprecedented flow in fund from one end of market spectrum to the other, and in the age of market globalization, the role of auditing and assurance cannot be overemphasized. Audits add to the value relevance of the information in the financial statements by providing a kind of certification to the truth and fairness of the figures presented. Although recent high-profile corporate crises, and more recently the banking crisis, have highlighted concerns over the current regulatory structure for auditing globally, there is a covert consensus on the importance of this function for the improvement of market confidence and therefore enhanced market performance. Similar note is applicable in the case of Corporate Governance. Although the term is relatively new, it is now widely used in the corporate environment and deserves all the attention due to the frequency and magnitude of the corporate misbehaviours that have been reported globally. This section of the book is essentially intended to enumerate the national and international regulatory framework for auditing and Corporate Governance. The objective of this approach is to draw a distinction and at the same time present a clearer picture of the interrelatedness of auditing and Corporate Governance. This is against the backdrop of almost immediate aspersion and blame on the auditing profession the moment another Corporate Governance issue comes to the fore. While this may be correct, and it is often the case that auditors have had some questions to answer in almost all cases of corporate misbehaviours, the regulatory requirement for the two are different. While auditing has a legal backing, Corporate Governance in the UK is strictly speaking voluntary.

The auditing profession has a multi-layered regulatory framework that is geared towards independence and objectivity. The role of the auditor in the corporate environment enjoys statutory backing in the form of legislation. The Companies Act 2006 guarantees the rights, duties, responsibilities of the auditor and specifies the requirement for entities that should be audited as well as the frequency of this. In addition to this, there are a number of court cases that have been established which also form part of the regulatory framework that impact on the profession. These court rulings in some cases become the frames of reference and benchmarks against which auditors' performance are assessed. The third layer of guidance and regulation comes from the regulatory authorities. For example, in the UK the Financial Reporting Council (FRC) provides a regulatory oversight on the auditing profession through the Audit Practice Board and the Audit Inspection. The professional accountancy body also regulates the members' behaviour through regulated examinations, a continuous professional development programme and disciplinary measures.

In terms of Corporate Governance, the FRC, through its Corporate Governance unit, is now charged with oversight function of the governance requirement of companies in the UK. This is in addition to specific industry requirements. For example, listed companies in the UK are required to comply or explain non-compliance with the Corporate Governance guidelines. Similarly, firms operating in certain sectors, for example banks and financial institutions regulated by the Financial Service Authority, are subjected to further governance requirements. Recently, the FRC produced the Stewardship Code for institutional investors and shareholders. It was anticipated that with such a document, institutional investors may become more responsible and that it may enhance their interactions with their investee companies. The continuing financial crisis has also seen more emphasis on tightening the rules on rewards and compensation so that firms and their management are seen to be more responsive and transparent in the ways that they are run.

The Literature

We will now examine the relevant literature on corporate governance and the role of the audit committees and auditor independence. The first part of this section considers the Audit Committee and a number of related themes. The second part of this section reviews the literature on auditor independence, starting with a definition of independence and the threats to it. A distinction is made between independence in appearance and in fact and the aspect that is most appropriate to this investigation is identified.

The third section focuses on the audit profession and the debate about audit and non-audit fees in the context of auditors providing non-audit services to their audit clients.

At the end of this chapter the arguments are synthesized and the main points summarized. The approach focuses mainly on literature from the UK supplemented by that from other parts of the globe. Figures 3.1 and 3.2 below summarize some of the key literatures used in the review.

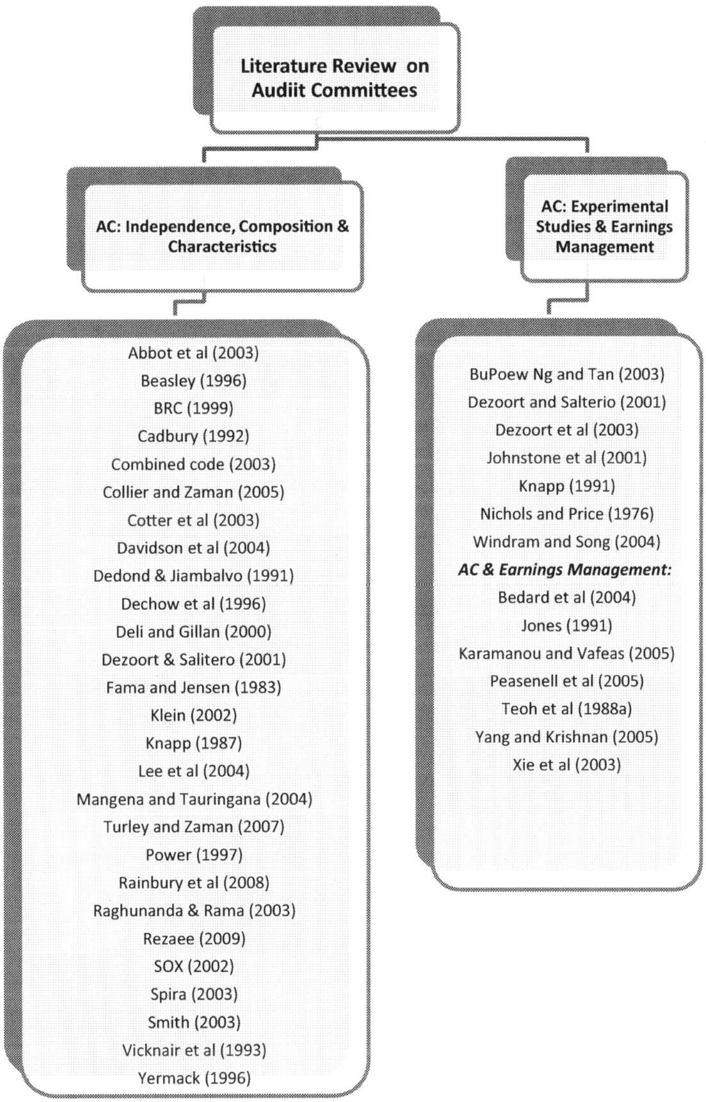

Figure 3.1 Key literatures on Audit Committees

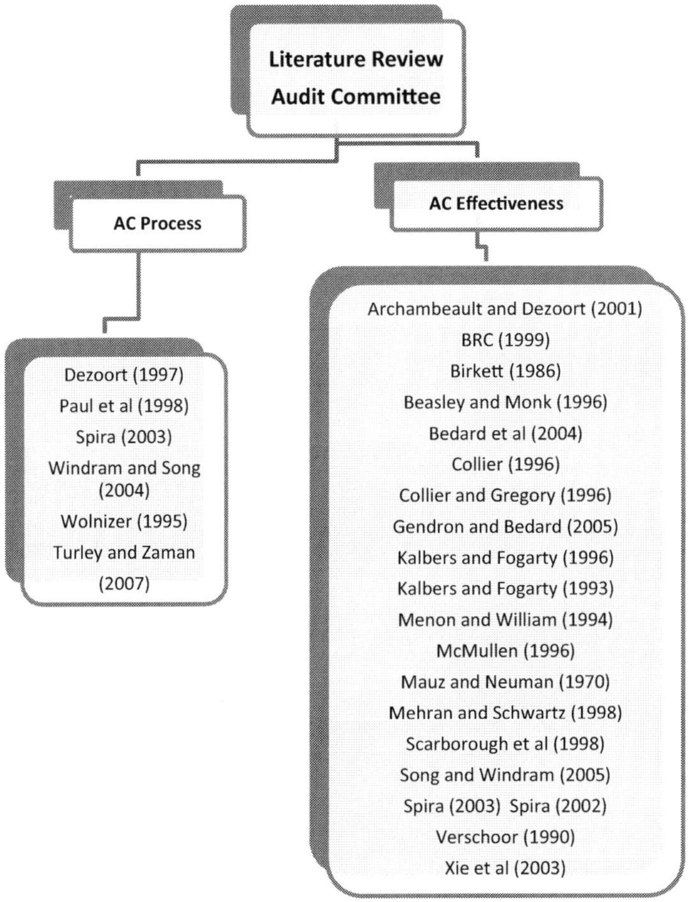

Figure 3.2 Key literatures on Audit Committees

Audit Committee Independence, Composition and Characteristics

An important concern relating to Audit Committees' performance centres on their independence. The presence of the Audit Committee should alleviate agency problems associated with moral hazard and adverse selection (Rainsbury et al., 2008: 394) through monitoring and oversight functions in reporting and auditing (Reinstein and Weirich, 1996: 28). With remits to provide oversight functions on financial matters and communications between the management and the external auditor (Zaman and Collier, 2005: 761), the Audit Committee needs to be independent to be able to function properly (Zaman and Collier, 2005: 758). Independence is just as important to the Audit Committee as it is important to the auditor (Deli and Gillan, 2000; Power, 1997). This will allow them to deal with the company's issues in an objective manner without any form of bias.

The Cadbury Report in section 4.12 provides that non-executive directors should be independent and it explains independence to mean:

> *... that apart from their directors' fees and shareholdings they should be independent of management and free from any business or other relationship which could materially interfere with the exercise of their independent judgement.*

The Blue Ribbon Committee (BRC) on 'Audit Committee effectiveness' defines independence as the exclusion from the Board of current and former employees, relatives of management and persons receiving compensation from the company (except directors' fees). The BRC also recommended the exclusion of directors who are partners in, controlling shareholders or executive officers of any for-profit business organization to which the corporation made or from which the corporation received significant payments in the last five years (BRC, 1999).

The Sarbanes Oxley Act defines independence in the context of the Audit Committee in section 301 to mean:

> *... in order to be considered independent for the purpose of this paragraph, a member of an Audit Committee of an issuer may not, other than in his or her capacity as a member of the Audit Committee, the BOD or any other board committee:-*
>
> *Accept any consultancy, advisory or other complementary fee from an issuer or be an affiliated person of the issuer or any subsidiary thereof.*

The importance of the Audit Committee's independence is highlighted by the nature and scope of its expected roles. Audit Committees are expected to enhance public confidence in the corporate system with regard to their transparency, adequacy in reporting and a reassurance of sufficient safeguards against fraudulent reporting and creative accounting (Rezaee et al., 2003: 536; Cadbury, 1992; DeFond and Jiambalvo, 1991: 651). It is also anticipated that the Audit Committee should buffer the relationship among many governance organs within the firm as well as external organs (Rezaee, 2009: 121) The Audit

Committee is crucially important in enhancing the relationship between the external auditor and management not only during the course of their duties but also in cases of disputes between them (Rainsbury et al., 2008: 394; Knapp, 1987). The Audit Committee should also enhance the relationship between the external auditor and the internal audit function (Wolnizer, 1995: 47). This is achieved through regular review of the activities of both organs and by determining the extent and scope of their work as well as by reviewing the audit process and making informed modifications (Fama and Jensen, 1983; Knapp, 1987; Dezoort and Salterio, 2001). In order to discharge their oversight functions effectively, it is important that the committee is independent of management. Lack of independence from the management may inadvertently turn the members of the Audit Committee into an extension of the management team itself and this will defeat the objective of having the Audit Committee in the first place. Independence entails having sufficient scope in taking decisions relating to their functions, having access to adequate and timely information to enable them to function, having the enabling environment in which to operate including the requisite resources and access to professional advice and training required to discharge the expected functions of the committee (Combined Code, 2003).

A considerable number of studies have also focused on examining Audit Committee composition and characteristics. In terms of committee composition, most Corporate Governance guidelines provide that the Audit Committee should be composed of mainly independent non-executive directors with at least three members. The Cadbury Report in section 4.11 states that:

> *... the calibre and number of non-executive directors on the board should be such that their views will carry significant weight in the board's decisions. ... all boards will require a minimum of three non-executive directors, one of whom may be the chairman of the company provided he or she is not also its executive head, additionally, two of the three should be independent in the terms set out in the next paragraph (4.12).*

The question of the composition of the Board has been the focus of several studies and three types of directors are known to serve on the Board of directors in a single-tier Board system. These are outside directors (completely independent of the management), the insider director (director but also an employee of the organization) and affiliated or grey area directors (outside director but with a commercial or other form of relationship with the firm, a recent employee of the firm or someone external but with a substantial shareholding in the firm) (Deli and Gillan, 2000). While the outside directors are considered independent (Fama and Jensen, 1983) the other two are not considered to be independent. For instance, Vicknair et al. (1993) recognized the problem of affiliated or grey area directors. These are directors who, though they might appear to be independent of the management and of the organization, still have some connections with the company or its Board and are thus capable of undermining the Board's independence. They also enjoy, either directly or indirectly, a financial interest in the firms on whose committees they serve. Therefore the presence of grey area directors on the Board has the propensity to reduce Board independence. Fama and Jensen (1983) observed that the executive director is an internal manager of the organization and has privileged information about the firm, while the external directors are independent and so should be able to resolve disagreements between internal managers and exercise independent judgements in cases of conflict of interest between management and shareholders including situations relating to reward and compensation for senior executives and to the review of financial statements.

Against the background of the national and international requirement for the Board of directors to be composed mainly of independent non-executive directors, Clifford and Evans (1997) examined the level of independence of Boards in Australian listed companies. Of relevance is the finding that the presence of grey area directors or affiliated directors may corrupt and confuse the independence perceptions of the Boards. This is because, although the number of non-executive directors on the Board may appear higher than the number of executive directors, as required by most Corporate Governance guidelines and which may signal good Corporate Governance practices, not all the non-executive directors are strictly independent of management, due to the presence of grey area directors. The grey area directors still have some commercial or other forms of affiliation with the management which may compromise their independence. The study population was the Australian top 500 companies based on market capitalization, listed on the Australian Stock Exchange as at 30 December, 1993. A sample size of 100 was used, but this was reduced to 90 because ten companies were trust companies or companies domiciled outside Australia. Of the remaining 90 companies, 43 did not provide sufficient information to allow classifications of their non-executive directors and so were excluded from the investigation. Thus the study was based on information on non-executive directors from 47 companies out of the 90 in the sample. Data on firm size was proxied by turnover and total assets which were collected from companies' annual reports. Three main questions were asked to determine the presence of affiliated directors on the Board: (1) is a non-executive director involved in transactions with the company other than those required to fulfil the role of director? (2) Is a non-executive director a substantial (shareholding greater than 5 per cent of the issued ordinary capital) shareholder in the company? And lastly, (3) is a non-executive director a previous employee of the company?

The authors found that 35 per cent of non-executive directors in 47 of the top 90 Australian listed companies were involved in transactions with their companies which places them into the category of grey area directors and such connections and interests may threaten their independence posture. They implied that the combination of the insider non-executives and grey area directors would constitute the majority of the Board for most of the companies involved in the study and this may give a wrong impression of the apparent independence of these Boards. Despite a majority of seemingly non-executive directors, there is considerable control and influence from the management due to the commercial relationship they maintained with the company. 3.2 per cent of non-executive directors were found to have substantial shareholdings in the companies in which they served as independent non-executive directors and around 1.4 per cent had been previous employees of the companies in which they served as independent non-executive directors. Although they reported similarities in their findings with other studies, the greatest limitation of this study is in the sample size. Given the importance of the subject matter (Audit Committee independence and the grey area directors) and the huge attention Corporate Governance has generated in recent times, it is necessary that reported findings are fairly representative of the reality in terms of the relevance of the research question and the scope of the study for which this survey is inadequate.

Studies have also suggested that the method of committee members' appointment is an important determinant of their independence and how independently they can be seen to act. Where members of the committee are appointed by management they are to perform oversight functions on, their objectivity and independence becomes a subject of concern. It will be more likely that their independence will be compromised and their views become biased (Verschoor, 2002, 1993; Klein, 2002; O'Sullivan and Diacon, 1999). And where the Board is composed of a greater number of executive directors than independent non-executive directors this may have adverse effects on the firm as can be implied from the following studies. Beasley (1996) reported that firms in which fraud is committed have fewer independent directors than firms where fraud is not committed.

Although statutorily the appointment of the external directors is the preserve of the shareholders exercised at the annual general meeting (AGM), in practice the executive directors recommend these appointments. However, the Cadbury Report section 4.30 requires the establishment of a nomination committee charged with the recommendation and appointment of directors to the Board. Following on from this recommendation, the Higgs Report reiterated this requirement and provided an outline of the expected duties and structure of the nomination committee. It is now within the remit of the nomination committee to undertake the selection and appointment of directors which is then ratified at the AGM. The Smith Committee Report provides in sections 3.3. and 3.4 that:

> *3.3. Appointments to the Audit Committee should be made by the board on the recommendation of the nomination committee (where there is one), in consultation with the Audit Committee chairman.*
>
> *3.4. Appointments should be for a period of up to three years, extendable by no more than two additional three-year periods, so long as members continue to be independent.*

Closely related to this, is the selection of the auditor and the impact of the Audit Committee members in this regard. It is thought that if the recommendation for appointment of the external auditor is within the remit of the independent Audit Committee it is more likely to enhance their independence than if the recommendation to shareholders is made by the executive management. The Smith Report (2003) provides that the appointment, retention and determination of the independence of the auditor are now within the remit of the Audit Committee acting on behalf of the main Board of directors. If auditors' appointments and the determination of their remuneration continue to be the preserve of the management (purportedly acting on behalf of the shareholders) it puts the auditors in a difficult situation in the context of their independence and objectivity (DeAngelo, 1981).

Although there are regulatory safeguards in terms of maximum percentages of a firm's fee that can be earned from a client or group of related clients, recent corporate collapses indicate that auditors are still susceptible to fee dependence. This may in part explain reasons for the recommendation that the selection, appointment and determination of the auditor and audit fee as well as the scope of the services to buy from the auditors be within the remit of the Audit Committee (Cadbury Report, 1992; Smith Report, 2003). However, this may not be over stressed as it has been shown that Audit Committee members may equally become biased in their selection process.

For instance, Reinstein and Weirich (1996) examined the conscious or unconscious bias exhibited by Audit Committee members when deciding on auditor selection and/or retention. In this US Study of 247 New York Stock Exchange listed firms, they reported a significant relationship (5 per cent level of significance) between certified public accountant (CPA) firms selected by Audit Committees and by the CPA firms which audit the Audit Committee member's own organization. For instance, of the 77 Audit Committee members that selected Arthur Andersen (this research was carried out before the ENRON debacle and the eventual collapse of Arthur Andersen) as their auditor, 19 of these committee members (24.7 per cent) also had a 'home employer' audit relationship with Arthur Andersen which may be thought to have biased their selection or choices. They concluded that a business relationship existing between the members of the Audit Committee and the audit firms they appointed signalled the absence of independence in the committees' selection process. However, they pointed out that such bias can only have a positive impact on auditor independence. Since the preference for the Audit Committee member's affiliated company auditor may be due to their quality and given that Audit Committee members tend to support the auditors in disputes between the auditor and management. On the other hand, such bias questions the objectivity of the Audit Committee towards the auditor especially now that the Audit Committee determines the scope, type and volume of services purchased from the auditor, their fees as well as reviewing their independence.

This is an important study in the context of the independence of the Audit Committee especially against the background of their increased responsibilities; however, one area the study could have examined is the switching decision of the auditee and the role of the Audit Committee in this. Although the study pointed out that Audit Committee members' selection bias can only lead to improvement in auditor independence, this may not always be the case. Lack of objectivity and transparency in the auditor selection process has the potential to compromise auditor independence and thereby affect auditing and reporting quality. It is important that members of the Audit Committee remain independent not only of the management but also of the auditors so as to be objective in their assessment of the auditors' independence (Abbott et al., 2000).

Deli and Gillian (2000) in a US study of Audit Committee independence examined factors associated with Audit Committee composition and its importance in the contracting process in organizations (the contracting process refers to the steps involved in entering into the nexus of contracts that subsist among many stakeholders in the corporate environment). Their study is consistent with the general theme that suggests that firms with higher demand for accounting certifications are more likely to have high-quality auditors and form Audit Committees. They tested four main hypotheses which investigated the relationship between the probability that a firm has a completely independent and active Audit Committee and the level of firm growth opportunities, firm size, Managerial Ownership and firm leverage. They also controlled for some other factors that may affect Audit Committee independence and composition such as regulatory pressure and trading venues (stock exchanges).

Deli and Gillan (2000) posit that firms with growth opportunities tend to have fewer observable assets and will therefore demand fewer accounting certifications, unlike firms that comprise mainly of 'assets-in-place' who have greater demand for accounting certification. Growth opportunities were measured as the ratio of firm size to the book value of assets while firm size was calculated as the sum of the market value of equity, book value of debt and the book value of preferred stock. Managerial ownership was measured as the sum of the percentage ownership of all employee directors. Leverage was measured as the ratio of long-term debt to firm size.

They reported the result of their multivariate logit regression and found a significant negative relationship between the probability of the existence of an independent and active Audit Committee and firm growth opportunities, since there is little demand for accounting certifications. Managerial ownership was also found to be negatively related to independent and active Audit Committees. As insider executive directors' shareholding increases the demand for Audit Committee activity falls since Managerial Ownership will probably align management's and owners' interest. Also since increased Managerial Ownership may mean a higher presence of management on the Audit Committee, this would serve to dilute the Audit Committee's independence. Further, Audit Committee independence and activity was found to be positively related to firm size and leverage. Bigger firms require more monitoring and accounting certifications just as do firms that have significant amounts of borrowing.

Although the study achieved its set objectives, those objectives were limited as the study could have examined other related issues pertaining to the role of the Audit Committee in the contracting process. The impact of the Audit Committee in moderating the cost of equity capital could have been examined especially in view of the fact that a number of governance codes envisage improved financial reporting and auditing as a result of Audit Committee activity. The role of the Audit Committee in debt contracting could have been examined extensively. Using the sum of market equity, debt and preferred stock to measure firm size is unusual. It is usual to use the natural logarithm of total assets or natural logarithm of turnover in a period. These are more stable and reflect the long-term performance of the organization more than volatile measures such as equity and debt.

In a related study, Klein (2002) examined whether Audit Committee and Board characteristics are related to earnings management by the firm using a sample of 692 publicly traded US firm-years. The main hypothesis was that more independent Audit Committees and Boards are associated with a lower incidence of earnings management which was proxied by abnormal accruals. The study considered three definitions of independence. Firstly, independence was interpreted as the percentage of outside (non-executive) directors on the Audit Committee or on the main Board. Secondly, a committee was only considered independent if and only if all its members are outside non-executive directors. Thirdly, a committee was considered to be independent if a majority of its members were independent of the management. The study found the third definition to be more feasible to operationalize.

The authors would have preferred the second definition, that is, to have 100 per cent non-executive directors on the Audit Committee. This is the requirement of most Corporate Governance guidelines. However, while this may be possible in the case of the Audit Committee it is not likely in the case of the main Board to be composed of only outside directors since there will be a need for inputs from the executive directors relating to the strategic and operational functions of the organization (Fama and Jensen, 1983). The study noted that the difference in the definition of independence can potentially affect Board structure and size. Achieving a 100 per cent independent Audit Committee may imply additional costs for the firm in terms of recruitment and associated costs. It is also important to balance the size of the Board and committee since Yermack (1996) posits that firms with a smaller Board size tend to attain better performance.

The paper reported the results of both univariate and multivariate models. It found that the magnitude of abnormal accruals is more pronounced in firms with Audit Committees which did not comprise of a majority of independent directors. It also reported a negative relationship between abnormal accruals and the percentage of outside non-executive directors. This implies that the higher the percentage of non-executive directors the lower the level of abnormal accruals. It also showed that firms with Boards and/or Audit Committees that move from a majority-independent to a minority-independent structure experience large increases in abnormal accruals in the year of the change compared to their counterparts. However, using abnormal accruals to capture the effectiveness of the Audit Committees in constraining fraud and earnings management remains debatable. This is because there is no single acceptable accurate measure of abnormal accruals and this exposes findings from this study to measurement bias. This limits its implications and power of generalization in respect of the roles and effectiveness of the Audit Committee. Additionally, the study reported its result with a caveat to the effect that the result did not measure causality between the variables; rather it only indicates a form of relationship.

Cotter and Silvester (2003) examine the relationship between Board structure, independence and firm value. With Agency Theory as their theoretical framework, they examined the impact of other mechanisms used to control agency conflict on full Board and committee independence (audit and compensation committees) and the association between independence and firm value in 109 large Australian companies. They documented a strong association between the proportion of independent non-executive directors on the full Board and its audit and compensation committees. They observed that both committees tend to have a greater proportion of independent directors than the full Board. They also found that greater full Board independence is associated with low management ownership and an absence of substantial shareholders. Greater Audit Committee independence is associated with reduced monitoring by debt-holders when leverage is low and that the low level of these other monitoring mechanisms seems to be compensated for by a higher level of Board and Audit Committee independence.

Their study was unable to provide evidence that firm value is enhanced through stronger monitoring committees or full Board independence. Equally, their result may not be generalized for smaller companies and for companies that do not have both audit and compensation committees. This is because the study was based on large Australian companies. They stated that their poor result may be due to problems with cross-sectional tests, but they failed to elaborate on the nature and reasons for the problems with cross-sectional tests. Furthermore, associating greater Audit Committee independence with reduced monitoring by debt-holders when leverage is low is just stating the obvious. The researcher would expect debt-holders to be interested in enhanced monitoring if leverage is high since this increases their risk exposure and it is against this type of scenario that the study should have measured the independence of the Audit Committee rather than when leverage is low and the risk and consequences of default are minimal.

In a study analyzing the effect of Audit Committee and Board of director characteristics including independence on auditor resignation, Lee et al. (2004) conducted a comparative analysis of 190 auditors' resignations with 190 auditor dismissals during the period 1996–2000 and found that when Audit Committees and Boards of directors are independent, auditors are less likely to resign but where they did resign, they are more likely to be replaced with an audit firm with a perceived higher profile and hence a higher perception of audit quality. They also found that the degree of Audit Committee member's financial expertise to be negatively related to the occurrence of an auditor's resignation. A similar result could not, however, be found with respect to the main Board. These results have important implications for the auditor selection process and audit quality. It confirms the expectation that an independent Audit Committee reinforces the auditing functions through their inputs in the audit planning process with respect to both internal and external audit functions.

Equally it provides an alternative communication route to the auditor which may prolong the auditor's tenure through governance requirements (Combined Code, 2003) that the Audit Committee should have closed-door meetings with the auditors. This type of meeting provides additional opportunities to the auditor to discuss important issues relating to the auditor's function and independence. Further, the result of the study fits the context of the Audit Committees enhancing auditing quality, for example, by replacing a resigning auditor with an auditor of perceived higher quality. The importance of the financial literacy of the Audit Committee member was also reinforced by this study. Overall, the study may be seen in the light of the enhanced roles of the Audit Committee. For example, in the UK, Audit Committees now play more active roles in the auditor selection process, determining the scope of the audit and in assessing the independence of the external auditors (Combined Code, 2003).

Abbott et al. (2003a) examine the impact of some Audit Committee characteristics identified by the Blue Ribbon Committee (BRC, 1999) on improving the effectiveness of corporate Audit Committees on the likelihood of financial restatement. They studied 88 US-based companies with restatement of annual results (without allegations of fraud) in the period 1991–1999 and a matched pair control group of firms of similar size, exchange listing, industry and auditor type with no restatement. Using Audit Committee independence and activity to proxy for committee diligence, they reported a significant and negative association between Audit Committee diligence and the occurrence of restatements. They also documented a significant and negative relationship between an Audit Committee that includes at least one member with financial expertise and restatement. This suggests that firms that do not have financial experts on their Audit Committees are more likely to experience the incidence of earnings restatements. The study adopted the BRC definition of independence and defined an outside non-executive director as being independent if he or she is not a current or past employee of the company and does not have any other affiliation with the firm or its management except in the normal discharge of their Board functions.

Their study may not be generalized due to certain limitations. For example, the sample size of 88 firms appears to be too small to allow a meaningful generalization on an important and sensitive issue such as earnings restatement. A study with a bigger sample would give more comfort as the consistency and power of the findings would be enhanced. Another limitation in this study was the subjectivity involved in the judgement between financial literacy and financial expertise and deciding on their suitability. What level of knowledge will qualify for financial literacy and how many years and the precise nature of the experience gained by an individual will be acceptable in order to meet the code of best practice's requirements that at least one member of the committee should be financially literate. The study could have used the distinction between Accounting Financial Expert (AFE) and Supervisory Financial Expert (SFE) (Hoitash et al., 2009). While AFEs have an accounting qualification gained through experience (for example, Chief Financial Officers), SFEs are those individuals who have qualifications suggestive of knowledge obtained through supervising accounting tasks (for example, Chief Executive Officers).

Similarly, Abbott et al. (2003b) examined the relationship between audit fees, non-audit fees and Audit Committee characteristics for a sample of US companies. Using a sample of 538 companies based on proxy documents submitted to the Securities and Exchange Commission (SEC) between 5

February, 2001 and 30 June, 2001, they found that Audit Committees that are more independent and that meet at least four times in a year tend to have lower non-audit fees ratio to audit fees. They argued that their result supports the move and expectations by the SEC in the US regarding the increased oversight functions of the Audit Committees. While suggesting a number of areas for future research, they noted that lack of statistical significance of some of the agency cost based variables may be connected to their data. They observed that their study used data from periods when SEC required registrants to disclose information about fees paid to the auditor for both audit and non-audit services, the result may be different if management have had enough time to adjust to the requirement of the new regulations by buying less non-audit services from their incumbent auditors.

One study that seems to play down the impact of financial literacy on the perception of Audit Committee performance is Raghunandan and Rama (2003). This study examined the impact of Audit Committee composition on shareholders' action with a specific focus on shareholders' voting patterns during auditor ratification. It does this by examining shareholders' voting patterns in ratification of external auditors in 199 US companies. The authors hypothesized that the proportion of shareholders not voting for ratification of the auditor in the presence of high non-audit fee ratios will be lower at companies that have: (1) solely independent non-executive directors on the Audit Committee; and (2) have at least one member with accounting or financial expertise on the Audit Committee. These hypotheses were developed following suggestions by the SEC that the composition of the Audit Committee can influence the monitoring of the auditor–client relationship and hence influence shareholders' perceptions about auditor independence.

They found that the presence of an Audit Committee with wholly independent non-executive directors is capable of explaining why shareholders are less likely to vote against or abstain from ratification of the auditor even when non-audit fees are relatively high. They suggested that Audit Committee composition is associated with shareholders' perceptions of the independence and performance of the auditor and provide a direct test of the association between Audit Committee composition and shareholders' actions. Their study also suggested that financial expertise does not provide a good explanation for shareholders' voting actions. The study carried a caveat warning that its results should be interpreted with caution due to the very low shareholders' vote against auditors' ratification which was less than 2 per cent in the sample studied. These could be because shareholders are not sophisticated enough to be interested in such voting, it may simply indicate lack of interest in such issues by the shareholders believing that their vote would not count and lastly it may be that the shareholders are already convinced that the big auditing firms symbolize quality and thus would not be motivated to vote against them

Davidson et al. (2004) studied stock market reaction to the announcement of the appointment of a director with financial expertise to the Audit Committee. The study examined 136 voluntary appointment announcements for the period from 1990–2001 and found a significant positive relationship between stock price movements and the appointment of a director with financial expertise. A number of regression analyses were run to test the hypotheses controlling for the state of the Audit Committee before the appointment and for alternative definitions of financial expertise.

Davidson et al. (2004) concluded that the market rewards firms that appoint financial experts to their Audit Committees and their findings are supportive of other studies that have documented a negative relationship between the proportion of 'experts' on Audit Committees and earnings management (Abbott et al., 2004; Bedard et al., 2004). The result from the study raises fundamental questions regarding its internal validity. The study proposes measuring the reaction of stock price to the appointment of a financially literate non-executive to the Audit Committee but did not indicate how it controlled for other noise effects on the stock price. Since it is known that stock prices vary due to a variety of noise or news (Verma and Verma, 2006) the increase in stock price may not be totally due to the announcement of the appointment of a financially literate non-executive director to the Audit Committee; it could just as easily be due to other announcements or other positive effects or noises that just happened to coincide with such an announcement.

Mangena and Tauringana (2008) examined the relationship between Audit Committee characteristics and voluntary external auditor involvement in UK interim reporting. Specifically they used Audit Committee shareholdings, expertise and size as the proxy for Audit Committee characteristics, in addition to other main Board characteristics and control variables such as company size, gearing and profitability. They used a logistic regression on data from 259 listed companies in the UK and reported an increase in the likelihood of the external auditors' involvement in the interim report when the Audit Committee has experts and less likelihood of external auditors' involvement with Audit Committee shareholdings. Audit Committee size was not found to be significant in the involvement of the external auditors in interim reporting.

The Audit Committee and Experimental Studies

Audit Committees are set up to enhance communications between management and auditors and to provide further assurance regarding firms' internal control procedures and especially their roles in respect of financial oversight on management (Nichols and Price, 1976; Johnstone et al., 2001). Both roles require that members of the committee should be able to make reasoned financial judgements. This is indicative of the requirement set out in most Corporate Governance guidelines that at least one member of the committee should be financially literate. In order to test the efficacy of this requirement, several experimental and judgement-based studies have been conducted.

Knapp (1991) investigates the degree to which three key audit context variables (audit firm's size class, length of tenure and general audit strategy) affect Audit Committee members' assessment of audit quality. He used a full-factorial, 2x3x2, ANOVA in which a sample of Audit Committee members responded to cases describing a problematic audit setting. The result of the study suggested that Audit Committee members' assessments of audit quality are significantly influenced by auditor size and length of auditor tenure. Audit Committee members believe that auditors from the (then) Big 8 audit firms are more likely to discover and disclose material errors than auditors from non-Big 8 firms.

In addition, Audit Committee members' opinions concerning the detection and disclosure of material error by auditors are also a function of their exposure to both Big 8 and non-Big 8 audit firms. Committee members that have interacted with auditors from both classes of audit firm do not think that non-Big 8 auditors will not disclose material error detected during the audit. Furthermore, he reported a positive relationship between length of tenure of the auditor and audit quality in the early years of an auditor–client relationship and an inverse relationship in the subsequent years due probably to auditors' complacency, familiarity and over reliance on the client's internal control. Finally, Knapp (1991) did not find that Audit Committee members ascribe a higher level of audit effectiveness to a structured audit approach compared to an unstructured audit approach. This particular finding may have implications for the requirement that members of the Audit Committee should be financially literate. Structured audit approaches pre-suppose proper audit planning and may be expected to enhance the audit process and, more importantly, should contribute to audit quality compared to unstructured audit approaches which are not properly planned.

DeZoort and Salterio (2001) studied the reaction of 68 representative Canadian Audit Committee members to a 'form vs. substance' dispute between the auditor and corporate management over a material accounting policy choice issue, specifically the timing of revenue recognition and associated expenses. They set out to test whether there are systematic differences in support for the auditor among committee members with varying degrees of independence and financial knowledge. They identified two threats to Audit Committee members' independence. Firstly, the amount of Board experience as an independent director. They suggested that a positive association is likely to exist between members' Board experience and independence. Thus more Board-level experience is crucial for members' independence. Audit Committee members that have served longer on the Board may exhibit better confidence in handling issues related to their functions, compared to inexperienced independent non-executive directors. The second threat was whether combining roles as a member of the committee and as a member of senior management in the same firm could affect members' independence. They argued that a negative association exists between role combination and independence of a committee member. Finally they tested the financial-reporting and audit-reporting knowledge of committee members through an accounting policy dispute task, knowledge and ability test and an experience questionnaire.

They created the experimental task with the assistance of four audit partners from the (then) Big 6 firms, a Big 6 national office accounting consultation partner, a corporate director with significant Audit Committee experience and four accounting professors. The task was also pre-tested on 12 MBA students with significant work experience. They reported that more independent Board membership experience and higher audit-reporting knowledge is associated with greater support for the auditor in the dispute with client management.

Furthermore, they found that concurrent Board and management membership is associated with higher levels of support for management in the dispute scenario. They reported no relationship between financial-reporting knowledge and Audit Committee members' judgement. Their study re-echoed the call for a committee that comprises wholly of independent members and also decried directors' duality. A committee that comprises mainly of independent non-executive directors has the potential to protect the interests of the shareholders and act independently of the management and question their decisions and strategies in a constructive manner compared to an Audit Committee on which the management is represented. This restrains the independence of the committee and compromises their effectiveness.

BuPoew Ng and Tan (2003) conducted an experimental study that investigated the effect of two contextual features – (1) 'availability of authoritative guidance; and (2) the effectiveness of the client's Audit Committee – on auditors' perceived outcome of auditor–client negotiations concerning an audit adjustment that affects the client's ability to meet analysts' forecasts'. The study involved 113 audit managers from a Big 4 audit firm and these auditors were required to provide a judgement relating to a proposed audit adjustment that is quantitatively immaterial but that will affect the client's ability to meet or beat analysts' consensus forecast. They manipulated the availability of precise authoritative guidance and Audit Committee effectiveness between subject variables allowing them to gain further insight into issues relating to audit adjustment and Audit Committee communication. They also used 'an audit adjustment context that relates to the potentially inappropriate choice of revenue-recognition method that has prompted the release of authoritative guidance on revenue recognition using a 2x2 between subject factorial design with Guidance Availability (absent, present) and Audit Committee Effectiveness (low, high) as the independent variable'.

They found that the availability of authoritative guidance has a greater effect on auditors' perceived negotiation outcome when the client's Audit Committee is ineffective rather than when it is effective. They also found that Audit Committee effectiveness has a greater effect on auditor's perceived negotiation outcome in the absence of authoritative guidance than in its presence. This suggests that authoritative guidance and effective Audit Committees are potential substitutes/compensating mechanisms for enhancing auditors' effectiveness and financial reporting quality. Furthermore, their study suggested that Corporate Governance mechanisms such as effective Audit Committees may prevent the potentially adverse effect of imprecise accounting rules by bolstering auditors' position during negotiations with clients and provide support for continuing efforts to enhance the effectiveness of the Audit Committee. The study also has implications for financial expertise on the Board and showed that Audit Committee effectiveness makes up for inadequacies in authoritative guidance thereby providing a buffer for the auditors during negotiations.

Although the study was meant to be an experimental study in actual fact it was not. The laboratory setting was lost because the study was eventually conducted online. The choice of the participants is also a likely deficiency in the study. The use of audit managers rather than audit partners who are actually more involved in negotiations with clients leaves the results from this study unclear. All the participants from the study were from just one audit firm and the result may have been different if the participants had cut across auditing firms.

DeZoort et al. (2003) examine how accounting and auditing issue characteristics affect Audit Committee members' judgements in an auditor–management disagreement. Two characteristics – (1) materiality justification ('a quantitative justification that only addresses the magnitude of the item versus a qualitative consequences-oriented justification that highlights the interruption of the company's earnings trend if the adjustment is recorded') and (2) precision of accounting issues (subject to precise measurement or imprecise estimate) – were tested.

The study was set up using Audit Committee members in public companies. Due to difficulties in gaining responses from Audit Committee members in very large companies, DeZoort et al. (2003) used Audit Committees in small and medium-sized companies. Information about Audit Committee members was gathered from The KPMG Audit Committee Institute (ACI) and after adjusting for 38 undeliverable and 34 respondents who failed a manipulation test they were left with 55 usable responses from a sample of 362. DeZoort et al. (2003) tested the hypotheses using a 2x2 between subject design where materiality justification and accounting precision were the experimental variables and Audit Committee members and auditors were the control variables. Respondents were asked to complete a case study focusing on whether a company should record an adjustment to 'write-off' a customer's accounts receivables balance. Participants were requested to indicate whether they supported the auditor's view (proposed adjustment should be recorded) or the management view (proposed adjustments should not be recorded).

They found that auditors enjoyed more support from the Audit Committee members if their materiality justification included both qualitative and consequences-oriented factors and when the accounting issue was subject to precise measurements. They also documented a relationship between Audit Committee members' experience and professional qualification and support for auditors in an auditor–management dispute. Specifically, more experienced Audit Committee members were more likely to support the auditor and CPAs among Audit Committee members were also shown to be more supportive of auditors in such dispute.

The study has important implications for improved communications between the auditor and Audit Committee members. It underscores the importance of experience and expertise as invaluable characteristics for Audit Committee members. The limitation of the study lies in its choice of small and medium-sized companies. The reality is that small and medium-sized companies are not statutorily required to form an Audit Committee and they could also seek exemption from audit. This is not the case with bigger companies and therefore the choice of small and medium-sized companies limits the practical usefulness of this study. Furthermore the study examined the behaviour of individual committee members, but the reality is that the committee acts and sees itself as a group and the result may have been totally different had a group setting been used such as a focus group approach.

Song and Windram (2004) reported their findings on the current level of activity within major UK Corporations in respect of Audit Committees. Their study provided further insights into the roles, responsibilities and characteristics of non-executive directors and the operations of UK Audit Committees. Their postal survey of Financial Times 500 companies focused mainly on the Audit Committee chairmen. With a 40 per cent response rate they found that there is a significant shift in Audit Committee function from the traditional financial reporting role to a greater focus on internal control and risk management. They also found that independence is seen as a very crucial feature of Audit Committee members. Lack of time, pressure from executive directors and an unclear remit are documented as major impediments to the effectiveness of the Audit Committee. On the other hand they observed a positive relationship between meeting frequency and number of non-executives on the Board.

The Audit Committee and Earnings Management

A number of studies have examined the impact of the Audit Committee on constraining earnings management.

Xie et al. (2003) examined the role of the Board and especially the Audit Committee in constraining earnings management. Their objective was to find out if there are relationships between Board composition and characteristics and the extent of earnings management in organizations. Specifically, they wanted to know if members' financial sophistication or background and frequency of Board meetings could explain smaller discretionary current accruals. Current accruals were defined as the change in non-cash current assets less the change in operating current liabilities. Since accruals can either be discretionary or non-discretionary, they had to deconstruct total accruals. This was done using the methods adopted by Teoh et al. (1998) and Jones (1991). In line with Teoh et al. (1998), they deflated the variables in the model by the book value of total assets from the prior year due to heteroskedasticity in the error terms. One hundred and ten firms from the S&P 500 index as listed in the June Standard and Poor's directory for 1992, 1993 and 1994 generated 330 observations out of which 48 firms either had insufficient or missing information leaving 282 firm-year observations. Data on Board composition and structure for these companies was gathered from the proxy statements nearest to but preceding the date of announcement of annual earnings in each year.

Xie et al. (2003) ran a univariate ordinary least squares regression with discretionary current accruals as the dependent variable and overall company and total Board characteristics variables as the independent variables. At 10 per cent significance levels, they found an inverse relationship between meeting frequency and discretionary accruals. They also documented a negative relationship between the percentage of independent outside directors and discretionary current accruals. The coefficient for the proportion of outside directors with a corporate background in relation to the total Board was found to be negative and significant at a 0.05 (5 per cent) level. Their study has implications for the proposal that Boards should have members that are financially literate and have sufficient experience at Board level in order to constrain creative accounting and earnings management. Boards that have more experienced and financially literate members are more likely to identify transactions or accounting treatment that has to do with creative accounting or/ and earnings management.

Bedard et al. (2004) examined the effect of Audit Committee expertise, independence and activity on aggressive earnings management measured by the level of income-increasing and income-decreasing abnormal accruals. They used two groups of US firms, one with relatively high and one with relatively low levels of abnormal accruals. They reported that the presence of at least one Audit Committee member with financial expertise and the level of governance expertise on the committee generally are associated with a lower likelihood of aggressive earnings management. Their results also suggest that share option schemes for non-executive directors compromise their independence since such stock options can be exercised in the short term and option schemes are positively associated with the likelihood of aggressive earnings management. Audit Committee expertise, firm size and frequency of committee meetings were not related to the likelihood of abnormal accruals. The major deficiency in this study is the likely measurement errors in the estimation of the abnormal accruals.

Peasenell et al. (2005), as part of a study examining the relationship between earnings management in UK firms and Board monitoring, reported an absence of evidence to support the assertion that the presence of an Audit Committee directly affects the extent of income-increasing adjustments to meet or exceed a threshold. They also found that Audit Committees do not impact directly on the degree of downward adjustments when pre-managed earnings exceed thresholds by a large margin.

Karamanou and Vafeas (2005) examined the association between Board and Audit Committee characteristics and management earnings forecasts (their occurrence, precision and accuracy) for 1995 Fortune 500 listed companies. Using Audit Committee independence, meeting frequency and expertise as characteristics of the Audit Committee, they found that firms with more effective Audit Committees (effectiveness was operationalized using BRC-suggested criteria) make or update an earnings forecast and that, while their forecast is less likely to be precise, it tends to be more accurate and receives a more favourable market response than companies with ineffective Audit Committees. They pointed out that less precision in forecasts from well-governed firms is only with respect to bad news, noting that such practice is compatible with minimizing chances of disclosing misleading information to the shareholders, especially in a litigious environment.

Yang and Krishnan (2005) studied the relationship between seven Audit Committee characteristics and quarterly earnings management. They argued that effective Audit Committees should not just focus on annual earnings management but rather such committees should also constrain earnings management contained in quarterly reports. Their study used a sample of 250 publicly traded companies for the period from 1996–2000 drawn from 10,386 US firms listed on the 1997 COMPUSTAT database. Audit Committee characteristics used include committee independence, expertise, meeting frequency, shareholding, number of outside directorships, experience and number of independent non-executive directors. They found that quarterly earnings management is lower for firms with more financial experts on the Audit Committee; a positive relationship was documented between likelihood of earnings management and Audit Committee members' share ownership. In other words, the more shares owned by Audit Committee members, the higher the likelihood of occurrence of quarterly earnings management and, lastly, more experienced Audit Committee members constrain quarterly earnings management. As with most earnings management studies, measurement bias and lack of causality are the major drawbacks of this study.

AUDIT COMMITTEE PROCESS

Studies have also examined the Audit Committee working process. The communication and relationship between the members of the committee on the one hand and between the committee and other organs of the organization on the other are important in assessing its effectiveness. It has been shown in Chapter 2 that the Audit Committee now has enlarged responsibilities in the wake of the corporate collapses that have occurred and the need to restore confidence in the market by signalling transparency in reporting and audit quality. Committee responsibilities now extend far beyond the traditional financial and auditing oversight to include internal auditing, risk management and 'relational' management at least between the external auditor and management. These duties require the right type of skills and expertise to discharge them effectively. The importance of inter-personal skills cannot be overemphasized especially when working as a small group such as the Audit Committee.

DeZoort (1997) studied Audit Committee oversight responsibilities from the actors' reflective perspectives of their expected roles and duties. Five hundred Audit Committee members selected from a random sample of 134 US companies participated in the study. The study has relevance against the backdrop of the increasing concern that Audit Committee members do not seem to appreciate the extent, nature and scope of their roles as corporate monitors charged with oversight functions on accounting, auditing and Corporate Governance in general (Wolnizer, 1995). DeZoort's study built on the work of Wolnizer (1995) and explores Audit Committee members' appreciation of their oversight responsibilities. The study used qualitative research methods which involved two elements, namely descriptive and exploratory components. The descriptive component provided insight into Audit Committee members' prowess in recognizing their assigned committee responsibilities; their thoughts about having sufficient expertise and experience in providing oversight in accounting and auditing, self-assessment of expertise in oversight areas and their attitudes towards expanding the scope of their responsibilities.

DeZoort (1997) employed two methods to gather exploratory information for the study. Firstly, open-ended questions were used to gather information about the Audit Committee's tasks and the issues facing them. Secondly, members were asked to rank their committee's five most important objectives in line with Wolnizer's (1995) list from the most important to the least important.

The study found that Audit Committee members surveyed were generally unable to recognize their assigned responsibilities as contained in the proxy statements with the exception of their roles relating to the review of internal audit and review of internal and external auditors' work.

The study reiterated the importance of clearer definitions of the roles and responsibilities of the Audit Committee and the need to ensure that they are actually discharging these responsibilities. This will involve members being aware of their duties in the first instance. This study re-echoed the caution raised on the ability of the committee to perform the 'mega' duties now being expected of it. It has to be observed that this study was conducted before the ENRON and other recent collapses and that the requirements in terms of the composition and duties of the Audit Committee have changed. Audit Committee members are now expected to be financially literate and the scope and nature of disclosure required has increased significantly. However, the positive impact of these changes has not yet been investigated especially in the wake of the recent corporate collapses and the subprime market crises.

Raghunandan et al. (2001) examined the association between Audit Committee composition and their interaction with internal audit. This interaction is measured in terms of the involvement of the Audit Committee in decisions to dismiss the chief internal auditor, meetings between the Audit Committee and the chief internal auditor, Audit Committee review of the internal auditing programme and the results of internal auditing in 398 Canadian manufacturing companies with turnover in excess of $50 million Canadian dollars. The study used questionnaires mailed to the chief internal auditors of these companies after stratifying them into large and small companies. They reported that the Audit Committee was involved in the dismissal of the chief internal auditor in only 48 per cent of the cases studied, while only 59 per cent of Audit Committees met three or more times with the chief internal auditor during the financial year, 79 per cent of Audit Committees studied granted private access to the chief internal auditor and 69 per cent of the Audit Committees studied reviewed both the internal audit programme and the results of internal audit.

This study is limited by the fact that it assumes a narrow purview of the internal auditing roles of the Audit Committee when their roles now involve more corporate risk assessment. Furthermore, it is possible that the internal audit function may be influenced by other factors not accounted for in this study such as the chief internal auditor's personality, qualifications and experience, all of which will impact on the interaction between the Audit Committee and the chief internal auditor. But the study definitely showed the changing nature of the committee's tasks and re-echoed the call for members to be more appreciative of their roles (Song and Windram, 2004). This was also well articulated by Spira (2003) who questioned the potency of the Audit Committee against the backdrop of the complexity and vagueness that characterize their operations. She observed that Audit Committee members need to be able to ask relevant, tough questions and demand appropriate answers. She also observed that this requires a reasonable amount of skill so that the committee does not become bogged down in the rituals of corporate cultures and logistics.

Audit Committee Effectiveness

A very important dimension to the study of Audit Committees is investigating their effectiveness. Since the formation or mere presence of an Audit Committee may not be equal to its effective discharge of its oversight duties (Sommer, 1991), especially when studies have documented Audit Committee formation for reasons such as compliance, appearance and signalling best practice rather than for their intrinsic benefit (Menon and Williams, 1994; Collier and Gregory, 1996; Kalbers and Fogarty, 1996). Similarly some researchers have questioned the relevance of the Audit Committee as part of the panacea for corporate debacles (Birkett, 1986; Vershoor, 1990; McMullen, 1996; Spira, 2003).

However, considering the growth in formations of Audit Committees and the important recognition it has enjoyed in national and international Corporate Governance regulations and debates, most commentators suggest that the Audit Committee is better placed to provide important oversight functions on the management. This is expected to enhance the auditor's independence through improved communication, contributing to audit quality, transparent reporting and corporate risk management (BRC, 1999; Sarbanes-Oxley Act, 2002; Combined Code, 2003). It is therefore surprising to observe the low number of studies in this important area of Audit Committee activity. This situation has been noted in studies including Kalbers and Fogarty (1993), McMullen (1996), Scarborough et al. (1998) and Spira (2003).

A number of reasons may be responsible for this including, for instance, how to operationalize or measure effectiveness against the backdrop of the very many meanings construed for the word in different fields. It is also important to be able to differentiate effectiveness of a process from its outcome. Equally, distinctions exist between effectiveness and factors associated with effectiveness (Cameron, 1986). Unfortunately, previous studies have been unable to operationalize the term in such a way as to totally capture a comprehensive meaning for it. This difficulty has been observed in previous studies (Cameron, 1986; Collier and Gregory, 1996; Spira, 2002).

The earliest documented research into Audit Committee effectiveness was a study by Mautz and Neumann (1977). They set out to answer the following questions. Why do some businessmen find corporate Audit Committees highly useful while others find little good to report about their own experience of them? What is there about the committee that causes such strong differences of opinion? What are the major characteristics and patterns of operation of Audit Committees? What are their leading advantages and disadvantages from the standpoint of directors, operating executives and independent CPAs? Does experience show that an Audit Committee can make a valuable contribution to management and, if so, under what conditions?

This extensive study used both qualitative and quantitative research methods. Over 4,000 questionnaires were mailed to survey targets supplemented by 42 interviews. They concluded that the corporate Audit Committee can make a substantial contribution to Corporate Governance but it will do so only when it is properly constituted and competently staffed and when it exists within a corporate environment that encourages, rather than discourages, its activities. But, despite the extent and the ambition of this study it was flawed in both its approach and methodology. The study failed to operationalize effectiveness in the light of the Audit Committee but rather suggested a general definition of effectiveness as it relates to Audit Committees. Furthermore, the study also failed to test any hypothesis and this failing seriously limits its usefulness and contribution to knowledge about Audit Committee effectiveness. Kalbers and Fogarty (1993) have observed this particular weakness in a number of other studies on Audit Committee effectiveness.

Kalbers and Fogarty (1993) extended Mautz and Neuman's (1977) work by investigating the relationship between Audit Committee effectiveness and its power. Effectiveness was construed against the performance of Audit Committees' functions of financial reporting, external auditor liaison and internal control oversight. The study explored the definitions of power using French and Raven's (1959) suggested definitions with some modifications. According to French and Raven's (1959) typology of power, there are five power types viz: reward, coercive, legitimate, expert and referent power with a later addition of information power (Raven, 1974). All six power types apply to the Audit Committee. The Audit Committee has legitimate power because it is the product of delegated authority through the Board of directors from the shareholders and public expectations as well as through corporate codes of best practice. They have the power of reward through their activity and recommendations, some of the beneficiaries of their power of reward may include the external auditor, internal auditor and other corporate officers. They have informational power. This is because in order to discharge their functions Audit Committee members need to have access to confidential and top-level information about the organization such as the corporate strategy, information on financial performance before it becomes public knowledge and so on which may have consequences for many key players in the corporate environment. Audit Committees have expert power, because they are composed of highly skilled personnel whose knowledge and expertise can impact significantly on the strategic direction of the organization and, lastly, Audit Committees are thought to have referent powers due to the fact that individuals on the committee may have strong personalities that can influence others and make a difference within the group.

Kalbers and Fogarty (1993) used the Linear Structural Relation Model to test predicted behaviour between Audit Committee effectiveness and power. They concluded that the relationships between the power dimension and the effectiveness dimension are complex. Formal, written authority coupled with observable support from top management play the most important roles in Audit Committee power and its effectiveness. With regard to power sources, this was found to be dependent on the personal attributes of Audit Committee members and the will to act (diligence) which constitutes the most significant power source influencing effectiveness. Examining Audit Committee effectiveness from the view point of their power in the organization was indeed a novel idea limited only to the extent that it may not be generalized to all Audit Committees especially since there may be sampling problems and the use of Linear Structural Relationship (LISREL) is relatively unpopular in the literature, although not necessarily because it is ineffective.

Collier and Gregory (1996) was a study of Audit Committee effectiveness. Effectiveness was construed from the functional forms, that is, audit quality and internal control. They hypothesized that the roles of the Audit Committee in audit quality and sound internal control are capable of exerting a two-way pressure on audit fees. They showed that an Audit Committee is effective in improving audit quality as measured by the size-related audit fee and in improving internal control as measured by the risk and complexity-related audit fee. They control for other variables that may affect audit fees.

Their sample was drawn from the FTSE 500 with variables included for the presence or absence of an Audit Committee. They also developed a model to test whether there is a difference in the size of the audit fee between companies with or without an Audit Committee. Their study documented a positive relationship between the size-related audit fee and the presence of an Audit Committee but the relationship between risk and complexity-related audit fee and the presence or absence of an Audit Committee was ambiguous and inconclusive. They concluded that the Audit Committee is effective in its role of overseeing the external audit and ensuring that the scope of the audit is adequate but that there is no conclusive evidence to suggest that it is effective in engendering a stronger internal control environment that is reflected in reduced audit fees.

Beasley (1996) conducted an empirical analysis of the relationship between Board composition and financial statement fraud. Specifically the study tested the proposition that increased outside non-executive director ownership coupled with greater representation of outside non-executive directors on the Board constrained the occurrence of fraud. However, the presence of the Audit Committee was found to be inconsequential in constraining financial fraud in organizations. The study brought a new twist to the debate on the effectiveness of the Audit Committee by suggesting that the whole Board rather than just the Audit Committee has the potential to constrain fraud and material misstatements. This finding conflicts with results from Bedard et al. (2004) and Xie et al. (2003).

Samples for 'fraud firm' were drawn from two main sources. First, the Accounting and Auditing Enforcement Release issued by the SEC and the Wall Street Journal Index caption of 'crime – white collar crime' for the years between 1980 and 1991. This population provided 75 usable sets of data for fraud firms. This was matched with data from no fraud firms. Matching was performed in terms of characteristics such as size, industry, national stock exchange and time periods to allow comparisons between 'fraud and no fraud' firms to be made.

The research design involved the use of logit cross-sectional regression analysis. This was justified on the basis that the dependent variable is dichotomous and also because bias in the constant terms will not adversely affect the analyses and findings of the study especially when it is not meant to be a predictive model of fraud. A dummy variable was included in the logit regression to control for the presence of an Audit Committee and a further interactive variable was added to account for the bias that the inclusion of outside non-executive directors on the Audit Committee can have on Board composition.

Beasley (1996) concluded that the presence of the Audit Committee has no significant effect on the likelihood of financial statement fraud and that the interaction of the Audit Committee with Board composition does not impact on the likelihood of financial statement fraud. Furthermore, Beasley (1996) suggested that the Board composition rather than the Audit Committee is more likely to constrain fraud in organizations, this finding being similar to that of Peasnell et al. (2004) who found that the Board rather than the Audit Committee are effective in constraining abnormal earnings.

Collier and Gregory (1999) examined the relationship between Audit Committee activity and agency costs. Their research was a follow on from Collier (1993) and attempted to replicate Menon and Williams (1994), a US study, in the UK. On this basis they tested similar hypotheses as in Menon and Williams (1994) and explained to what extent Audit Committees' activities are influenced by agency variables such as leverage and firm size as well as other variables such as directors' shareholdings, proportion of outsiders' holdings and their representation on the Board, the degree of dominance of the chief executive (that is, whether the roles of the chief executive and chair of the Board are combined in one director) and the extent of shareholder diversity.

Their study was mainly quantitative with eight hypotheses tested using a sample of major UK companies listed on the London Stock Exchange. Their original sample consisted of the top 250 of the Times 1000 for 1989–1990. They eliminated companies which were not UK based and not listed on the London Stock Exchange and, of the remaining 167 companies; they received 142 usable replies giving a response rate of 85 per cent. Out of the usable 142 replies, 89 companies had an Audit Committee but one of them did not have the required accounting information, thus leaving a sample of 88 companies. Ordinary Least Squares, Poisson Regression and Heckman (1979) two-stage procedures were quantitatively used in the research. Collier and Gregory (1999) found a positive relationship between high-quality auditors (now Big 4), leverage and Audit Committee activity. Audit Committee activity was found to be inversely related to director duality and the presence of a dominant chief executive. Audit Committee activities were reduced in companies where the position of the chief executive and chairman of the Board are combined and firms with dominant chief executives constrained Audit Committee activity.

Song and Windram (2005) conducted a UK study on Audit Committee effectiveness. It examined the effectiveness of UK Audit Committees in their financial reporting oversight functions. Comparing 27 companies that have been subjected to a Financial Reporting Review Panel Investigation with a control sample that have not over the period 1991–2000, Song and Windram (2005) used a binary logit regression model analysis similar to Archambeault and DeZoort (2001) and found that independence rather than size of the Board enhances Audit Committee independence in their financial reporting oversight functions. Directors' share ownership and multiple directorships were found to undermine Audit Committee effectiveness. Although weakly associated, they found that director financial literacy and frequency of Audit Committee meetings contribute to Audit Committee effectiveness.

They defended the choice of their small sample size by citing evidence from Mehran et al. (1998), Maddala (1991) and Stone and Rasp (1991) and suggesting that the sample size is limited by the information provided by the FRRP on companies that have violated reporting practices. Although the study acknowledged that the period under review coincides with the production of a number of Corporate Governance guidelines, the impact of these was not taken into consideration in the design of the study.

Gendron and Bedard (2006), like Spira (2002), used qualitative research methods to study Audit Committee activity. Their aim was to find out how participants in Audit Committees in three Canadian listed companies gave meaning to their performance, how they internally developed and sustained a sense of effectiveness in their activities as members of a small group. They used a social constructivist approach to achieve this objective and concluded that attendees' reflective acts upon processes and activities surrounding Audit Committee meetings play a key role in configuring meanings of effectiveness.

The limitation of this study in the context of this review is its stated objectives. Gendron and Bedard (2006) pointed out that they were not interested in 'trying to objectively' assess whether the Audit Committees under study were indeed effective or in identifying factors that are positively linked to effectiveness. Instead they wanted to understand better the process by which meanings of effectiveness are internally developed and sustained within the small group of people who attended the Audit Committee meeting.

Turley and Zaman (2007) studied Audit Committee effectiveness from the perspectives of formal and informal processes, and power interplays within an organizational and institutional context. This study is novel in its approach and contributions. It used a case study of a UK public company to study the role of informal process and impact of power in enhancing Corporate Governance outcomes. It showed that Audit Committee activity and effectiveness need to be understood beyond the constructs of the quantitative measures, which often neglect the potency of the informal interaction within organization. These informal interactions (informal communication outside the organizational dictates) among key actors (including Audit Committee chair, financial reporting and internal audit functionaries, and the external auditor) in the corporate environments were found to enhance Corporate Governance outcomes more than formal processes (that is, as required by the governance codes in terms of disclosures and compliance with the broader requirements of such codes).

Three sources were identified for data collection. They conducted semi-structured interviews with relevant personnel affected by Audit Committee activities (such as the main Board members, external auditors, internal audit and financial reporting functionaries within the organization), internal documents, and publicly available information of the company were also used as sources of data for their analysis. In terms of the formal process, they found that the Audit Committee in their case study had limited impact on matters of internal audit and control, financial reporting and external audit. The Audit Committee was not proactive, and was very much a receiving and responding body.

Three episodes were narrated to show the impacts of the Audit Committee and how it influenced Corporate Governance outcomes through the informal processes. The first relates to contest over the allocation of resources within the organization, the second episode had to do with the discovery by the internal audit of reporting irregularities in the reports prepared by the Group finance director and lastly, a discovery by the internal audit of the misappropriation of the company assets by the a senior executive. Key participants involved in these episodes explored the informal communication channel through the Audit Committee to resolve these issues. Overall, Turley and Zaman (2007) suggested that the informal interaction and communication are important elements in the jigsaw towards understanding Audit Committee effectiveness. They suggested that the Audit Committee can be used as a threat, ally and an arbiter in resolving conflicts within an organization.

Although this study is novel in its approach and in highlighting the importance of informal processes and communication, as well as the role of power in enhancing governance outcomes in an organization, it is important to have a number of follow-up studies with more cases. This will enable a comparison of outcomes thereby influencing policy directions and improving our understanding of the factors that affect Audit Committee operations and outcomes as an important Corporate Governance mechanism. It may be difficult to appreciate fully the role of formal, informal and power in enhancing Corporate Governance outcomes on the basis of a single case study.

Effectiveness is a vague and difficult term to operationalize in both qualitative and quantitative research. Studies that have purported to study Audit Committee effectiveness have ended up studying factors that contribute to the effectiveness or performance of Audit Committees with respect to a particular function such as reporting quality. The construction of effectiveness has also been attempted qualitatively in terms of how members of the committee make meaning of their effectiveness with little success. This is not unconnected with the sensitivity involved in the issues addressed by the Audit Committee and therefore the reluctance of members of the committee to grant access for the purpose of qualitative research. The best that has been done remains a measure of factors that may account for effectiveness or at best a partial measure of effectiveness in the context of a particular function. It seems the practical first step to disentangle a measure of effectiveness and particularly the effectiveness of the Audit Committee is to determine what factors actually influence its effectiveness. This can be best achieved through a qualitative research approach but is nearly impossible to operationalize due to access and sensitivity concerns rightly or wrongly attached to the issue. Table 3.1 presents some key results from prior studies

Auditor Independence

Auditor independence is a topic of important concern to many stakeholders in the corporate environment. Auditors have a statutory duty to report on the truth and fairness of the stewardship report prepared by the management to the owners of the business. Further, stakeholders such as investors,

Table 3.1 Some key results from prior studies on determinants of Audit Committee activity

Author (s)	Focus	Hypothesized relationships	Findings
Kalbers and Fogarty (1993)	Relationships between Audit Committees (AC) effectiveness and power construct	AC effectiveness is related to six power constructs. AC functions such as financial reporting, external auditing and internal auditing functions are distinct dimensions of AC effectiveness. Each type of AC power is positively associated with each category of AC effectiveness. Organizational type of power is less directly related to types of AC effectiveness than power types	**Linear Structural relationship (LISTREL):** Found that the relationship between power dimension and effectiveness dimensions are complex. Formal, written authority and observable supports from top management play the most important roles in AC power and its effectiveness
Collier and Gregory (1996)	Audit committee effectiveness and fees	Effectiveness construed from the functional forms e.g. audit quality and internal control. Relationship between firm size-related audit fees and presence or absence of AC, relationship between complexity-related audit fees and presence or absence of AC and relationship between risk-related audit fees and AC	**Multivariate analysis:** Positive relationship between size-related audit fees and AC. But relationship between complexity and risk-related audit fees and AC are ambiguous and inconclusive
Collier and Gregory (1999)	Audit committee activity and agency costs	Relationship between AC activity and agency costs variables such as leverage, firm size, ownership, degree of executive dominance and shareholders diversity	**Multivariate analysis, Poisson regression, and Heckman model:** Found positive relationship between high-quality auditors, leverage and AC activity. AC activity is inversely related to directors duality and presence of dominant chief executive
Deli and Gillian (2000)	Factors associated with ACs' independence, compositions and importance	Independent and active AC is associated with firm's growth potentials, size, Managerial Ownership and firm leverage	**Multivariate analyses:** AC independence is negatively related to firm's growth potential and management share ownership but positively related to firm size and leverage
Klein (2002)	Effects of AC and Board characteristics on firms' earnings management	Independent AC is associated with lower incidents of earnings management proxy by abnormal accruals	**Multivariate analysis:** Earnings management is negatively related to AC independence

Table 3.1 Some key results from prior studies on determinants of Audit Committee activity *concluded*

Author (s)	Focus	Hypothesized relationships	Findings
Abbott et al. (2003a)	Effects of AC characteristics on improving AC effectiveness and impact on financial restatements	Using AC independence to proxy for its diligence, examined the effects of some AC characteristics on financial statements restatements	**Match sample and regression analyses:** Significant negative relationship between AC with experts and incidence of financial restatements also negative relationship between meeting frequency and financial restatements
Abbott et al. (2003b)	Relationships between AC characteristics and audit and non-audit fees	Do AC characteristics' impact on fees paid to the auditors?	**Multivariate analysis:** ACs that are more independent and diligence tend to have lower non-audit fees ratios to audit fees
Turley and Zaman (2007)	AC effectiveness from the formal and informal processes and power interplay within organizational and institutional context		**Case study:** Found that informal processes and structures enhance the Corporate Governance outcomes more than the formal process and structures. Also that AC undertakes important power functions within the organizational and institutional contexts in which they operate
Mangena and Tauringana (2008)	AC characteristics and external auditors involvement in interim reporting	Examined the effects of AC shareholding, expertise and size on external auditors involvements in interim reporting	**Logistic regression:** Positive relationship between the likelihood of external auditor involvement in interim reporting and AC expertise, negative relationship between the likelihood of external auditor involvement in interim reporting and AC shareholdings

financial institutions (including money and capital markets), governments and employees are often guided in many ways by the reports provided by the management in respect of the firm's financial position as certified by the auditor. Auditor independence is fundamental to public confidence in the reporting and auditing process as well as the reliability of the auditors' report. Audit reports add value to the financial statements provided by the

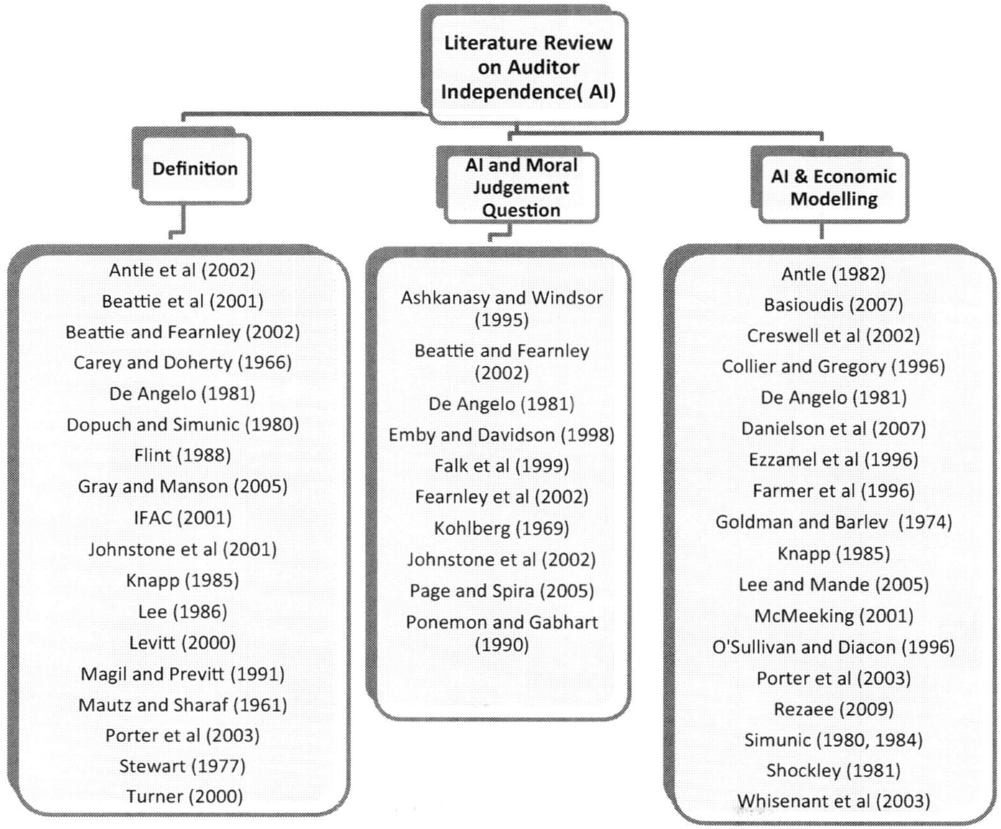

Figure 3.3 Key Literatures on Auditor Independence

management to shareholders since they provide independent verification of what has been reported (Johnstone et al., 2001) but they also reduce the cost of informational exchange for both sides (Dopuch and Simunic, 1980) and also benefit the management in providing a signalling mechanism to the market that the information so provided is reliable.

However, recent corporate fiascos, including those of early 2001–2003 and the recent crises triggered by the subprime market in the US, have heightened worries about threats to auditor independence and how best to safeguard it. It is difficult to give a definition of auditor independence that is generally accepted and all encompassing (Gray and Manson, 2005); however two suggested definitions are now presented.

Auditor independence has been defined as the conditional probability of reporting a discovered breach (DeAngelo, 1981). The International Federation of Accountants (IFAC) differentiates between independence of mind and independence in appearance. It defines independence of mind as the state of mind that permits the provision of an opinion without being affected by influences that compromise professional judgement allowing an individual to act with integrity, exercise objectivity and professional scepticism. Independence in appearance is defined by IFAC as 'the avoidance of facts and circumstances that are so significant that a reasonable and informed third party, having knowledge of all relevant information would reasonably conclude that a firm's or a member of the assurance team's integrity, objectivity or professional scepticism had been compromised' (IFAC, 2001). Knapp (1985) suggested that auditor independence is the ability to withstand client pressure while Magill and Previts (1991) concluded that independence is a function of character with integrity and trustworthiness being the key.

Furthermore, Carey and Doherty (1966) interpreted auditor independence in three ways: firstly in the sense of not being subordinate, secondly in the sense of avoidance of any situation which may even subconsciously impair the auditors' objectivity and lastly in the sense of avoidance of any relationship which to a reasonable observer may suggest a conflict of interest. Other words that have been used to describe auditor independence include 'completely objective', 'unprejudiced by previous involvement in the subject of audit', 'uncompromised by vested interest in the outcome or its consequences' and 'unbiased and uninfluenced by considerations extraneous to the matter at issue' (Flint, 1988).

Mautz and Sharaf (1961) distinguished between practitioner independence and professional independence. Practitioner independence refers to a state of mind and deals with issues that may affect or influence auditors' disinterestedness. They observed that practitioner independence may be evident in three major ways, namely: programming (where auditors have freedom to develop their own audit programme without undue influence from the client), investigative (this suggests that the auditor has unlimited access to relevant information for the purposes of the audit) and reporting independence (where the content of the report is related to the scope of the examination undertaken). They further suggested that professional independence has to do with the independence of the profession itself. The profession must have an aura surrounding it and in the way its representatives project and conduct themselves.

Although issues of auditor independence have been the subject of discussion for a very long time (and as early as 1900 according to Page and Spira, 2005), they have enjoyed varying degrees of attention depending on events in the global economy and the occasional spotlight due probably to events in which the auditors are expected to play a significant part or are found to have 'underperformed' (for example, the global economic downturn in the 1920s, the corporate collapses of the late 1980s and early 1990s and, more recently, the collapse of energy giant ENRON, the debacles of mortgage lenders, Northern Rock in the UK and similar happenings in the US with Fannie Mae and Freddie Mac).

Until the early 1990s the issue of auditor independence did not receive the kind of attention it has enjoyed recently. However, in 1991, with the establishment of the Financial Reporting Review Panel (FRRP) in the UK, the standard regulating bodies and the cooperation of the audit professional bodies, pronouncements on potential threats to independence and safeguards were released and these seem to have engendered a stream of discussions on the issues surrounding auditor independence. The difficulties in having a good grasp of the issues relating to auditor independence lie in the abstractness of the concept of independence (Gray and Manson, 2005). It seems that independence is largely a function of whether there is a dispute between the auditor and the client on the treatment of audit reporting issues or in the event of a fraud or financial misstatements (Beattie et al., 2001). Other than these, it will seem difficult to make assertions about auditor independence either in appearance or in fact. This is also compounded due to the problem that there is no formal theory of auditor independence (Johnstone et al., 2001; Beattie and Fearnley, 2002) leaving researchers and academics to rove around the ambiguity ingrained in the conception and framing of ideas about what constitutes auditor independence. This ambiguity has been eloquently described by Page and Spira (2005) in their analyses of the persistence of ambiguity in the framing of the concept of auditor independence. In their opinion this ambiguity allows room for manoeuvring and enhances the creation of further ambiguities.

However, various regulatory frameworks and professional body pronouncements seem to present possible situations that may constitute threats to independence and suggest safeguards which are to be observed to mitigate the risk to independence both in appearance and in fact. For instance, the UK regulatory framework on auditing (according to the Guide to Professional Ethics Statement (GPES) 1) identifies the following threats to auditor independence: auditor self-review, self-interest, advocacy, familiarity, intimidation and suggested safeguards which have been classified as those created by the profession (the practice environment), those created by legislation or regulations (regulatory safeguards and sanctions) and those involving third parties (client's Audit Committee, regulatory bodies or another firm).

In addition to the regulatory approach, academics have continued to devote attention to the issues of auditor independence especially against the background of corporate collapse and the reputational loss suffered by auditors. The adverse effects of these misbehaviours on the auditing profession cannot be overemphasized. If fund providers are to continue to invest in the capital market which is essential for the flow of production and generation of further wealth there is the urgent need for greater efficiency and transparency in the governance system in corporations. Investors need formidable protection for their funds. They need to be assured that the gatekeepers in the corporate palace are not careless in keeping a watch over the stewardship of management. Auditors need to be able to discharge their professional duties in an atmosphere that radiates confidence and guarantees their independence and objectivity. Failure to apply the necessary diligence and safeguards can end up with the total collapse of the audit firm as happened with Arthur Andersen over ENRON

The importance of the auditors' responsibilities can be appreciated in the context of providing essential certification in all situations where conflicts of interest potentially exist. Auditors act as intermediaries between the management of an enterprise and all those interested in the entity (Porter et al., 2003). Lee (1986) referred to the 'remoteness gap' to argue the need for an audit and indeed an independent auditor. He pointed out that where stakeholders are dispersed and are unable to observe their agent, in this case the management, it becomes imperative that the appointed auditor takes their place and asserts the authority granted to them to obtain necessary information to meet the requirements of the stakeholders.

Thus the importance of the auditor and the auditing profession in ensuring the smooth running of the market system and sustaining the confidence in it cannot be overemphasized and their independence is crucial to these roles. Auditors used to face a precarious situation in that the consequences of qualifying a report may include the termination of their engagement since their appointment and remuneration was largely decided by the management on whom they report. This has now changed, since the recommendation for their appointment and a host of other issues relating to the auditors are now effectively within the remit of the Audit Committee. This includes the scope of their audit, an assessment of their independence and an alternative communication channel (Combined Code, 2003). It is intuitive to expect that this will free the auditor from the fear of intimidation by the management, by reducing their dependence on their decision in terms of their appointment and remuneration, improve corporate communication, enhance audit quality and transparent reporting.

This recommendation has now been adopted by many other market regulators including those in the US who now require that the Audit Committee rather than the management should be responsible for the selection, appointment and review of the activities of the external auditors (SOX, 2002; Combined Code, 2003). A similar provision is true in the case of the UK where the Audit Committee recommends the appointment of the external auditor but the actual appointment is made by the shareholders voting in the general meeting. The Audit Committees effectively decides the scope of the audit, evaluates the independence of the external auditor and pre-determines the scope of non-auditing services to be bought from the auditors.

Auditor Independence: A Moral Judgement Question

Independence is a state of mind and, to the extent that it is a personal phenomenon, it is capable of being influenced by each individual's personality, moral and ethical dispositions (Page and Spira, 2005; Falk et al., 1999). However, in order to provide a framework through which to ensure the observance of a common and minimum acceptable level of professional behaviour, the accounting and regulatory bodies have provided a code of ethics and professional conduct. This is designed to regulate the profession and ensure that members conduct themselves in a professional manner that signals independence, objectivity and integrity (Auditing Practices Board, 1995). A number of studies have also established links between auditor independence and their level of moral cognition and some of these studies are now reviewed in this section.

Ponemon and Gabhart (1990) in their three stages of moral development model (based largely on the work by Kohlberg (1969) who identified three ethical cognition levels – pre-conventional, conventional and post-conventional) used this ethical categorization to examine the auditor's implicit reasoning in the resolution of hypothetical independence conflicts (Beattie and Fearnley, 2002). The pre-conventional stage refers to situations in which the individual places self-interest well above the common interest of society and is sensitive to penalty attributes. The conventional stage refers to the stage in which the individual conforms to the rules of society and is sensitive to affiliation attributes while the post-conventional stage refers to the situation in which the individual forms a judgement conforming to ethical principles and not to society's rules. They found that a systematic relationship exists between auditors' ethical cognition and resolution of independence conflict situations. Independent judgement was also found to be very sensitive to factors relating to penalties and less sensitive to affiliation factors. Auditors' moral cognition was also found to impact on the way they rank factors affecting their independence.

Windsor and Ashkanasy (1995) extended previous studies examining the impact of the theory of developmental stages of moral reasoning on auditors' moral judgements. Their study was unique in that it incorporated economic (clients' financial health and probability of tendering) and auditors' moral belief in a just world as part of the set of variables that affect their independence judgement. They identified three styles of auditor decision making (Beattie and Fearnley, 2002):

- Autonomous – this is where auditors are responsive to personal beliefs and are more likely to resist client management power.
- Accommodating – these are auditors who responded to both personal belief and client management power and who are least resistant to client management pressure.

- Pragmatic – these are auditors who are responsive to client management power irrespective of belief.

These three styles correspond to auditors with high, medium and low levels of moral reasoning respectively.

Falk et al. (1999) undertook an experimental study on auditor independence, self-interested behaviour and ethics. They studied auditors' decisions on whether to preserve or compromise independence in client–auditor dispute scenarios. The research also underscores the role of belief and economic incentives in auditors' decision-making processes. These are all reflected in their three research hypotheses which were:

- while maintaining or violating auditor independence is costless, the external auditor is more likely to maintain auditor independence;
- as the difference between the expected cost of issuing a qualified report and the expected cost of issuing an unqualified report rises, the frequency with which auditor independence is violated rises;
- the frequency with which auditor independence is preserved is greater for subjects with higher Defining Issue Test (DIT) scores than for subjects with lower DIT scores. DIT was developed by Rest (1979) as a tool for assessing a subject's moral development.

They found that increases in the probabilities of losing a client by disagreeing with their decision increases the frequency of independence violations irrespective of the monitoring on the individual auditor's behaviour. They also reported a moderating effect of monitoring and penalties on the frequency of violations of independence when the probability of losing a client is small, but the frequency of violation is not reduced when the probability of the loss of a client is high. And, finally, they found that subjects with low moral development scores violate independence more frequently than those who have higher scores. This study did not specify the type of disagreement and on what accounting and auditing issues the disagreement arose. It also failed to indicate whether there are specific regulations on the source of the dispute between auditor and management.

Emby and Davidson (1997) examined the effect of variations in engagement factors on auditor independence in Canadian companies. Factors such as the contractual arrangements, terms of audit engagements, conditions and the nature of services provided were manipulated in an auditor–client dispute scenario over an audit reporting issue. The paper hypothesized that a balance of power between the auditor and their client determines the extent of auditor independence.

They used a 2^4 between-subjects ANOVA approach to test five hypotheses:

- that auditors act as if they have relatively less power in conflict situations with their audit clients when clients have the ability to terminate the relationship;
- that auditors act as if they have relatively less power in conflict situations with their audit clients when clients have the ability to determine the audit fee;
- that auditors act as if they have relatively less power in conflict situations with their audit clients when clients have the ability to determine engagement working conditions;
- that auditors act as if they have relatively more power in conflict situations with their audit clients when the range of non-audit services services they provide to an audit client includes specialized services that are not easily available elsewhere; and
- that large audit firms act as if they have relatively more power in conflict situations with their audit clients compared to smaller audit firms.

They developed a hypothetical conflict situation between an auditor and their client on the treatment of a contingent liability. Variables in the case were manipulated at two levels with each subject receiving only one version of the case. A total of 140 cases were distributed, 92 usable responses were received giving a response rate of 66 per cent.

Emby and Davidson (1997) concluded that an auditor's power to insist on a judgement (disclosure of contingent liability) is reduced when a client's economic power is high. However, auditors that provide more specialised services to their audit clients are more able to insist on a judgement (disclosure of contingent liability) but they failed to document any relationship between the size of the client and their influence on an auditor's judgment. Their study has implications for the debate on whether the provision of non-audit services to audit clients impairs auditors' independence and also that communications between auditors and their clients in a conflict situation require a moderating mechanism in such a way that the shareholders are eventually adequately protected.

Johnstone et al. (2000) studied the antecedents and consequences of independence risk. Their study suggested a broad and complete view of the threats to independence and concluded that an independence risk framework that identifies and understands the relationships between the various incentives and situational factors that determine the actual and perceived audit quality should enhance the discovery of more potent mitigating factors to actual and perceived risks to independence. They suggested the following mitigating factors to independent risks:

- Corporate Governance mechanism;
- regulatory oversight;
- auditing firm policies (on achieving independence, for example, partner reviews, peer reviews and so on);
- auditing firm culture; and
- individual auditor characteristics.

Fearnley et al. (2002) examined the role of the FRRP in enhancing auditor independence and improving attitudes to compliance among UK listed companies. Their study underscored the importance of an effective regulatory framework with the ability to demand compliance and sanction non-compliance.

Though the remit of the FRRP is with the directors of listed companies and not the auditors, auditors have huge incentives to avoid such enquiries. The economic and social cost of such actions may be disastrous to the auditor. The auditor–client relationship may be adversely affected, leading to the loss of the client and other clients and, as the information about the action spreads, this may raise a reputational crisis and questions of competence and independence. Furthermore, auditors risk being investigated by their professional body causing personal embarrassment and threatening their professional careers. All these costs are better avoided by the auditor, especially auditors at the conventional and post-conventional stages of individual cognitive moral development.

Fearnley et al.'s (2002) qualitative study used semi-structured interviews and publicly available information on the FRRP's impact on audit firms. The financial directors and auditors of listed companies who had been investigated by the FRRP were interviewed. They made personal approaches to all potential interviewees from a population of 18 companies whose accounts had been criticized by the FRRP in the press. Five directors refused the interview and two dropped out later. Fearnley et al. (2002) thus interviewed representatives of 11 UK listed companies and four audit firm partners. The study highlights the importance of reputation to the auditing profession and to the individual auditor. The single most important drawback of the study is the small sample size and the inability to generalize its findings and the possibility that respondents are just following a line rather than giving their true thoughts.

Auditor Independence and Economic Modelling

An approach to studying auditor independence involves economic modelling of its implications and this requires decisions on the factors that may affect auditors' judgement in economic terms. It also touches on the modelling of the determinants of audit and non-audit pricing and the decisions by companies to buy their audit and non-audit services from the same audit firm and the rationale for these decisions. Model specification issues, including whether to endogenously model the relationship between audit and non-audit fees or to use single equation models and their implications have relevance here. It is important to note that the majority of studies modelling auditor independence in economic terms are from the US and are positivist in orientation.

DeAngelo (1981) argued that the level of economic bonding between the auditor and the auditee has a tendency to impact on auditors' independence. To the extent that auditors earn client-specific rent, he posited that auditors' independence is determined in terms of the joint probability that the auditor will discover (competence) and report a mis-statement (objectivity and independence). DeAngelo (1981) provided a multi-period analysis of the economic relationship between the auditor and the auditee, arguing that auditors are exposed to two main risks in situations where they earn significant client-specific rent and that there is a certain pressure to compromise independence in order to maintain the continuity of that rent. Firstly, auditors are under threat of losing a premium client if they fail to compromise independence as such a client may use the threat of switching to another audit firm in a very competitive and concentrated audit market. Secondly, where the auditor decides to compromise independence and the probability of being caught is high, auditors are at risk of losing all other client-specific rents due to the market's reaction. This happened in the case of Arthur Andersen when the problems at ENRON were discovered and eventually led to its collapse. This is because all other current and potential clients may now see the auditor as a reputational risk to their organization). Thus auditors may be inclined to consider independence on the basis of cost vs. benefit analyses depending upon which moral cognition level they fall into. These situations show that economic bonding imposes some limitations on auditor independence.

In a similar study, Antle (1982) reported a single period economic model that examines the auditor's behaviour in the presence of economic bonding with the client. Antle (1982) suggested that where management exhibit the tendency to misrepresent information in order to take advantage of the shareholders, the auditors have a tendency to be drawn in if the probability of being caught is considered to be remote and also where the auditor considers that the economic benefit of compromising independence outweighs the consequences of being caught. In such situations the auditor will have no incentive to either discover or report misstatements. On the other hand, Goldman and Barlev (1974), in the context of auditors providing non-audit services to their audit clients, had suggested that increasing economic bonding between the audit firm and the auditee may act to improve auditor independence as it may mean that the audit firm is becoming indispensable to the organization, so this reduces the possibility or the credibility of a switch threat.

Auditor Independence vs. Audit and Non-Audit Services

An area of auditor independence that has enjoyed much focus since the collapse of ENRON has been the debate about auditors providing non-audit services to their audit clients. Findings are inconclusive (Shockley, 1981; Knapp, 1985; Farmer et al., 1987; Craswell et al., 2002; Beattie and Fearnley, 2002). It has been suggested that such a practice may adversely affect the appearance of the independence of the auditor and may give rise to a situation where the auditors are auditing their own work (DeAngelo, 1981; Antle, 1982). Furthermore, it has been argued that auditors may become more financially dependent on their clients and that financial considerations may prevail and inhibit auditors' professional judgement. For instance, Arthur Andersen was reported to have earned $25 million in audit fees from ENRON while non-audit services brought in over $27 million from the same company in the same accounting period.

Supporters of the idea that auditors can provide NAS to their auditing client fail to see any real moral or professional threat to auditor independence. They argue that providing non-audit services to audit clients allows some economic benefits especially when knowledge of the business gained during the audit can be transferred in delivering efficient non-audit services and vice versa (Porter et al., 2003: 79; Simunic, 1984) This knowledge transfer may promote a more efficient utilization of resources and improve reporting quality from the auditors' perspectives. Whilst it may be appealing to suggest that provision of non-audit services may create a perception of dependence and thereby impair auditor independence especially in terms of self-interest, self-review and familiarity threats (Porter et al., 2003: 80), it is very important to note that perceptions are not reality and may not translate into actions (Beattie and Fearnley, 2002: 62). Perception of dependence is not the same as actual dependence.

However, the issues remain in the balance between academics and professionals. Although Beattie and Fernley (2002) concluded that there is very little clear support for the view that joint provision of audit and non-audit servicesimpairs independence they agreed that joint provision adversely affects the perception of independence. Many recent Corporate Governance pronouncements appear to tacitly support the idea that auditors should not provide non-audit services to their audit clients and this is evident in the Sarbanes Oxley Act (SOX) (2002) and the Combined Code (2003). This point is also emphasized by the requirements for the establishment of the Audit Committee in listed companies, regulating the provision of auditing and non-auditing services.

The regulatory framework in the UK in respect of auditors providing non-audit services to their audit clients requires that listed companies should disclose in their annual report the value of non-audit services bought in the period from their auditor (Beattie and Fearnley, 2002). This requirement has been in place even before the Cadbury Committee reported in 1992. It also restricts the non-audit services that can be provided by the auditor and institutes appropriate safeguards without compromising auditor independence. Furthermore, the Audit Committee is to pre-approve such services and the value of non-audit services that can be bought. Where the anticipated value of services is higher than the pre-determined level any changes must be approved by the Audit Committee. In addition, the EC Directive on auditors (2002) requires that non-audit services provided should be analyzed into their respective components, for example, assurance, tax, advisory and so on. Following on from the aforementioned, two strands of research into auditor independence are now considered. First, studies that have attempted to model determinants of audit and non-audit fees and, secondly, research that have established a relationship between audit and non-audit fees.

Determinants of Audit and Non-Audit Fees

The primary work in studying the determinants of audit and non-audit fees was conducted by Simunic (1980). This study compared audit fees and their determinants when they were bought alone and their determinants when they were bought along with non-audit services. Simunic (1980) found that audit fees are higher when both sets of services are bought from the same auditor compared to when they are not. He also found that the audit fee is a function of the auditee size, complexity, risk and relative elasticity of demand for both audit and non-audit services.

Collier and Gregory (1996) examined the relationship between Audit Committee effectiveness and auditors' fee and also found that auditors' fee is a function of auditee risk, complexity and size. Size was proxied by total sales, number of employees and total assets. Complexity was measured using the number of subsidiaries, the proportion of foreign subsidiaries to total subsidiaries and risk was measured using audit report qualifications, stock, debtors and their relationship to sales. Positive relationships were observed between size, complexity and audit fees. They also found some relationship between factors determining audit fee and the presence of Audit Committees. Specifically, they found that the audit fee associated with the client's risk and complexity tends to fall with the presence of Audit Committees although this finding is not significant at the 5 per cent though it is significant at the 10 per cent level.

Craswell et al. (2002) studied the relationship between auditor independence and fee dependence. Auditor independence was measured as the propensity of auditors to issue a qualified audit opinion which was represented by the ratio of audit fee to total national fee of the audit firm. They used both univariate and multivariate logit regressions with the square root of the number of subsidiaries to represent complexity, the natural log of total client assets as a measure of size and the ratio of current assets to total assets as a measure of complexity. They also controlled for auditor type and industry. Essentially, they reported that the level of economic dependence between the auditor and their client does not affect auditor propensity to issue a qualified audit opinion. They argued that their result showed that in a setting where public disclosure of audit and non-audit fees is mandatory, auditors appear willing to issue-qualified opinions irrespective of the economic importance of the client to the auditor.

Basioudis (2007), in the context of audit pricing, specifically explored the impact of audit firm alumni on audit fees in UK listed companies. This study is set against a background in which one in six directors of UK listed companies is a chartered accountant and in full knowledge of the fact that the big audit firms maintain a strong interaction and links with their former employees through social events and maintaining contacts through alumni directories which enables them to keep track of their progress and subsequent employment after leaving the audit firm. The study argued that audit firms exploit this alumni influence in gaining an insight into the boardroom of a client or a potential client. This type of insight becomes very important in making engagement acceptance and continuation decisions in the context of the auditor's engagement risk. Three hypotheses were tested which were stated to be:

- clients who take on alumni of the incumbent auditor as executive directors will pay lower audit fees than clients that do not employ such alumni;

- audit clients will not pay lower or higher audit fees when an alumnus of the incumbent auditor sits on the Board of directors as a non-executive; and

- audit clients will pay lower audit fees when an alumnus of the incumbent auditor sits on the client Board of directors as the chair, chief executive or finance director.

The sample comprised of all executives and non-executives of UK-quoted companies who are simultaneously Institute of Chartered Accountants in England and Wales (ICAEW)-qualified chartered accountants. As was the case with most other single-equation fee models in previous studies, the study used variables to capture size, complexity and auditee risk with additional variables including measures of alumni affiliation and used publicly available data in a multiple regression model to arrive at its findings. The study found that audit fees are significantly influenced by the audit firm's alumni among the executive Board members. Specifically, audit fees are reduced by as much as 21 per cent. In addition, non-executive directors who have qualified as chartered accountants with the incumbent auditor do not influence the level of audit fees in the UK audit market. Further they found a significant negative relationship between audit fees and chairs, chief executives or finance directors who are alumni of the incumbent audit firm. This implies having more audit firms' alumni on the Board results in downward pressures on the audit fees.

One major drawback of this study lies in its tacit approval of auditors maintaining business relationships with their clients on the grounds that the preventative steps instituted by both regulatory bodies and auditing firms should be sufficient as safeguards. Experience with Arthur Andersen has shown that regulatory frameworks either internally within an organization or even those instituted externally by professional bodies can be overridden and this has also been shown by the Credit Crunch where control mechanisms and regulatory frameworks have failed (Windsor and Warming-Rasmussen, 2009; Fraser and Pong, 2009).

Danielsen et al. (2007) in the context of audit pricing considered whether the auditor's insider knowledge of a client's situation is reflected in their pricing of services supplied to those clients. They tested for the effect of knowing each client's unique risk situation on the audit fees charged. Higher audit fees were found to be charged to clients who were considered opaque and consequently were judged to be high risk. To these sets of clients market-based measures of opacity are positively correlated with high fees. The second hypothesis considered the effects of a firm's decision to purchase reputational capital from their auditor and the subsequent effect on their audit fees. Firms will probably do this to signal better transparency and quality reporting since the market associates high audit quality with the Big 4 audit firms.

Audit and Non-Audit Fee Modelling

One other method that researchers have used to study auditors' independence in the context of their economic bonding with the auditee is to examine the determinants of the decision to purchase both audit and non-audit services by the client.

The debates have been firstly on the flow of the relationship between audit and non- audit fees. Do audit fees directly affect non-audit fees or is the relationship the other way round? Are there other factors moderating the relationship between audit and non-audit fees? A line of argument holds that audit firms use audit services as the 'loss leader' which allows them to gain a foothold in the client's organization and then negotiate the provision of non-audit services at higher rates to compensate for the losses incurred on the audit. They suggest that in such a situation an inverse relationship will be expected between audit and non-audit fees (Collier and Gregory, 1996; McMeeking, 2001). However, others argue that the relationship between fees may be explained in terms of auditors' specialization, knowledge spillovers and cost vs. benefit considerations by the client. They maintain that the audit market is highly concentrated (dominated by the big four audit firms) and that high-quality audit firms select themselves into clients rather than using the audit as a loss leader. The proponents of knowledge spillovers argue for a positive relationship between audit and non-audit fees due to economies of scope and cost vs. benefit analysis (Ezzamel et al., 1996; O'Sullivan and Diacon, 1996; Whisenant et al., 2003).

Secondly, there are debates about the most appropriate method through which to capture the relationship between audit and non-audit fees. There are researchers who have modelled the relationship using single equation models where either the audit or non-audit fee has been the dependent variable while the other has been part of the explanatory variable in addition to other variables (Beattie and Fearnley, 2002). However, others have suggested that such models may have been mis-specified due to endogeneity concerns between audit and non-audit fees (Whisenant et al., 2003; Lee and Mande, 2005). They contend that using single equation models in the face of endogeneity makes ordinary least square (OLS) inconsistent and biased. This will affect the results in such a way that the estimates will be spurious and the outcomes of most of the statistical tests will be biased.

They have suggested that audit and non-audit fees are jointly determined and, as a result, a simultaneous model will best capture the nature of the relationships between the two variables. They argued that results from such a model will be consistent and unbiased (Lee and Mande, 2005; Whisenant et al., 2003).

Auditor Independence and Audit Committee

Assumptions about the relationship between the Audit Committee and the external auditor have been made in the Cadbury Report (1992) and subsequent

Corporate Governance reports in the UK. Specifically, the Cadbury Report expected that auditors will be better able to discharge their responsibilities and ensure their independence through the existence of Board-level support from the Audit Committee. The Audit Committee is supposed to be the auditor's first point of contact in addressing concerns over auditing and reporting issues in the organization. The level and areas of envisaged interactions between these two important control mechanisms are many and have grown over time (Rezaee, 2009). Their importance in the smooth functioning of the market system, restoration of confidence in it and protection of the interests of its key players cannot be overemphasized. It has been proposed that the existence of the Audit Committee should bolster the position of the auditor in the area of their appointments.

This and the previous chapter have reviewed the anticipated functions of the Audit Committee and examined its responsibilities with respect to the auditors. Importantly, auditors now have another line of communication with those charged with governance in organizations. Their appointment, determination of the scope of their work and their remuneration are no longer at the mercy of the management on whose reports they are to form an opinion. Auditors now have meetings with those charged with governance in organizations without executive management being present giving them the opportunity to express their concerns far more easily than if those meetings were with management.

This chapter has also highlighted research activity documenting support for the auditors by Audit Committees in cases of disputes between the auditor and management. This has been argued to have a positive impact on auditors' independence. The Audit Committee is also to determine the independence of the external auditors with respect to the audit of the organization. Here, the issues of joint provision of audit and non-audit services are pertinent. In the UK, the Audit Committee is to determine the type and value of non-audit services that may be bought from an incumbent auditor and if the agreed level is to be exceeded it must be approved by the Audit Committee. In theory and for the reasons outlined above, it would appear that the existence and role of the Audit Committee should enhance auditor independence. However, empirically this has not been shown to be the case. The author also reported some of the doubts that have been expressed in the ability of the Audit Committee to discharge the 'mega' responsibilities now envisaged for it by regulators. Table 3.2 below presents results of some key prior studies on Corporate Governance and auditor independence.

Table 3.2 Some key results of prior studies on Corporate Governance and Auditor Independence

Author (s)	Focus	Hypothesized relationships	Findings
Collier and Gregory (1996)	Audit committee effectiveness and fees	Effectiveness construed from the functional forms e.g. audit quality and internal control. Relationship between firm size-related audit fees and presence or absence of AC, relationship between complexity related audit fees and presence or absence of AC and relationship between risk-related audit fees and AC	**Multivariate analysis:** Positive relationship between size-related audit fees and AC. But relationship between complexity and risk-related audit fees and AC are ambiguous and inconclusive
Abbott et al. (2003b)	Relationships between AC characteristics and audit and non-audit fees	Do AC characteristics' impact on fees paid to the Auditors?	**Multivariate analysis:** ACs that are more independent and diligence tend to have lower non-audit fees ratios to audit fees
Whisenant et al. (2003)	Joint determination of audit and non-audit fees	Non-audit fees are not associated with audit fees when joint determinations of fees are controlled for	**Multivariate analysis and simultaneous equation model:** The fees are jointly determined through their explanatory parameters. Positive relationship is found between the fees in a single equation but not when modelled jointly
Lee and Mande (2005)	AC characteristics with endogenously determined audit and non-audit fees	There is no association between Non-audit services purchased from the external auditors and measures of effective AC. There is no association between audit services purchased from the external auditors and measures of effective AC. There is no association between audit services and Non-audit services purchased from the external auditors	**Multivariate analysis and simultaneous equation model:** AC effectiveness is found to be positively related to audit fees. Also an inverse relationship is documented between effective AC and non-audit fees. However, when non-audit fee is modelled endogenously, the relationship between non-audit fees and effective AC fail to exist

Summary of the Literature

The focus of this section of the chapter has been the review of current literature on the three main objectives of the book in the context of discussions on Corporate Governance and its impact on auditors and their independence. The following questions have been focused upon: (1) the determinants of Audit Committee activity and effectiveness; (2) the relationship between the Audit Committee and auditors in respect of their independence; and (3) the debate about the relationship between audit and non-audit fees and their impact on auditors' independence.

The review showed the likely impact of committee independence, Board composition, expertise, ownership structure and precise definition of committee duties in determining the activity of the Audit Committee in the context of enhancing market confidence and in protecting the interests of the shareholders in a situation of separation of ownership from management. However, the results are inconsistent and inconclusive. A large number of these findings are US-based and may not be projected indiscriminately onto the UK situation. Apart from the work of Collier and Gregory (1996, 1999) which attempted to replicate the study by Menon and Williams (1994) in the US and the later work by Spira (2002, 2003) on Audit Committee effectiveness, there are very few UK-based studies that have empirically assessed the determinants of Audit Committee effectiveness using any recent data. Collier and Gregory (1996, 1999) are the closest to this study in terms of their objectives and approach. Spira (2002, 2003) provides the UK insight to the study although the approaches adopted there are different to those chosen in the current study.

The second objective of the review was to appreciate the gaps in the current knowledge stock of the relationship between Audit Committee activity and auditor independence. It showed that apart from Collier and Gregory (1999) there is a dearth of UK-based empirical studies that have directly examined this important relationship. As for effectiveness, the definition of independence was found to be vague, imprecise and ambiguous. This has been documented by Page and Spira (2005). The literature showed that independence is related to ethical and moral judgement and the stage of moral development of the individual auditor. The review also found that experimental studies have enjoyed prominence in testing auditor independence and in assessing the roles of the Audit Committee in this respect. Quantitative studies using questionnaires have not recorded reasonable success, while qualitative studies have been few and far between in examining either Audit Committee activities or their relationship with the auditor in terms of their independence. Only two UK-based studies used interviews with members of Audit Committees – Spira (2003) and Turley and Zaman (2007).

Simunic (1980) and DeAngelo (1981) provided other possibilities for examining auditor independence using economic modelling. This allowed independence in appearance to be captured by proxies such as ratio of audit to non-audit fees and the ratio of audit fee to total fees. Although they may not be a complete and precise measure of independence, these measures do provide an opportunity to measure indirectly the relationship between auditors' independence and Audit Committee activity. Many of the studies testing these relationships are US-based and positivist in orientation. This is not inappropriate but it is important that studies are undertaken in other environments that will provide alternative and richer views on the subject. The continued use of positivist approaches may be consequent upon the difficulty in negotiating access to conduct such qualitative research.

The debates surrounding audit and non-audit fees, their impact on auditor independence and the role of the Audit Committees in this respect have also been examined. The relationships between audit and non-audit fees are inconclusive. While some have found a positive relationship, others have documented negative relationships. Further methodological issues have also been debated. Some have criticized the use of single equation models as inadequate and misrepresenting the nature of the relationship between the fees, suggesting simultaneous equation models instead.

Finally, this review has shown that many areas of concern to the author deserve more attention and that there remain more questions than answers. For instance the researcher needs to identify the real determinants of Audit Committee activity, effectiveness or diligence. There are gaps in our understanding of the relationship between Audit Committee activities and how they actually impact on auditor independence. The debate about the nature of the relationship between audit and non-audit fees and their impact on auditor independence, as well as the role of the Audit Committee in these, needs more clarification and convincing evidence.

In the next chapter, the author explains the theoretical underpinnings of his own empirical investigations.

4

Theory and Corporate Phenomena – Concepts and Frameworks

Introduction

The role of theory in amplifying corporate phenomena and understanding interactions within and between organizations cannot be overemphasized. Theories shape meanings and help analyses of concepts and their implications (Riahi-Belkaoui, 2000). A number of theoretical frameworks have been used in studying the nature of the governance relationship that subsists in the corporate environment. This chapter of the book discusses the various theories that have shaped the meanings of Corporate Governance and that have been used in the book to achieve its objectives. Four main theories have been used to varying degrees in the book and are now discussed below and presented in Figure 4.1.

These are:

- Agency Theory
- Stakeholder Theory
- Stewardship Theory
- Signalling Theory

Figure 4.1 The theoretical framework for Corporate Governance

Agency Theory

This seems to be the dominant theoretical paradigm in the discussion of the firm and its activities, and has been used widely in different aspects of corporate finance and certainly in Corporate Governance studies and analyses (Davis et al., 1997; Dedman, 2004). The theory is rooted in the work of Berle and Means (1932) on the separation of firm ownership from management. It is also often credited to the landmark work of Jensen and Meckling (1976) and Fama and Jensen (1983). They suggested that agency problems will arise in any circumstance where the principal (owners, shareholders) employs the agent (management) to undertake a number of duties on their behalf for a reward. Thus management acting as agent to the Principals owe them a fiduciary duty of care to run the organization in the best interests of the owners for a stipulated reward (Berle and Means, 1932; Jensen and Meckling, 1976; Pratt and Zeckhauser, 1985). However, Jensen and Meckling (1976) argue that conflicts of interest do inevitably exist between the management and owners of businesses in cases where owners are not managers. This is because the theory assumes a model of man (manager) that is self-serving, individualistic and opportunistic in nature, who prefers to maximize his own utility functions at the expense of the owners. As a result, the theory is built on the assumption that there is almost always a divergence of objectives between the goals of the management and those of the shareholders.

Agency problems may also arise due to moral hazards and adverse selections (Meckling and Jensen, 1976; Eisenhardt, 1985). Moral hazard refers to a situation where due to imperfections in the contract between the agent and the principal, management may take sub-optimal decisions and may be opportunistic. An example of such sub-optimal decisions includes investment in assets or projects that give negative net present value (NPV) or consumption of private perquisites rather than investing in a project that will give a positive NPV. While moral hazards tend to happen after the contract, adverse selection may occur both before and after the contract between the principal and the agent. Adverse selection refers to the possibility of shareholders hiring agents who do not have the right type and kind of skills that may enable them to deliver expected returns. This may be due to the existence of information asymmetry between the parties or inherent imperfections in the contracting process (Gomez-Mejia and Wiseman, 2007).

Furthermore, given that shareholders have different risk attitudes compared to management (Jensen and Meckling, 1976), the continuous existence of information asymmetry may impose on the principal the need to institute some forms of controls. These control mechanisms require the allocation of resource and have the tendency to increase the costs of operations, often referred to as the agency cost. Agency problems may exist in a number of instances within the organization. They are known to exist in diversification and investing decisions and in decisions relating to mergers and acquisitions (Lane et al., 1998). This may relate to management's tendencies to prevent suitable offers in furtherance of their own interests at the expense of the shareholders' (Kosnik, 1987; Buchholtz and Ribbens, 1994; Lane et al., 1998). The agency problem is not limited to the relationship between management and shareholders alone, although this seems to have enjoyed the most attention. It may also be exhibited in the relationship between management and debt-holders (Jensen and Meckling, 1976; Myers, 1977; Shleifer and Vishny, 1986; Stulz, 1990). Often the primary concern is how to reduce or minimize the agency cost of operations and thereby increase the returns available for sharing among the residual claimants.

However, in the context of increasing separation of ownership from management, as the ownership base becomes more dispersed, management tend to become less accountable and their activities less observable, at least to the shareholders (Fama, 1980). While management are involved in the operational decision making of businesses, owners are either so numerous that they cannot all be involved in the management of the firm or they do not possess the right type of skills to manage the enterprise successfully (Morck and Steier, 2005). However, management is more closely involved in the business and for a longer time, in terms of daily operations,than the owners and thus has more information about the business than its owners individually. This creates the classic case of information asymmetry (Aboody and Lev, 2000). Differences in the nature and scope of information between the two parties exacerbate the agency problems. For reasons mentioned earlier, shareholders are often at a disadvantage: this gives management an unbridled opportunity to consume perks or take sub-optimal decisions that affect the organization (Murphy and Zimmerman, 1993), conflicting with shareholders' wealth maximization objectives.

A number of mechanisms have been devised to reduce conflicts of interest and their impacts on organizations. These include incorporating in the contract between the contracting parties as many clauses as possible that simulate possible scenarios and attempt to provide for them in the contract. Other methods of control include incentivising the management and linking management compensation to performance, reducing the free cash flow available within the organization through debt financing which reduces the possibilities of consumption of perquisites. Also increasing management's stake in the equity of the company has been suggested. Jensen and Meckling (1976) have argued that increasing managements' share ownership should bring their interests more closely in line with those of other shareholders. However, the risks of management entrenchments have also been identified (Lane et al., 1998; Shleifer and Vishny, 1989). This refers to a situation where management's share ownership is so substantial that they can wield significant power and hence influence the composition of the Board of directors. This may facilitate management shirking and excessive consumption of perks.

Agency Theory is very important in the context of a broader discussion of Corporate Governance and in the formulation of governance mechanisms and policies. Governance structures in the 'Anglo–American countries' favour the agency model of governance. This explains why shareholders' value maximization objective seems to be the overriding aim of firms in these economies and this is aptly reflected in the monitoring devices. For instance, since the composition of the Board of directors is aimed at protecting the interest of the shareholders, it does not generally tolerate the representation of other stakeholders on the Board. This is not the case in other governance models such as the Japanese and German models, where other stakeholders' interests are represented on the Board and their representatives take active part in the Board proceedings. In Germany, such representation is provided for by law. Basically, the existence of a number of committees such as the Audit Committee, the Remuneration Committee and the Nomination Committee, among others, aims to ensure firm continuity and the protection of firm values (Vafeas, 1999) for which equity holders are the residual claimants.

In the context of this book , Agency Theory plays a fundamental role in the design and execution of the investigation. The book adopts the main variant of Agency Theory (Jensen and Meckling, 1976). This relates to agency problems in a 'modern' firm where the shareholders are separate from the management and where the equity base is dispersed, unlike the alternative variant that examines agency problems in family-owned enterprises (Tosi et al., 2000). Agency Theory provides the main theoretical underpinning of the book and determines to a great extent the approach used in the book. It influences the formulation of the study hypotheses, informs the research methodology and statistical techniques used in the book. Popular agency cost variables relevant to the study will now be examined. Relationships between variables are explained first in the context of Agency Theory and then other theories.

Stakeholder Theory

One of the criticisms of Agency Theory is that it provides a short-term perspective and explanation of the purpose of the firm (Freeman, 1984; Freeman, Wick and Parmar, 2004). Also, critics argue that its scope is narrow, since it projects the activities of the firm from the perspective of the shareholders only. An alternative proposition known as the Stakeholder Theory suggests that a firm's activities should be projected on longer and broader perspectives (Freeman, 1984). The theory posits that the essence of corporate activity is not only for the benefit of the shareholders, but also for the benefit of all relevant stakeholders (including the shareholders) and it is all these relevant stakeholders who should be the main remit of the 'modern' firm (Freeman, 1984; Cadbury, 1992, Jensen, 2001). It argues that firms should be managed in such a way that they coordinate the diverging interests of their numerous stakeholders including employees, shareholders, customers, suppliers, the government and society in general. This consideration should thus impact upon the formulation of the corporate strategy of the organization as a whole (Marcoux, 2003).

The arguments for the stakeholders' view of the corporation have often been premised on moral and business ethics (Phillips, 1997). However, as pointed out earlier in the discussion of Agency Theory, the perception of the interaction and the nature of the relationship between the firm and society are greatly influenced by our own points of view on what the main purpose of the firm is. One such view is that of the classical economist, summed up succinctly in Carr (1968). Although his views might not be totally representative of all classical economists, a good number of them share his notion of 'pure profit making' as the only objective of the firm. So much so that he suggested that businesses have a lower standard of ethics compared to society as a whole and therefore an abdication of all moral or ethical concern is consistent with the achievement of the firm's 'pure profit making' goals. A modified classicalist view suggests that whilst businesses pursue the main objective of shareholder value maximization, they should be aware of their responsibility to society by being obedient to the law and being ethical, this is the 'constrained profit making' view of the firm (Freeman, 1998 in Branco and Rodrigues, 2007).

However, even if the author assumes that businesses have a duty to protect the interests of all stakeholders, the author will still be confounded by the problem of tradeoffs involving the conflicting interests of all the stakeholders. Lack of measureable objectives with respect to each of the stakeholders still provides opportunity for management to be less accountable and to consume perquisites (Mallin, 2004). Jensen (2001) has observed that proponents of the Stakeholder Theory have been unable to provide realistic resolutions of the numerous conflicting interests of stakeholders that businesses need to protect. He therefore suggested a strand of Stakeholder Theory which he referred to as the 'enlightened Stakeholder Theory' or the 'enlightened shareholders maximization theory'. The theory posits that in order to maximize stakeholders' value, businesses should focus on maximizing shareholders' returns and this in itself would ensure the maximum return to all stakeholders. He further explains that a business would not be able to maximize shareholders' value if any stakeholder is ignored or mistreated.

Stakeholder Theory is very important in the context of a spectrum of discussions on Corporate Governance, not least the form of the control mechanisms adopted, and the possibility of control mechanisms playing substituting and/or complementary roles. The continental European model of Corporate Governance is known to favour the stakeholder perspective of the firm (Moerland, 1995). This is evident in the structures and composition of the Board of directors and in the roles played by other stakeholders. For example, it is normal for financial institutions to own substantial stakes in companies in Germany or France and it is also usual that they have a representative on the governing Board of such companies, in addition to the earlier mentioned roles of the employees in the firm's management (Goergen and Renneboog, 2008). This governance arrangement has been argued to provide financial stability for these firms and also to ensure closer monitoring from the financial investors (Goergen and Renneboog, 2008). And these may explain the rarity of hostile takeovers in these markets.

The stakeholder model approach to Corporate Governance has been criticized for being inadequate as a complete theory of the firm, but rather no more than a logical presentation of a series of techniques (Key, 1999: 320). Furthermore, Key (1999) wrote that:

> *Freemans' theory as presented can be criticised in four ways: 1) inadequate explanation of process; 2) incomplete linkage of internal and external variables; 3) insufficient attention to the system within which business operates and the level of analysis within the system; and 4) inadequate environmental assessment.*
>
> *(Key, 1999: 321)*

Another criticism that has been levelled against the Stakeholder Theory of the firm is that it is unrealistic. The notion that the firm exists to benefit all stakeholders who do not directly have a stake in the firm appears bogus and at best superficial and this perhaps explains the complexity or near impossibility of a mechanism that will effectively allocate residual returns of the firm to all its stakeholders (Jensen, 2001; Carr, 1968). It thus seems to have limited empirical applicability in Corporate Governance as it lacks specificity and is difficult to operationalize. This is especially so since it is not measurable and observable. Unlike the Agency Theory of the firm, it is not suggesting a set of measurable variables that can proxy for stakeholders' interest or power in the firm. However, proponents of the theory see it as being the most apt and feasible explanation of the relationship between the corporation and the society. They consider this relationship to transcend the mere capital contributions by owners to a more embedded and intertwined interaction between the two.

For the purpose of this book, the author has used Stakeholder Theory to provide alternative explanations (Brenner and Cochran, 1991) for the nature of interactions between the business and its stakeholders. Although there are variants of the Stakeholder Theory (Donaldson and Preston, 1995; Jones, 1991; Jones and Wicks, 1999) its use has been restricted to only the Primary Stakeholders theory as enumerated by Freeman (1984). This is to enhance the quality of the discourse in the book. Consequently, rather than being diffused, the discussion focused more directly on the core understanding of the theory. It has also thrown up some concern about the suitability of Agency Theory and why it still assumes a dominant feature in Corporate Governance discourse. Table 4.1 adapted from Kochan and Rubinstein (2000) summarizes the important differences between the Agency Theory and the Stakeholder Theory of the firm.

Table 4.1 Distinctions between the Shareholder's and the Stakeholder's Perspective of Corporate Governance

	Shareholder Perspective	**Stakeholder Perspective**
Purpose	Maximize shareholders' wealth	Pursue multiple objectives of parties with different interests
Governance structure	Principal–agent model (managers are agents of shareholders)	Team production model
Governance process	Control	Coordination, cooperation and conflict resolution
Performance metrics	Shareholder value sufficient to maintain investors' commitment	Firm's distribution of value created to maintain commitment of multiple stakeholders
Residual risk holder	Shareholders	All stakeholders

Stewardship Theory

Stakeholder theory provides an alternative paradigm to the Agency Theory. It provides an alternative theoretical paradigm to the Agency Theory of the firm. Unlike Agency Theory, it adopts a Sociological and Psychological explanation for the relationship between the shareholders and management in an organization. The theory starts from the assumption that the management is essentially a steward rather than an agent of the principal. It further posits that management is not comprised of the 'bad guys' as they are portrayed under Agency Theory, since it is assumed that there will almost always be a conflict of interest between the shareholders and management for reasons mentioned earlier in the discussions of Agency Theory.

On the other hand, Stewardship Theory holds that management is inherently honest and their major concern is running the business to achieve set corporate objectives. They are not self-centred individuals and seek collective goals rather than individualistic objectives (Davis et al., 1997). They are pro-organizational rather than opportunistic. Further, the theory assumes that there is a convergence between the interests of shareholders and management (Van Slyke, 2006; Donaldson and Davis, 1991, 1993). It suggests that this convergence can be achieved through trust between the parties and not through the imposition of the monitoring and control mechanisms in the organization suggested by Agency Theory. The model of man under Stewardship Theory is essentially different from that assumed under Agency Theory. Table 4.2 summarizes the important features and differences between Agency and Stewardship theories.

Although the main difference is in the model of man, this singular difference permeates the perceptions and attitudes to corporate objectives and operations. For instance, while Agency Theory uses 'control' as the basis of the relationship between the agent and the principal, Stewardship Theory uses 'trust' as the basis of the relationship. Furthermore, while Agency Theory adopts a structured arrangement that monitors and controls divergence in the objective functions confronting shareholders and their agents, this is unlike Stewardship Theory which adopts a structural arrangement that empowers management and facilitates interest congruence between management and owners of business.

The relevance of Stewardship Theory in Corporate Governance discourse includes the alternative perspectives that it enables in the relationship between management and shareholders. Imagine a corporate arrangement where there is no conflict of interest, where there is congruence of objectives. It would mean that the problems of adverse selection and moral hazard may not exist and agency costs will more or less be nil. Donaldson and Davis (1991) showed that, with Stewardship Theory as the theoretical frame, duality of roles can lead to improved firm performance, measured as Return on Capital Employed. In this book, Stewardship Theory has been used in the explanation of the alternatives to Agency Theory in the development of Corporate Governance. Although it is not the basis for the formulation of the hypotheses tested in this study, it is important in the conjectures arrived at in some of the findings of the study.

Signalling Theory

Spence (1974) developed Signalling Theory during his doctoral studies at Harvard, as part of the device to understand how to deal with information

Table 4.2 The Domains and Dimensions of Agency and Stewardship Theories

Theory	**Agency**	**Stewardship**
Manager as	Agents	Stewards
Approach to Governance	Economic	Sociological and Psychological
Model of Man	Individualistic	Collectivist
Behaviour	Opportunistic/self serving	Pro-organizational/trustworthy
Manager motivated by	Their own objectives	Principal's objectives
Manager's and principal's interests	Diverge	Converge
Structure that	Monitors and controls	Facilitates and empowers
Owner's attitude	Risk aversion	Risk propensity
Principal–manager relationship based on	Control	Trust
Psychological mechanisms	Agency Theory	Stewardship Theory
Motivation	Lower order needs Extrinsic needs	Higher order needs Intrinsic needs
Social comparison	Other managers	Principal
Identification	Little value commitment	Great value commitment
Power	Institutional	Personal
Situational Mechanisms	Agency Theory	Stewardship Theory
Management philosophy	Control oriented	Involvement oriented
Dealing with risk and uncertainty	Great control, more supervision	Training and empowering people. Redesigning jobs to be more challenging and motivating
Risk orientation	Control mechanisms	Trust
Time frame	Short term	Long term
Objective	Cost control	Performance enhancement
Cultural differences	Individualism, larger power distance	Collectivism, small power distance
Manager's choice	Principal's choice Agent	Principal's choice Steward
Agent	Mutual agency relationship Minimizes potential costs	Agent acts opportunistically Principal feels angry and betrayed
Steward	Principal acts opportunistically. Managers feel frustrated and betrayed	Mutual stewardship relationship. Maximizes potential performance

Source: Adapted from Vargas Sánchez, 2004

asymmetry in an imperfect market. He defines a 'signal' as those 'activities or attributes of individuals in a market which, by design or accident, alter the belief of, or convey information to, other individuals in the market' (1974: 1) He used this theory to address the problem in the labour market, where information asymmetry exists between employers' perception of employees' ability and employees' knowledge of their own skills and ability. He suggests that in order to portray the acquisition of the required set of skills, potential employees send out a number of signals to the employer hoping to impress and thereby gain employment. For example, potential employees may signal this ability through additional qualifications or education. It is important that the right signal is projected so that it is able to convey the information required which ordinarily is not observable (Ndofor and Levitas, 2004).

Although the theory was developed originally to address the problem of adverse selections due to information asymmetry in labour markets, it has enjoyed wide application in other fields of study including Anthropology (Bird and Smith, 2005), Marketing (Riley, 1975) and Strategy (Perri, 2002) among others. For example, in the field of Strategy, Porter (1980) has interpreted the idea of the 'signal' to include 'market signals' which he defines as 'any action by a competitor that provides a direct or indirect indication of its intention, motives, goals or internal situation' (Porter, 1980: 75) the implication of this being that a signal could now include conduct either direct or indirect projected into the market to elicit a certain envisaged reaction from a targeted audience.

In the context of Corporate Governance, its relevance is in providing a partial solution to the problem of information asymmetry which is one of the fundamental causes of agency problems in organizations. In the context of this book, Signalling Theory provides significant insight into directors' behaviours and provides important explanations of the relationship between control mechanisms. The theory has been used in this book to provide explanations and improve our understanding of the behaviours of the non-executive directors in discharging their Corporate Governance responsibilities (Shivdasani, 1993).

Summary

The objective of this chapter was to highlight the relevant theoretical divides and to identify their suitability for the discourse that the book engendered. Theories are crucial for allocation, ascription and progression of meanings. The theoretical background for the discourse in Corporate Governance is highly diverse and often confounding. The most obvious theoretical argument, but not necessarily the most eloquent in explaining the nature of the interaction in the firm, as least, in the world of its critics, is the Agency Theory. Other theories have important roles in our quest for a better and more complete understanding of the nexus of factors that impact on and are influenced by these interactions that subsist in the firm and its internal and external constituents. For all these, the role of theories remains highly essential. In the next chapter, the author presents the report of the empirical investigations guided by the Agency Theoretical frame. It details the methods used, findings and their significance.

5

Audit Committees and Auditor Independence – The Research Evidence

Introduction

In this chapter the author describes the main empirical research in the book and presents its findings. A number of propositions are offered in the form of testable hypotheses. These account for the determinants of Audit Committees in listed companies in the UK, the relationship between Audit Committee activity and auditor independence and the relationship between audit and non-audit fees in the presence of Audit Committee activity. In the hope of facilitating readers' access to the empirical components of the book without being either too technical or over simplistic, the chapter provides an overview of the functions of Audit Committees, followed by a brief account of the sources of data, the definition of variables and explanations of the research approach. The chapter concludes with the research outcomes and a discussion thereof.

Functions of the Audit Committee

In the wake of the corporate failures that spread across the global economy in the late 1990s and the early twenty-first century, most of the codes of governance produced have envisioned a large and important role to the Audit Committee, although there are some academics that have expressed their reservations about the seemingly hyped expectations of these committees (Spira, 2002; Zaman and Collier, 2005). Under current governance requirements, the committee is to provide oversight functions on the management in respect of auditing, financial reporting, internal control and risk management in organizations and thereby expect to protect the interests of the shareholders. While this is a laudable idea, what is now important is to be able to assess the performance of this committee as a basis for determining the appropriateness of the responses to corporate failures. Further, Audit Committees as sub-Board committees are to ensure transparent reporting and reporting quality among other responsibilities, so an appreciation of the activity of the Audit Committee would stem from an understanding of their expected roles and responsibilities. The Combined Code (2003), and specifically the Smith Committee (2003), focused attention on the roles of the Audit Committee. Previously, the Treadway Commission of 1987 in the US stated the expected roles of the Audit Committee and the importance of these roles in the corporate environment in which market confidence is to be sustained. Further, the Blue Ribbon Committee Report (BRC) of 1999 in the US emphasized the importance of the role of the Audit Committee and provided a list of factors that may enhance the committee's functioning. In the following section, the chapter will summarize the proposed functions of the Audit Committee and measures that have been suggested to enhance the activity or functioning of the committee.

A division of the roles of the Audit Committee can be categorized into two main periods namely the pre-Cadbury and post-Cadbury activities of Audit Committees. These time-related roles depict the importance attached to the activities of this sub-Board committee most probably as a result of corporate misbehaviours and their effects on investors in terms of their lost investments, drastic falls in the value of their shares and also the effect on the market in respect of loss of confidence in the market system to protect investors. Pre-Cadbury Audit Committees do not seem to enjoy as much attention as the post-Cadbury Committee. For instance, in the UK there was no high-profile report on the activities of the Audit Committee prior to the Smith Committee Report of 2003. In the US the Sarbanes-Oxley Act (SOX) only came into effect in 2002. Although there have been reports such as the Treadway (1987) and BRC (1993) none of these enjoyed the congressional backing that SOX has. Post ENRON, Audit Committee activities are well defined and 'enforced' (in the case of US companies, compliance is compulsory and non-compliance is sanctioned with exceptions given only for foreign registrants). The Audit Committee enjoys both corporate and social legitimacy and is an important feature of modern Corporate Governance mechanisms. Their roles as well as their expected contributions to corporate stability and sustainability are well codified. Prior to the Smith Report, a number of academics and professionals have tried to articulate the functions of the Audit Committee. These include the Cadbury Report (1992), Collier and Gregory (1999), Wolnizer (1995), Spira (2002, 2003), and later we had Dedman (2004), Mallin (2004), The Combined Code (2003) and Rezaee (2009). According to Wolnizer (1995), Audit Committee functions can be categorized under three main headings: Auditing, Financial Reporting and Corporate Governance functions. This categorization by Wolnizer fits well with the Smith Report (2003) in the UK as well The Combined Code (2003).

Two prominent British academics have authored works on the activity of the Audit Committee. First there was the work by Collier and Gregory (1996) on Audit Committee effectiveness and reporting quality and, secondly, the audit fee, Audit Committee activity and agency cost (Collier and Gregory, 1999). They defined Audit Committee activity to mean the diligence with which the committee carries out its work. Essentially they used the frequency of Audit Committee meetings to stand for committee activity and examined the relationship between the frequencies of Audit Committee meetings on other variables which were the explanatory variables.

In these two studies, Audit Committee activities were defined in relation to the number of meetings held within the year and hours spent in meetings within a year. What is not known is the duration of each of the meetings and what was discussed during the meetings, the level of the discussions and their effects on reporting quality or indeed their effect on other variables of interest are not known. These are not observable except through access to the minutes of committee meetings. Spira (2003) provided a deep insight into the internal working of the Audit Committee and how they make meaning of their functions. Here she emphasized the difficulty in determining the effectiveness or activity of an individual let alone the effectiveness of a group and also highlighted the difficulty in conducting research in this area because of the exclusivity of the members of the Board and issues with access and sensitivity.

Others have also identified the real difficulty encountered in defining the effectiveness of the performance of an individual or a group (Kalbers and Fogarty, 1993; Grendon and Bedard, 2006). This is because it has many domains and spheres through which it may be examined and there is no universal definition of effectiveness. However, it is possible to identify factors that may account for the committee's effectiveness or activity and these may be referred to as the determinants of the effectiveness of the committee. The BRC in the US provided indicators of an effective Audit Committee which include committee independence, composition and structure of the committee, the presence of an expert on the committee and the presence of a committee's terms of reference or charter to provide a basis for the assessment of the committee.

Previous literature suggests the predominance of quantitative studies in Corporate Governance compared to qualitative studies especially because of the nature of the subject. Corporate Governance spreads across disciplines touching on accounting, finance, economics and law. These are fields that are traditionally quantitative in orientation, with the exception of law. Although there are behavioural aspects to these disciplines, the overriding influence of positivist trends is clearly observable. Further, existing literature on Corporate Governance from an Agency Theoretical framework perspective has identified some base variables and likely control variables depending on the subset of the subject that is being examined. A synthesis of previous literature revealed that an Audit Committee's activity or diligence is determined by variables such as committee composition, structure, expertise and charter. Also, firm specific variables such as firm size, complexity and risk have been used in previous studies (Collier and Gregory, 1999, 1996, 1999; Kalbers and Fogarty, 1993; Spira, 2002; Peasnell et al., 2005).

Development of Hypotheses

BOARD AND AUDIT COMMITTEE COMPOSITION AND COMMITTEE ACTIVITY

A significant body of existing literature (Cotter and Silvester, 2003; DeZoort et al., 2003; Klein, 2002; Song and Windram, 2004) suggests that a unique trend underlies the relationship between the Board and Audit Committee composition and firm activity level which may include performance and other positive indices of financial and non-financial performance. The theoretical framework suggests that Audit Committees that are composed of independent non-executive directors tend to be more active than those composed of mainly executive or grey area directors. Grey area directors are directors that are not totally independent of the management. This may be by virtue of their recent employment with the company or their shareholdings and affiliations (Vicknair et al., 1993). Denis et al (1997) reported a positive relationship between an increase in the number of outside non-executive directors and the average stock price return. The announcement of the appointment of an additional outside non-executive director on the Board had a positive effect on stock price increase (Rosenstein and Wyatt, 1990), while the presence of an Audit Committee has been related to a reduced incidence of reporting irregularities and material misstatements (Carcello and Neal, 2000). Thus Audit Committees are associated with improved reporting quality (McMullen, 1996). Dechow et al. (1996) suggested that firms subjected to enforcement actions by regulators are less likely to have an Audit Committee. Klein (2002) documented negative relationships between Board and Audit Committee independence and earnings management. Board composition was documented to be an important determinant of corporate reporting quality. Beasley (1996) examined the role of the Audit Committee in constraining financial statement fraud. Comparing fraud and no-fraud companies, he found that no-fraud firms tend to have more outside independent non-executive directors than fraud firms, which underscored the importance of the Board and Audit Committee structure. Current literature seems to indicate that higher numbers of independent non-executive directors on the Board could enhance the protection of shareholders' interests.

The a priori theoretical expectation is that there is a positive relationship between Audit Committee activity and the proportion of independent non-executive directors on the Board and on the Audit Committee. In other words, Audit Committee activity is an increasing function of the proportion of the independent non-executive directors on the Board. This suggests that in line with the expectations of the BRC, the Smith Report and the SOX Act, a higher proportion of outside non-executive directors on the committee should translate into a higher level of diligence and performance of the Audit Committee in discharging their oversight functions. This a priori statement is not a measure of the nature of the increased activity or what causes it; rather it is a statement predicting a relationship between increased committee activity and the increased presence of outside non-executive directors on the committee. The author would thus expect the beta co-efficient sign to be positive. This may indicate that an increase in Audit Committee activity is partly explained by an increase in the number of independent non-executive directors.

The first set of the null hypotheses will investigate the relationship between Board and Audit Committee composition and Audit Committee activity. This is stated as:

> *H1: There are no relationship between Audit Committee activity and the proportion of independent non-executive directors on the board.*

AUDIT COMMITTEE AND OWNERSHIP STRUCTURE IN ORGANIZATION

Studies have documented relationships between the ownership structure of companies and the Board structure as well as the structure of the Audit

Committee (Jensen and Meckling, 1976; McConnell and Servaes, 1990; Dechow et al., 1996). Where the Audit Committee is structured in such a way that it reflects ownership distribution in the organization, it may have implications for corporate transparency and reporting. In the Anglo-American model of Corporate Governance, ownership is dispersed unlike in the Continental European and Japanese models of Corporate Governance where stock ownership is concentrated. In market-led governance, shareholders' interest is best protected by an independent Board (BRC, 1999; SOX, 2002; Combined Code, 2003) and consequently by an independent Audit Committee that is composed mainly of outside directors (Smith, 2003).

However, where management share ownership is significant, information asymmetry may be constrained and this may alleviate agency problems (Jensen and Meckling, 1976). This is because increased management share ownership may reduce management consumption of perquisites and management interests may coincide with those of the shareholders. Kaplan (1989) reported a positive effect of management buyouts on firm performance and a similar finding was reported by Smith (1990). Alternative arguments indicate that the relationship between Managerial Ownership and firm performance is not always positive and may not always be linear.

McConnell and Servaes (1990) and Hermalin and Weisbach (1998) suggested that the relationship is positive to certain levels of Managerial Ownership (between 0–5 per cent ownership) and that after certain levels (between 5–25 per cent ownership) increases in Managerial Ownership will result in negative performance indicating that the increased presence of management on the Board and on the Audit Committee may negatively affect firm performance depending on the definition of performance used. Bondholders favour firms that have more non-executives on their Board than executives (Anderson et al., 2002). For instance, creditors and loan providers may indicate a preference for Boards that are more transparent. Cotter et al. (2003) found a negative relationship between committee independence and Managerial Ownership, which suggest that firms with lower management shareholdings tend to have more independent Audit Committees, compared to firms with significant share ownership by management.

Further, institutional ownership is also important as a determinant of the activity or diligence of the Board and Audit Committee. For instance, Agrawal and Mandelker (1990) provided evidence of a positive relationship between institutional investors and firm performance but Faccio and Lasfer (2000) could not report such a relationship. Mitra and Hossain (2007) suggested that the presence of institutional shareholders impact upon the effectiveness of stockholder monitoring of corporate affairs including for example audit and non-audit management process. An increase in institutional stock ownership was associated with a decrease in non-audit fee ratios. Extending this line of thought, it is expected that institutional investors play monitoring roles and are better informed than individual investors (Balsam et al., 2002), and so they actively monitor the financial accounting process (Venkatachalam, 1998) which supports the conjecture that they are an important variable in the explanation of the activity or diligence of the Audit Committee.

This inconsistency in the findings provides a basis for further examination of the relationship between ownership structure (both institutional and managerial) and Audit Committee activity or diligence. It may well be that the Board and Audit Committees are more active if Managerial Ownership is high and vice versa. The author thus set up a second hypothesis tested in the book on the relationship between ownership structure and committee activity.

> *H2: There are no relationships between ownership structure and Audit Committee activity.*

AUDIT COMMITTEE EXPERTISE

One of the propositions of most post-ENRON Corporate Governance provisions globally requires that the Audit Committee be composed of persons that have recent and relevant financial experience, thereby implying that they should be able to, at a minimum, read and understand the financial statements which include the income statement, balance sheet, cash flow statement and the notes to the accounts. Further, most of these provisions also require that at least one person among the members should have recent relevant financial qualifications. The definition of recent relevant financial qualification is ambiguous and there has not been a clear interpretation of this requirement. One suggested definition provided in the SOX is presented below:

> *A financial expert is any member who has the education or experience of a public accountant, auditor, principal financial officer, comptroller or principal accounting officer of an issuer, or has been in a position requiring the understanding of generally accepted accounting principles and financial statement experience in the preparation and auditing of financial statements of comparable issuers, experience in*

> *the application of such principles in connection with the accounting for estimates, accruals and reserves; experience with internal accounting control and an understanding of Audit Committee functions.*
>
> *(Dey, 2008: 1151; Woodlock, 2006: 52)*

The central issue to this provision is the need for the members of the Audit Committee to *have between them* the required skill and experience to be able to discharge their specific oversight functions effectively. They need to be able to ask relevant, probing and tough questions (Spira, 2003) in order to ensure that management are above Board in their activities and in order to fulfil their duty of protecting the interests of the shareholders. The business environment is very dynamic and requires individuals that can keep up with the various dimensions of growth in the business world especially in a globally competitive market where confidence needs to be sustained and correct signals in respect of corporate accountability and transparency need to be projected (Cadbury, 1992). Lack of transparency may be taken to imply poor accountability and investors are sceptical of such organizations. Even at a national level, countries that have a history of suppression and anti-democratic practices have often been seen to be unaccountable and unsuitable for serious investment (La Porta et al., 2002).

Abbott et al. (2003a) documented a significant negative relationship between the presence of a member of a Board with financial expertise and the incidence of financial statement restatement. Similar findings were documented by Raghunandan and Rama (2003), when they found that shareholders support the ratification of auditor appointment even when the ratio of non-audit fee to audit fee is high so long as there is a financial expert on the Board. Davidson et al. (2004) found positive stock price reaction to the announcement of the appointment of financial expertise to the Audit Committee. These findings gave the sense that the presence of an expert on the Board may imply increased committee vigilance and increased internal control and enhanced risk management functions of the committee. With such increases in the oversight function, all things being equal, it should reduce the vulnerability to internal control override by management, for example, and it may also mean better reporting quality and thus better protection for the shareholders and other relevant stakeholders such as the bondholders (Anderson et al., 2003).

From the foregoing, it is intuitive to envisage an a priori relationship between Audit Committee activity and the presence of a financial expert on the Board. If there are experts on the Board, the Board should function more effectively and this should explain increases in its activities. In terms of signs of the co-efficient of this relationship, the author envisages a positive relationship between the presence of an expert on the Audit Committee and its activities. The author proposed a third hypothesis in this regard:

H3: Audit Committee activity is not related to committee expertise.

AUDIT COMMITTEE CHARTER

One of the provisions of the BRC in the US, the Smith Committee Report and the Combined Code in the UK on the effectiveness of the Audit Committee is the requirement that every Audit Committee should have terms of reference defining their scope of operations, their functions, process and procedure and, importantly, as a basis for their evaluation. Every committee is unique and should have a charter drafted specifically for their needs. It is imagined that the availability of a charter provides clarification of the roles and expectations of the Audit Committee. It is not proposed that this charter should be static or fixed but rather should be reviewed on a regular basis to determine its appropriateness and whether it needs to be modified in the light of current requirements and exigencies. The charter should provide a benchmark against which the committee and its personnel will be evaluated.

This study therefore suggests an a priori theory that the availability of a committee charter making clear and stating the scope of the committee functions, resources, methods and basis of evaluation, all things being equal, should increase the activities of the committee in the discharge of its oversight responsibilities. In terms of the direction of the relationship, the research will expect a positive relationship between the presence or availability of a committee charter and the activity of the committee. In other words the co-efficient is expected to be positive. The null hypothesis here is stated as:

H4: Audit Committee activity is not related to committee charter.

The following control variables are thought to be of importance in determining Audit Committee activity and have also been used in previous empirical studies. Furthermore, the complexity of the organization is also a factor that may affect the activity of the committee. Here, complexity is not in terms of the nature of the operations alone but also in terms of structure and number of subsidiaries. The complexity brought about by complex ownership structures and modes of operation may spread across geographical boundaries. For such organizations complexity will impact upon the activity of the committee. Number of subsidiaries, proportion of the subsidiaries that are based in overseas jurisdictions and the ratio of current assets to total assets has been used as a proxy for firm complexity (Goddard and Masters, 2000; Collier and Gregory, 1999).

In all, this study anticipates relationships between these control variables and the level of activity of the Audit Committee. From the foregoing, the following a priori theories are suggested: firstly, that a complex structure will exercise the Audit Committee more and hence a positive relationship should subsist between Audit Committee activity and organizational complexity. Secondly, bigger organizations should require closer monitoring and this should imply greater activity for the Audit Committee. These expectations are based on an agency cost theoretical framework. The following null hypotheses are therefore examined:

H5a: Audit Committee activity is not related to firm complexity.

H5b: Audit Committee activity is not related to firm size.

Diligence

An alternative definition of Audit Committee activity termed diligence is also examined in this book. In this study, DILIGENCE was defined as the linear sum of the number of Audit Committee meetings per annum, the binary value of the presence of a financial expert on the committee and the presence of a charter. Audit Committees that meet a minimum of three times in a year are awarded a point and committees with less than three meetings a year are awarded zero. Further, the Combined Code (2003) requires that Audit Committees should have at least one member with recent and relevant financial expertise (the Code was not specific in terms of qualification or number of years and nature of experience that would qualify as recent and relevant. However, Dey (2008) used the definition provided in SOX). For the purpose of this study, expertise was defined as a committee member who is a qualified accountant or a committee with at least one member that meets this requirement; such committees were awarded a point and zero for committees that fail to meet this definition. Lastly, the Combined Code requires that Audit Committees should have terms of reference that detail their expected responsibilities and procedures. The author expects that this should enhance committee effectiveness by providing a benchmark against which Audit Committees and their members are evaluated. The presence of a set of expected responsibilities and terms of reference serves as a target for the Audit Committee. Therefore, committees that have terms of reference or a charter were awarded a point and zero for committees that do not have such terms of reference or a charter. Based on this scoring method, the author derived a composite dependent variable and examines how much change in this variable is explained by the researcher's set of independent variables.

In arriving at the choice of multiple regressions using ordinary least square (OLS), the study considered the nature of the investigation and data availability. It may have been possible to use a binary logistic or probit regression but these would have been inappropriate for this type of investigation. Logistic regression is most suitable in estimating relationships where the dependent variable is dichotomous in nature although the independent variables could either be categorical or continuous variables (Maddala, 2001). Logistic regression applies maximum likelihood estimation by transforming the dependent variable into a logit variable which is the natural log of the odds of the dependent occurring or not. Although similar to OLS in that it relates the changes in the dependent variable to the independent variables, logistic regression finds the changes in the log odd of the dependent variables and not the changes in the variables themselves (Maddala, 2001)

Further, making the dependent variable dichotomous in OLS violates its core assumptions. Specifically, the assumptions of normality and homoscedasticity are violated since normality is impossible with just two values (for example, yes or no; 1 or 0 and so on) Homoscedasticity is also violated because with two values 1 and 0, variances will not be equal, they will probably be low at both extreme ends of the regression line when Y=0 and Y=1 but will be high in the middle violating the assumptions of constant variance across the whole length of the regression line (Wooldridge, 2000). The same reasoning applies in the case of probit regression. On the other hand, using OLS is suitable for this investigation since none of the properties or assumptions on which OLS is based is violated. Despite this reassurance, pre- and post-estimation tests were performed to confirm the validity of some of the OLS assumptions especially violation of constant variance assumption or the perfect collinearity between two independent variables.

Data

This investigation uses cross-sectional data from the FTSE 350 companies listed on the London Stock Exchange for the year 2005/2006 based on the report of the survey of the Accountancy Age magazine 2006 to answer the relevant research questions. Data to test these hypotheses were sourced from the Accountancy Age magazine, FAME database and from the annual reports of companies. It is normal to use the entire population in certain types of investigation. For example, studies focusing on Fortune 500, S&P 500 companies, FTSE 100 or FTSE 350 companies are all 'population'-based investigations. Sampling is appropriate where the population frame is so large that it is impossible to investigate it (Saunders et al., 2007: 216), while random sampling allows an equal chance to all events but, where the population is not too large (as is the case with FTSE 100 and FTSE 350) a more focused investigation can be undertaken. The following studies have used population based studies. O'Sullivan (2000) used the Times 1000, Klein (2002) used the S&P 500, Song and Windram (2004) focused on the UK top 500, Xie et al. (2003) used the S&P 500 index and Collier and Gregory (1996) used the FTSE top 500 companies as the focus of their studies. In this study the author will be using the UK FTSE 350 companies. These represent the UK top 350 companies based on their market capitalization. The FTSE 350 combines the membership of the FTSE 100 and FTSE 250. Using the FTSE 350 reduces the problem of changes in index membership which would have been a difficult issue if the investigation were focusing on just the FTSE 100 or just the FTSE 250.

Firm-specific information such as the variables proxying for size, complexity and risk were sourced from the database, Corporate Governance information was collected by hand from the annual reports and accounts of companies both from the hard copies and online reports. Some of the variables were transformed: for example, the sales and number of employee figures were both used to proxy for organizational size. This was done by taking their natural log to avoid the problems of heteroscedasticity and the possible distorting effect of such problem on the estimations of parameters. Cross-sectional investigations such as this often involve both very small and very big variables with differences in their variations. These differences are capable of influencing the regression results, for example, they inflate the correlation among all variables and could also be a source of heteroscedasticity, transforming them reduces these problems.

Although this study is based on the FTSE 350, the actual number of companies in the investigation is less than this for two reasons. Firstly, the FTSE 350 is normally stated in two ways, one which includes investment companies and one that excludes them. The author uses the variation that excludes investment companies. FAME and Accountancy Age Magazines and most other stock exchange-based studies also use the index that excludes investment companies. Excluding these companies normally leaves the FTSE 350 with 314 companies indicating that 36 companies are categorized as investment companies. Secondly, a number of companies' studies do exclude companies from the financial sectors and companies in regulated industries. This is due to the additional governance requirements of these companies as well as the complexities involved in the way they prepare and present their accounts which are industry specific. Including them in the sample may bias the results of the investigation. Another reason for a smaller sample size compared to the total number of companies on the index is the non-availability of governance and other variables needed for the investigation. This leaves the author with 245 companies in the sample.

Table 5.1 shows the sector distribution of the companies in the study; the classification was based on the UK Primary Standard Industrial Classification (2003). There are new classifications now being used. The 2003 edition relates to the data in this investigation. It shows that the surveyed companies are spread across various sectors in the economy, the highest contributing sector being the industrial and manufacturing sector with 36 companies.

The first regression has the number of Audit Committee meetings as the dependent variable (Collier and Gregory, 1996; Song and Windram, 2004). This is based on the view that the frequency of meetings is one of few and reliable observable measure of committee activity. Although it is not a perfect measure of all the dimension of the committees' activity, it gives a sense of the commitments and responsibility of the committee to its functions.

The regression result presented in Table 5.2 shows an R^2 of approximately 27 per cent and an adjusted R^2 of 23 per cent. Both measures are used to determine the explanatory power of the model. This result indicates that the model specified above (equation 3) explained 27 per cent of the variation in the meeting frequency. The adjusted R^2 is usually lower than the R^2 and this is because it penalizes the introduction of additional variables into the model.

The F-statistic is significant with a value of 5.29 and significant at the 1 per cent level. While the t-statistic is used in testing individual parameters in the model for their significance, the F-test is a model test statistic that investigates the significance of the model as a whole. These results show that the model has a reasonable explanatory power of the relationship between the dependent and independent variables.

Table 5.1 Industry description

	Number
Aerospace and Defence	6
Agriculture	1
Automotive	2
Biotechnology	2
Building and Construction	14
Business and Support Services	7
Chemicals	3
Computer, Technology and Internet	10
Consumer and Retail Products	19
Electronics and Engineering	15
Food Manufacturing and Products	10
Healthcare and Pharmaceutical	9
Industrial and Manufacturing	36
Leisure and Entertainment	18
Metal and Mining	15
Oil, Gas and Energy	13
Publishing and Media	16
Real Estate	19
Telecommunications	7
Transportation	13
Others	10
Total	245

BOARD SIZE (BOSIZE)

The governance variables are the variables of concern. The variable that measures the Board size (BOSIZE) showed a positive sign between Audit Committee activity and Board size although it is not statistically significant. The regression produced a co-efficient value of 0.41 and a t-value of 0.55. These results show that an increase in Board size may produce an increase in Audit

Table 5.2 OLS results with frequency of Audit Committee Meetings as dependent variable

Variable	Co-efficient	R.Std Error	t-stat	p-values	VIF
Constant	0.745	1.152	0.65	0.519	
BOSIZE	0.041	0.075	0.55	0.582	3.17
NONEXEC	0.246	0.098	2.49	0.013***	3.47
BOARDMET	0.178	0.039	4.55	0.000***	1.18
INVESTOR	-0.069	0.042	-1.67	0.096*	1.25
MGTOWNER	0.033	0.175	0.19	0.847	1.07
AUEXP	-0.114	0.182	-0.63	0.531	1.04
AUSIZ	0.055	0.109	0.50	0.618	1.42
AUCHAT	-0.329	0.219	-1.50	0.136	1.09
LNNOEMPLOY	-0.118	0.070	-1.68	0.094*	1.49
LNSUB	-0.039	0.112	-0.35	0.726	1.30
LNTOVER	0.138	0.107	1.29	0.198	3.25
ROC	0.003	0.004	0.07	0.945	1.07
R^2	0.2734				
Adj R^2	0.2358				
F-statistics	5.29	0.000			
n=245					

*, **,*** represent statistical significance at 10 per cent. 5 per cent and 1 per cent two-tailed.

Committee activity. Put another way, Audit Committees tend to be more active the larger the Board size. But this result is weak statistically as it may be totally due to chance. It has been reported for completeness only.

INDEPENDENT NON-EXECUTIVE DIRECTORS (NONEXEC)

The study also found a significant positive relationship between the proportion of non-executive directors and measures of Audit Committee activity. It implies that the H1 alternative hypothesis, which states that the higher the number of independent non-executive directors there are on the Board the higher the activity of the Audit Committee, should be accepted as against the null hypothesis. NONEXEC produced a co-efficient of 0.25 and a t-value of 2.49, which is higher than the 1.96 critical region thresholds for a 95 per cent confidence level, giving a p-value of 0.013. This allows us to reject the H1 null hypothesis which states that there are no relationships between the proportion of non-executive directors and Audit Committee activity. This result is very important as it confirms the crucial role of the number of non-executives in increasing the activity levels of the Audit Committee. Similar findings have been documented by Collier and Gregory (1996) and Abbott et al. (2003a). This indicates that increasing the number of independent non-executive directors on the main Board improves the activity of the Audit Committee.

BOARD MEETING (BOARDMET)

Another variable used to proxy for the Board activity was the frequency of the Board meetings (BOARDMET). This variable showed a significant positive relationship with the measure of Audit Committee activity. It produced a co-efficient of 0.18 and is significant at the 1 per cent level with a t-statistic of 4.55. These findings indicate that the activity levels of the Audit Committee are enhanced by the frequency of the meetings of the main Board itself. This could also be interpreted to mean that more meetings of the Audit Committee invoke more meetings of the main Board or vice versa.

The plausible explanation for this could be that, because the Audit Committee is a sub-set of the main Board, it would be expected that an active Board should impact positively on the activity of the Audit Committee. Especially in view of the fact that the main Board has delegated its financial and auditing reporting oversight functions to the Audit Committee, it could be that more frequent meetings of the main Board generate issues that need further consideration and deliberation by the Audit Committee, which could explain the fact that main Board meetings drive Audit Committee meetings. Furthermore, Audit Committee meeting frequency could also be due to fulfilling their reporting functions to the main Board, which could also explain the fact that the main Board meetings drive the number of Audit Committee meetings in the year. The result that suggests that the frequency of the main Board's meetings determines Audit Committee activity does not in any way imply that the independence of the Audit Committee is impaired or compromised.

OWNERSHIP STRUCTURE (INVESTOR AND MGTOWNER)

H2 measures the relationship between Audit Committee activity and ownership structure in a firm. This was measured using two variables in the model. These are, first, management ownership (MGTOWNER) and, secondly, substantial outside ownership (INVESTOR). With respect to Managerial Ownership, theoretically, the author was unable to decide upon the expected direction of the relationship. This is because of the conflicting indications from the literature. A strand of evidence from the literature suggests that Managerial Ownership could constrain consumption of perquisites, thereby aligning the interests of the shareholders with those of management. As a result, there is a tendency for Managerial Ownership to substitute for Corporate Governance functions of the Audit Committee, hence the potentially negative relationship between these variables. However, a positive relationship may also exist indicating that, despite Managerial Ownership, the Audit Committee still performs an important monitoring function in order to protect the interests of other stakeholders. These show that it was not possible to be definite about the actual direction of the relationship between Managerial Ownership and Audit Committee activity. The regression result in this respect produced an insignificant positive relationship between this variable and Audit Committee activity, with a co-efficient of 0.037 and a t-value of 0.19. This result is similar to that obtained by Collier and Gregory (1999) who failed to document any significant relationship between Audit Committee activity and management shareholding. Similar results were found by Bradbury (1990) and Collier and Gregory (1999).

For INVESTOR, the author tested a two tailed null hypothesis which suggest that Audit Committee activity is not related to ownership structure, that is, substantial outside shareholders holding more than 3 per cent of a company's shares. This is because extant literature suggests that substantial shareholders could play both active and passive monitoring roles within the corporation. Thus, if the active hypothesis holds, a positive relationship could be expected. On the other hand, if substantial investors are passive, a negative relationship would subsist between Audit Committee activity and substantial shareholdings. However, the regression produced a result that showed a significant negative relationship at the 10 per cent level two tail between these variables, which implies that Audit Committee activity is not enhanced by the presence of more substantial shareholdings. The co-efficient was -0.069 and a t-statistics of -1.67.

However, a possible explanation of the researcher's finding could be that there is a form of substitution taking place between the Audit Committee and institutional investors. A more active Audit Committee may elicit less attention from institutional investors, who might not consider it necessary to duplicate intervention roles being played by the Audit Committee. This interpretation favours the institutional investors' passive hypothesis. Further, the documented negative relationship between Audit Committee activity and substantial investors can also be explained on the basis that some substantial shareholders consider intervention and monitoring roles as counter-productive and costly. Black (1990) and Admati et al. (1994) suggested that substantial investors weigh the cost of intervention against its benefits. They tend to be passive if the marginal cost of intervention is greater than its marginal benefits. A face off between major investors and the management would most probably result in bringing negative publicity for the company and may drive down the net worth of the company as its share price falls. Equally, if substitution is assumed between control mechanisms, it could be that Audit Committee activity substitutes for substantial investors' monitoring. Mitra and Hossain (2007) examined the relationship between ownership structure and their monitoring activity with respect to auditing. They found that when institutional investors are active in monitoring, this exerts a downward pressure on firms' agency costs of operation, specifically the cost of auditing.

FINANCIAL EXPERTISE (AUEXP)

H3 tested the relationship between committee expertise (AUEXP) and levels of Audit Committee activity. The results of the regression showed an insignificant negative relationship between the presence of at least one member with financial expertise and increased levels of committee activity. The co-efficient value is -0.114 and a t-statistic of -0.63. The result showed a negative co-efficient sign which suggests that an increase in Audit Committee activity could be partly explained by a fall in the number of experts on the Audit Committee. The author would have expected that in line with the provisions of the Combined Code (2003) and BRC (1999), more financial expertise on the Board would increase the activity levels of the Audit Committee. This could be because the Audit Committee is responsible for the auditing and financial reporting oversight functions of the Board; therefore more experts on the Audit Committee should have bolstered the monitoring and oversight functions of the committee in terms of quality and scope. Abbott et al. (2003a) find a negative relationship between Audit Committees that have financial experts and restatements, Abbott et al. (2004) and Bedard et al. (2004) also documented a negative relationship between Audit Committee expertise and earnings management. These studies suggest that the presence of financial experts on the Audit Committee constrains restatements and earnings management.

On the other hand, this result may be indicative of the inconsistency and lack of clarity in Corporate Governance guidelines on the definition of what constitutes a financial expert. It could be that the availability of more precise guidance on, for example, what criteria fulfil the definition of financial literacy and how many years of financial expertise qualifies for financial literacy, will enhance the use of appropriate variables to proxy for committee expertise and thereby improve research findings on the importance of financial expertise in enhancing Corporate Governance in general and the Audit Committee in particular.

AUDIT COMMITTEE CHARTER (AUCHAT)

With respect to H4, the author tested a null hypothesis that there is no relationship between Audit Committee activity and the presence of an Audit Committee charter. It may be expected that Audit Committee activity is enhanced by the availability of a well-defined Audit Committee charter and terms of reference, so that a positive relationship between the existence of a charter and the frequency of Audit Committee meetings could be envisaged. However, the regression result produced a negative but insignificant relationship between these variables. The co-efficient was -0.329 and t-value of -1.50. The t-statistic falls within the acceptance ratio for the null hypothesis indicating that we cannot accept the alternative hypothesis which suggests that Audit Committee activity is enhanced by having a well-defined Audit Committee charter and terms of reference. The result is similar to the findings from the exploratory study by Carcello et al. (2002) who found that what the Audit Committee members say they are doing is different from what their charter expects them to be doing.

FIRM SIZE AND COMPLEXITY (LNNOEMPLOY AND LNSUB)

H5a measures the relationship between Audit Committee activity and firm complexity while H5b measures the relationship between Audit Committee activity and firm size. These hypotheses were tested on the basis of a two tail test. Although Agency Theoretical expectations suggest that the bigger the firm the higher the associated agency costs of monitoring and control, thus, bigger organizations could exercise the Audit Committee more. But, it might also be the case that smaller firms pose greater challenges to the Audit Committee giving rise to greater activity in both situations. However, the regression result suggests that a significant negative relationship exists between firm size and

Audit Committee activity. The co-efficient was -0.118 with a t-statistic of -1.68. These results indicate a significant negative relationship between these variables at the 10 per cent level. The results show that an increase in Audit Committee activity is explained by a reduction in the size of the firm, or that the smaller the organization the more active the Audit Committee. However, another variable that proxy for firm size was natural log of total assets. Although this showed a positive relationship with Audit Committee activity, it was statistically insignificant. Collier and Gregory (1999) also found an insignificant positive relationship between Audit Committee activity (they used total meeting hours as their proxy for activity) and firm size.

In terms of H5b, this examines the relationship between firm complexity and Audit Committee activity. The regression result produced a co-efficient of -0.039 and a t-value of -0.35, once again showing a negative relationship between firm complexity and Audit Committee activity. These results indicate that we cannot accept the alternative hypotheses, that firm complexity affects Audit Committee activity in a statistically significant way. This finding is similar to the findings in Collier and Gregory (1996).

These results are unanticipated, as it would be expected that bigger organizations should exercise the Audit Committee more frequently; equally, complex organizations should require greater monitoring and therefore should increase Audit Committee activity. A negative relationship, though statistically insignificant, suggests that smaller organizations drive Audit Committee activity. A plausible explanation from this finding could be that Audit Committees in smaller firms have to do more in order to achieve their corporate objectives. It could also be that such organizations would need to show more transparency and quality in their financial and audit reports compared to larger, more established and, possibly, older organizations who could have built a reputation for corporate transparency and quality reporting. This result conflicts with the findings in Menon and Williams (1994) who found a positive relationship between Audit Committee activity and the size of the firm.

Alternative Specification of Dependent Variable

The author also examined the sensitivity of the findings reported in Table 5.2 above to the alternative definition of Audit Committee activity, by using a composite definition discussed earlier. This is the basis for the second regression performed in this investigation. Table 5.3 presents the results of the regression with Diligence as the dependent variable.

Table 5.3 Regression result with diligence as the dependent variable

Variable	OLS	Std Error	t-stat	p-values	VIF
Constant	0.936	1.126	0.83	0.407	
BOSIZE	0.074	0.073	1.01	0.314	3.15
NONEXEC	0.215	0.105	2.05	0.041**	3.61
BOARDMET	0.195	0.036	5.44	0.000***	1.17
INVESTOR	-0.046	0.041	-1.10	0.271	1.25
MGTOWNER	-0.004	0.207	-0.02	0.985	1.06
AUSIZ	0.072	0.115	0.63	0.530	1.42
LNNOEMPLOY	-0.124	0.079	-1.55	0.122	2.74
LNSUB	0.035	0.082	0.43	0.671	1.28
ROC	-0.002	0.006	-0.27	0.790	1.08
R^2	0.2654				
Adjusted R^2 n= 245	0.2340	F-statistics	8.45	0.000	

*, **,*** represent statistical significance at 10 per cent. 5 per cent and 1 per cent two-tailed.

Results and Discussion

Although defining committee activity as a composite measure of committee size, expertise and the presence of a charter/terms of reference does not show a great deal of increased statistical benefit over the frequency of meeting measure, it reinforces some of the findings in the initial measure. For example, the regression result shows a positive and significant relationship between the presence of independent non-executive directors (NONEXEC) and diligence. It produces a co-efficient of 0.215 and a t- statistic of 2.05. This is well above the 1.96 critical values for the acceptance of the null hypothesis. This is consistent with the result in the previous regression which used frequency of meeting to proxy for Audit Committee activity.

This result reinforces the initial findings (H1) that allude to the importance of the non-executive directors in enhancing Audit Committee activity. Improvement in Audit Committee activity is a necessary requirement towards achieving an effective Audit Committee. Since effectiveness may not be possible without being active (Collier and Zaman, 2005).

Equally, BOARDMET maintains its positive sign and statistical significance under the researcher's alternative definition of Audit Committee activity. The co-efficient was 0.195 and the t-statistic was 5.44. Variables that proxy for ownership structure and the control variables remain statistically insignificant. The model explains 26 per cent of the variation in the dependent variable and the F-statistic is significant at the 1 per cent level with a value of 8.45.

Section Summary

This is the first empirical section in this chapter of the book and five main hypotheses were tested. Essentially, these hypotheses have been used to examine the determinants of the activity of the Audit Committee in the UK's largest companies in the reporting period 2005–2006. Importantly, the study found a significant positive relationship between Audit Committee activity measured as the number of meetings in the year and the proportion of independent non-executive directors on the Board. In addition, it also found a positive relationship between the main Board meeting frequency and the activity of the Audit Committee. Audit Committees were found to be less active in companies that have substantial outside investors, owning more than 3 per cent of ordinary shares in the company. It indicates that the higher the numbers of this type of investor in a firm, the lower the activity of the Audit Committee. This result may indicate a likely substitution between these control mechanisms. Size and firm complexities were not found to be important determinants of Audit Committee activities. Although these results find backing in the literature they were unexpected, as was the negative relationship found between the presence of a financial expert on the Audit Committee and its apparently reduced levels of activity.

The alternative definition of Audit Committee activity also confirmed the strong positive relationship between Board independence, as measured by the proportion of non-executive directors to executive directors on the Board, and Audit Committee activity. This is interpreted to be indicative of the importance attached to the presence of more independent non-executive directors on the Board which could impact on the independence of the Audit Committee, since there is an inextricable link between presence of independent non-executive directors on the Board and Audit Committee independence, which ultimately could enhance their activity. Recent Corporate Governance discourse and guidelines have envisioned important monitoring and oversight functions for the non-executives on the Board of directors as the representatives of the interests of the shareholders. Frequency of meetings could be indicative of

Audit Committee activity and a higher number of non-executive directors on the Board have been found to increase Audit Committee activity. The Audit Committee is the part of the Board that has the remit to ensure auditing and reporting quality; therefore this result is very important in indicating that an increased number of non-executive directors enhance Audit Committee activity which may enhance auditing and reporting quality in firms.

Following on from the outcome of the first empirical study above, the author presents in the remaining part of this chapter two additional empirical investigations that are the natural progression of the findings in the reported findings above. These investigations relate to a central issue addressed in the book – auditor independence. The next section presents the empirical investigation on the relationship between Corporate Governance and auditor independence.

The Relationship between Corporate Governance and Auditor Independence

The investigation in this part of the chapter focuses on the relationship between Corporate Governance, proxy by Audit Committee activity, and auditor independence (external auditors' fee). One of the expectations of the Cadbury Report was that an improvement in Corporate Governance would impact upon auditor independence and indeed upon the communication between the external auditor and management by opening up another route for the auditor to be able to express concerns via the Audit Committee (Page and Spira, 2005). Initially, the committees' oversight was concentrated mainly in the area of financial reporting and auditing but, as Rezaee (2009) and Mallin (2004) show, these roles have increased tremendously to include firms' internal control and risk management oversight functions. Indeed, the Audit Committees now play an important role in the appointment, determination of the remuneration, scope of activities and review of the independence of the external auditors (Combined Code, 2003; SOX, 2002). This reiterates the importance of empirically studying the nature of the relationship that exists between the Audit Committee and external auditors.

Audit Committee Activity, External Auditors' Fees and Auditor Independence

Different measures of perception of auditor independence have been explored by researchers; these approaches used the economic bonding argument (DeAngelo, 1981; Simunic, 1984) as a basis. This involves 'capturing' independence by reference to the fees paid to the auditors. With the debate on auditors' provision of non-audit services to their client ongoing, albeit low-keyed now, the ratio of non-audit services to audit fee (Frankel et al., 2002) has been used to proxy for independence, so also has the ratio of non-audit fee to total fees been used (Ashbaugh et al., 2003). Association between these measures and surrogate for client's auditing or reporting qualities are then examined. Measures such as frequency of litigation against the auditor (Palmrose, 1999), propensity to qualify audit report (Lennox, 1999; DeFond et al., 2002), earnings restatements (Raghunandan et al., 2001), earnings management using abnormal accrual (Frankel et al., 2002; Ferguson et al., 2004) have been used as surrogates. Another approach has been to use event studies by examining the effects of proxy for auditor independence on share prices (Frankel et al., 2002) and bond prices (Brandon et al., 2004). These methods have produced largely conflicting results with most finding lack of relationship or insignificant relationship between proxy for auditor independence and surrogate variables (Beattie and Fearnley, 2002; Ruddock et al., 2006).

However, the author contends that the concern should be more on the interactions between auditors and Audit Committees, rather than on surrogate for compromised independence. Focus needs to be more on the effects of the Audit Committee on auditing and how these impact on auditor independence. What are the effects of Audit Committee activity on auditing and on auditor independence? These deserve empirical investigation. Spira (2003) reinforced this perception when she observed that the relationship between audit and Audit Committees is assumed rather than proved, and that very little evidence are available outside North America that proves or supports the value of the Audit Committee. Equally, Turley and Zaman (2007) observed that the impact of Audit Committee on external audit is under researched.

Building on the findings reported earlier in this chapter, the author uses frequency of meetings to proxy for Audit Committee activity and a number of alternative specifications of external auditors' fees to proxy for the economic bonding between the auditor and the auditee. The author adopts Reynolds et al. (2004) and Ashbaugh et al.'s (2003) arguments that suggest that total fee rather than the ratio of non-audit services to audit fee is a more realistic measure of the economic bonding between the auditor and their client. However, in addition to this, the author also examined the effect of using client importance, measured as the ratio of the total fee from a client to the total income of the auditor, as another proxy for the level of economic bonding between the auditor and their clients. This is referred to as the Total Relative Income (TRI) in this study. This measure has its basis in the economic theory of auditing suggested by DeAngelo (1981). Thereafter, and to test the consistency of the results from using the methods above, the author also uses audit fee, non-audit fees and fee ratios as proxies for economic bonding between the auditor and auditee. These measures are summarized below.

Alternative Definitions of External Auditors' Fee

- Natural log of total fees paid to the auditor (LNTOTFEE).
- Total Relative Income of the auditors (TRI).
- Natural log of non-audit fee (LNNOAUFEE).
- Natural log of audit fee (LNAUFEE).
- Fee ratios.

Development of Hypotheses

BOARD COMPOSITION AND EXTERNAL AUDITORS' FEE

The motivation for the first research hypothesis in this study develops from the requirement by most recent Corporate Governance guidelines (Combined Code, 2003; SOX, 2002) that Boards of directors should be composed mostly of independent non-executive directors, who are expected to be able to protect the interests of all stakeholders in the corporation especially those of the shareholders. The presence of more independent non-executive directors should reduce agency costs through their monitoring and decision control functions (Fama and Jensen, 1983). Dahya et al. 2002 documented an increase in the proportion of independent non-executive directors in UK listed companies. Song and Windram (2004) found an increase in the nature and scope of the work of non-executive directors on the Board. Enhanced activity of the Board has been found to reduce agency costs associated with financial fraud and with sanctions from regulating authorities (Beasley, 1996; Dechow et al., 1996). These findings support the conjecture that a higher proportion of independent non-executive directors on the Board enhance Board monitoring and controlling functions some of which may relate to auditing and reporting activities.

However, the implications of these changes on auditing and related functions may not be clear cut. To the extent that independent non-executive directors are keen on projecting an appearance of high reporting quality, the author expects a positive relationship between external auditors' fees and the proportion of independent non-executive directors on the Board. This suggests that the more independent non-executive directors on the Board there are, the greater the likelihood of demanding more services from the external auditor and consequently, the higher the external auditors' fees. On the other hand, it could well be that an increased number of independent non-executive directors on the Board would enhance monitoring, leading to improved internal control within the organization. This may translate into a reduction in auditors' time used in completing their audit and related assignments, with the effects being a reduction in the total fees earned by the auditor from the client. From these analyses, the author suggests the hypothesis below:

> *H6: There are no relationship between the external auditors' fees and board composition.*

AUDIT COMMITTEE ACTIVITY AND EXTERNAL AUDITORS' FEES

Further, a number of governance studies have examined the possibilities of the Audit Committee failing to discharge its enlarged responsibilities. Although, as already noted, it is extremely difficult to measure committee effectiveness, studies have tried to measure the activity and diligence of the Audit Committee (Collier and Gregory, 1996; Kalbers and Fogarty, 1996; Stewart and Munro, 2007) by using its meeting frequency. Collier and Gregory (1999) used the number of hours of meetings in a year as the measure of the extent of work undertaken by the committee.

The Audit Committee of the Board has the primary responsibility of ensuring auditing and reporting quality in the corporation. This has been unequivocally supported in many Corporate Governance codes, although there are academics that question the level of expectations placed on the committee. The Cadbury Committee Report and the Smith Committee reports envisaged an important role for the Audit Committee in ensuring corporate auditing and reporting quality. To achieve this, Audit Committees are required to be composed of mainly independent non-executive directors. They are also required to meet at least three times in a year to deliberate on reporting and auditing issues. Rezaee (2009) showed that the scope of the activity of the committee has increased significantly to include internal control, and risk management functions.

While it may be expected that diligent Audit Committees may mean lower audit fees being charged by the external auditor, at the same time members of the Audit Committees may be interested in signalling efficiency and may be keen on preserving their reputation (Riahi-Belkaoui, 2004) and human capital worth in which case they may buy more services from the external auditor (Collier and Gregory, 1996). The human capital preservation argument holds that members of Audit Committees are appointed due to their knowledge, skills and experience which are referred to as their human capital (Livingstone, 1997). This capital is preserved by reducing exposures to factors that can deplete it.

Previous studies have found conflicting results regarding the relationship between Audit Committee activity and external auditors' fees. While Abbott et al. (2003b) did not find any significant association between Audit Committee meeting frequency and audit fees, Stewart and Munro (2007) found a significant positive relationship. In this study, using more recent data, the author tests the relationship between Audit Committee diligence proxied by meeting frequency and external auditors' fees and perceived auditor independence proxied by the extent of economic bonding between the auditor and the auditee.

> *H7: The external auditors' fees are not related to Audit Committee activity.*

Ownership structure and External Auditors' Fee

Consideration of this aspect falls into two parts in this book. That is, substantial outside shareholdings and substantial management shareholdings. These are now discussed.

SUBSTANTIAL OUTSIDE SHAREHOLDINGS

Previous studies (Jensen and Meckling, 1976; Short and Keasey, 1999) have suggested that ownership structure in organizations matters in respect of corporate monitoring and controls. While individual stockholders may find it costly to monitor management, it may be more economical and efficient for investors with substantial shareholdings in a firm to monitor management action in ensuring reporting and auditing quality (Mitra and Hossain, 2007). It has also been shown that substantial shareholders have access to important firm disclosures before they are made public (El-Gazzar, 1998) which may indicate their influence in a corporation. They could also observe and identify earnings management earlier than individual shareholders and are more likely to intervene where they perceive that such earnings management is capable of affecting the firm's value (Balsam et al., 2002). Kane and Velury (2004) suggested that substantial shareholders can influence management for two main reasons. First, because of the size of their holding they have real influence over security trade and can thus affect the firm's stock prices and, secondly, they can affect management through their impact on the strategic direction of the organization. Taken together, substantial shareholders play Corporate Governance functions in organizations by constraining agency cost. The author anticipates a negative relationship between substantial stock ownership (INVESTOR) and external auditors' fees.

SUBSTANTIAL MANAGEMENT SHAREHOLDINGS

Jensen and Meckling (1976) suggested that substantial Managerial Ownership may constrain management from consuming perquisites, thereby reducing conflicts of interest between directors and other stakeholders. Others have suggested that the relationship between management share ownership and measures of agency cost may not be linear (McConnell and Servaes, 1990; Short and Keasey, 1999). Thus, this relationship is positive up to a certain range of management shareholding and negative thereafter. For this reason the author is unable to anticipate the direction of the relationship between substantial management shareholdings (MGTOWNER) and external auditors' fees.

OTHER GOVERNANCE VARIABLES

The following governance control variables were also used in the study.

Expert

This control variable relates to the Audit Committee. Its relevance is motivated by the Corporate Governance requirement that at least one member of the Audit Committee should be a financial expert. This is to enhance the effectiveness of the Audit Committee in discharging its financial oversight functions. However, previous studies have proved inconclusive with respect to the effect of the presence of a financial expert on auditing and reporting quality. While Abbott et al. (2004) found that firms with financial experts on their Audit Committees are less likely to experience financial reporting restatement or fraud, Carcello and Neal (2003) found that financial experts on the Audit Committee do not protect auditors from dismissal following the issuance of a going-concern report. In this study, the research used a dummy variable (EXPERT) with a value of 1 if the Audit Committee has at least one financial expert and 0 if otherwise.

Charter

The Smith Report and the BRC reports as well as other Corporate Governance reports require that the Audit Committee should have a charter that guides its activities. This is supposed to be reviewed annually. The author anticipates a negative relationship between the presence of a charter on the Audit Committee (CHARTER) and the external auditors' fees. This is because having a charter can contribute to the effectiveness of the Audit Committee in discharging its financial oversight functions which should result in a reduction in external auditors' fees as a result of the reduction in agency cost and increased diligence on the Audit Committee's part.

Committee size

The Cadbury Committee Report suggested a minimum of three independent non-executive directors on the Audit Committee; this is also the suggestion of the BRC in the US. Abbott et al. (2004) were of the opinion that the requirement to have a minimum number of non-executive directors on the Audit Committee was an attempt to elevate the status and organizational importance of this governance mechanism. Turley and Zaman (2007) have shown that Audit Committees have organizational influence and power. Similarly, Kalbers and Forgarty (1993) enumerate the importance of Audit Committee legitimacy and power which may be reflected in the size of the committee. The author anticipates a positive relationship between the Audit Committee size (COMMSIZE) and their activity and, by extension, the author expects a negative relationship between Audit Committee size and external auditors' fee.

Board meetings

Board meeting was used as a measure of Board activity. The author expects that increased Board activity should constrain external auditors' fees. A negative relationship is anticipated between this variable (BOARDMET) and the external auditors' fees.

CONTROL VARIABLES

Previous studies have identified a number of control variables that are important in determining external auditors' fees. These have been categorized into variables that measure firms' profitability, audit risk, complexity of operation, and size. These are now discussed.

Profitability

The effect of profitability on audit fees can be bi-directional. To the extent that a client is profitable may imply more audit effort for the auditor in order to ensure that the assertions made in the financial statements are true, complete and accurate. This may require substantial audit work which invariably exerts an upward pressure on the fees paid to the external auditor. However, a profitable firm may be seen as a less risky client in terms of going concern assessments and, where a business risk approach is used in auditing the client, it may mean that the audit is completed more quickly thereby exerting downward pressure on external auditors' fees. Lee and Mande (2005) used return on assets (ROA) as a measure of profitability. This was measured as net income divide by total assets. Mitra and Hossain (2007) used net income divided by average assets to measure ROA. The author adopts Lee and Mande's (2005) definitions of ROA because it is more complete and more widely used in previous studies.

Risk and complexity

Intuition suggests that a positive relationship should exist between variables that proxy for firm riskiness and complexities and external auditors' fees. The more risky and complex a client is the more the audit effort and time required to gather the necessary audit evidence that could aid in the formation of an appropriate audit opinion and consequently the higher the external auditors' fees. A number of variables have been used in previous studies to proxy for risk and complexities of the auditee, including natural log of subsidiaries and the number of employees. For example, Goodwin-Stewart and Kent (2006) used the ratio of receivables plus inventory to total assets, while Lee and Mande (2005) used the square root of the number of employees in addition to other variables such as dummy variables that assume a value of 1 if a client has a pension scheme and 0 if otherwise, an indicator variable which is equal to 1 if a firm restates its earnings in the year and 0 if otherwise. In this study the author uses the natural log of the number of subsidiaries as a measure of client complexity.

Firm size

Previous studies have shown that client size is a major determinant of the external auditors' fees both for audit and non-audit services. The intuition is that bigger organizations require more time to complete their audit compared to smaller ones. They may also involve more visits and more sites than smaller firms. All these build up audit time and are reflected in increased fees. A positive relationship is expected between auditee size and the value of the external auditors' fees. Mitra and Hossain (2007) used the natural log of total assets to proxy for firm size, a similar measure used by Goodwin-Stewart and Kent (2006) and Lee and Mande (2005). In line with previous studies, the author used the natural log of turnover (LNTOVER) as well as the natural log of number of employees (LNEMPLOY) to proxy for firm size.

Regression Results and Discussion

The third regression reported uses the natural log of total fee as the dependent variable explained by all other variables as detailed above in the hypotheses development. The regression result is presented in Table 5.4.

Table 5.4 Natural log of total fees as the dependent variable

Variable	OLS	Std Error	t-stat	p-values	VIF
Constant	1.658	1.221	1.36	0.176	
BOSIZE	0.084	0.079	1.08	0.291	3.18
NONEXEC	0.224	0.114	1.96	0.050**	3.72
BOARDMET	-0.094	0.041	-2.30	0.023**	1.32
AUSIZ	0.096	0.124	0.78	0.436	1.43
AUACT	0.210	0.663	3.16	0.002***	1.45
AUCHAT	0.149	0.239	0.62	0.534	1.11
AUEXP	-0.119	0.209	-0.57	0.568	1.05
INVESTOR	-0.059	0.045	-1.31	0.191	1.29
MGTOWNER	-0.389	0.224	-1.74	0.083*	1.07
LNNOEMPLOY	0.428	0.086	4.98	0.000***	2.78
LNSUB	0.277	0.135	2.06	0.041**	1.28
LNTOVER	0.363	0.117	3.1	0.002***	3.25
ROC	-0.023	0.006	-3.58	0.000***	1.08
R^2	0.6434	F-statistics	31.92	0.000	
AdjustedR^2	0.6232	n =244			

*, **,*** represent statistical significance at 10 per cent. 5 per cent and 1 per cent two-tailed.

The main regression used the natural log of total fees (LNTOTFEE) paid to the auditor by a firm. This represents the sum of both audit and non-audit fees, where non-audit fees implies all fees for non-audit engagements. The natural log of total fee was used as the dependent variable in line with previous studies which have used the natural log of total fee (Ashbaugh et al., 2003; Reynolds, Deis and Francis, 2004). They argued that this measure is more indicative of the economic bonding between the auditor and the auditee than ratio of non-audit service.

BOARD COMPOSITION AND EXTERNAL AUDITORS' FEES

Hypothesis H6 examines the relationship between external auditors' fees and Board composition. The study established a significant positive relationship between the proportion of non-executive directors (NONEXEC), a measure of Board composition, and total fees paid to auditors. The regression produced a co-efficient for NONEXEC of 0.224 and a t-statistic of 1.96. This is significant at the 5 per cent level. This result indicates that the higher the number of independent non-executive directors there are on the Board, the higher the total fees (both audit and non-audit) that are earned by the auditor from their client. This result is statistically significant, indicating that the null hypothesis will be rejected and the alternative hypothesis, which suggests a positive relationship between these variables, will be accepted.

This result is quite important and interesting. Its importance relates to the expected role of the independent non-executive directors in protecting the interests of the shareholders. The need to have more independent non-executive directors on the Board is to ensure that management pursue to a greater extent the interests and objectives of the shareholders. This is achieved by reducing or constraining agency costs associated with management expropriation of the shareholders' wealth by improved monitoring and control mechanisms. The result is interesting in the sense that it could provide some explanations of the likely behavioural patterns of the independent non-executive directors. Such explanations can be found in theories such as the signalling, reputation and human capital theories.

In line with theoretical expectations, the result is consistent with the underlying reasoning of Signalling Theory (Spence, 1973) as well as the human capital preservation concepts of the Human Capital Theory (Fleischhauer, 2007). It is not the objective in this book to empirically prove these theories. The result suggests that rather than reduce the value of services purchased from the external auditors, non-executive directors will signal preferences for auditing and reporting quality and for auditing coverage by buying more services from the auditors in order to signal transparency to the market and boost market confidence in the reports of the firm. Furthermore, maintaining or buying more services from the auditors may help non-executive directors to preserve their jobs and consequently their human capital worth. This is because more services bought from the external auditors may aid early detection of financial misstatements and errors or fraud and so prevent corporate misbehaviours. Serving on the Board of a distressed or misbehaving company has adverse effects on the human capital worth and reputations of the directors associated with such a company. The effects of such reputational damage could be seen in the reduced appointments such independent non-executive directors will be awarded subsequently, as other companies become cautious in associating their firms with such independent non-executive directors. Similar findings were documented in O'Sullivan (1999) and Mitra et al. (2007) in terms of finding a positive relationship between the proportion of non-executive directors and auditors' fees although they reported statistically insignificant positive relationships. Carcello et al. (2002) also found a positive relationship between Board characteristics and higher audit fees. On the other hand the result conflicts with the findings in Tsui et al. (2001) who found a negative relationship between Board independence and audit fees.

The result could also be explained in the context of its effect on auditor independence and the auditing process. Given that there is an inextricable link between the presence of non-executive directors on the Board and the Audit Committee (Collier, 1993), the author contends that the presence of more independent non-executive directors on the Board in the current Corporate Governance climate, notwithstanding recent corporate lapses, could increase auditors' independence by encouraging auditors to increase their audit work and coverage and also that such increase in audit efforts could be encouraged by the independent non-executive directors NONEXEC in an attempt to minimize the risk of future financial problems or frauds. This consequently leads to increased total fees accruing to the auditors for both auditing and non-auditing services. In the meantime, total fees paid to the auditor will reflect the extensive work performed by the auditor without much reliance on the work of internal personnel such as the internal auditors or indeed the effectiveness of the Audit Committee. Thus, the null hypothesis of no relationship is rejected and the alternative hypothesis of a positive relationship between Board composition, measured as the proportion of non-executive directors on the Board, and external auditors' fee is accepted.

BOARD MEETING FREQUENCY AND EXTERNAL AUDITORS' FEES

Another indicator of the main Board's activities is the variable measuring the relationship between Board meeting frequency (BOARDMET) and external auditors' total fees. The regression result shows a negative and statistically significant relationship with a co-efficient of -0.094, a p-value of 0.023 and a t-statistic of -2.30. The result indicates that frequent Board meetings are associated with a fall in total fees paid to the auditors. Thus it shows that if all other variables are held constant, an increase in Board meeting frequency has a negative effect on the total fees paid to the auditor. This could also be interpreted to mean that the main Board constrains the scope and volume of services bought from the auditors. It could be argued that the result reinforces the perception that the main Board has delegated its audit and financial oversight functions to the Audit Committee. It will be unlikely that the main Board would require more audit coverage or additional testing or indeed adjustment to the scope of the audit. These requirements are more the preserve of the Audit Committee. Thus this result supports the opinion that the main Board focuses more on the general monitoring oversight function and also that more Board meetings and size of the Board could translate into more effective monitoring which could be responsible for the negative relationship found between these variables. This result conflicts with findings from Carcello et al. (2002) who found a positive relationship between board Independence, diligence and expertise and audit fees.

AUDIT COMMITTEE MEETING FREQUENCY AND EXTERNAL AUDITORS' FEES

H7 examines the relationship between Audit Committee activity (proxied by meeting frequency) and external auditors' fee. This study found a positive and statistically significant relationship between the measures of Audit Committee activity (AUACT) and external auditors' total fee. This indicates that the higher the level of Audit Committee activity, all other things being equal, the higher the total fee earned by the auditor from their client. The beta co-efficient for the Audit Committee meeting frequency showed a value of 0.21, a t-value of 3.16 and p-value of 0.002: these show that this result is significant at the 1 per cent level. This means that the null hypothesis is rejected and the alternative hypothesis of a positive relationship between Audit Committee activity and total fees paid to the external auditor is accepted.

A positive relationship could indicate that the Audit Committee supports buying more services or will not allow the value of services bought from the auditors to fall. This could be because Audit Committee members are keen to signal their desire to maintain or ensure improvement in auditing and reporting quality (Collier and Gregory, 1996). It could also be because Audit Committee members are conscious of the effect of poor reporting quality on their human capital worth (Goodwin-Stewart and Kent, 2006) and subsequent Board appointments (Fama and Jensen, 1983; Coughlan and Schmidt, 1985; Denis and Denis, 1995; Franks et al., 2001). All these could mean more meetings for the Audit Committee which could in effect mean more oversight function being carried out by the Audit Committee. It is expected that improved oversight activities by the Audit Committee could actually lead to more being expected from the external auditors in the form of auditing and other assurance services. There could be increases in compliance and due diligence engagements for the auditors. These additional services requested would have an impact on the overall fees paid to the auditor. Equally, expectations placed on the performance of the enlarged roles of the Audit Committee may mean that members of the Audit Committee need to be aware of these expectations and their consequences for their reputation, personal liability and reporting quality. The researcher's findings are in line with Abbott et al. (2003a), who argued that the presence of an Audit Committee could improve external auditors' bargaining power with the client, especially now that Corporate Governance guidelines require that auditors' remuneration and engagements should no longer be at the mercy of the management. Most Corporate Governance guidelines require the Audit Committee to be responsible for making recommendations on the scope and appointment of the external auditors and an assessment of their independence (Combined Code, 2003; SOX, 2002) although the final approval of auditor choice still vests in the shareholders exercising this power at the annual general meeting.

Stewart and Munro (2007) also found a similar result. They suggested an explanation for the positive relationship between Audit Committee meeting frequency and external auditors' fees in Australian companies. They argued that the increase in external auditors' fees may be due to additional time spent by auditors in preparing for and attending meetings with Audit Committee members and not necessarily as a result of any increase in core audit work. The frequency of committee meetings and attendance at those meetings by auditors could build up auditors' hours worked and consequently be reflected in the fees paid to the auditor (although it has to be noted that most guidelines do not require auditors to attend all meetings of the Audit Committee but rather by invitation of the committee only). This explanation is open to criticism. For instance, it could be argued that attendance at such meetings is crucial to transparent reporting and has an impact upon improving audit and reporting quality. It could also be argued that auditors' meetings and engagements with Audit Committee members are an integral part of the audit process and should count in the determination of the independence of the auditors. The rationality and importance of such interactions can be better appreciated considering that one of the anticipated benefits of having an Audit Committee in organizations is the provision of an alternative medium of communication to the auditors especially in cases of conflict between the auditors and management. Improvements in the communication process between the external auditors and those charged with governance in organizations should impact positively on auditors' independence, this is because auditors could now enjoy more support from Audit Committee members and not be under pressure or intimidation from seeking re-appointment from management. Therefore suggesting that an increase in audit fees could be down to attendance at the meetings is true, but suggesting that this is not part of the core audit function may not be correct in the context of the required level of interaction between the auditors and the Audit Committee and the increased Audit Committee oversight function.

The positive relationship could also be explained in the context of the expected negative relationship between the measure of perception of auditor independence and Audit Committee activity. Increases in total fees paid to the auditor, all other things being equal, should lead to increases in the perception of compromised auditor independence and consequently lead to increases in Audit Committee activity as they are exercised to ensure that perceptions of compromised auditor independence arising from increased total fees paid to the auditor are contained by the increase in Audit Committee activity.

Abbott et al (2003b) argue that better performing Audit Committees will demand higher audit quality in order to avoid personal monetary or reputational losses. Also it has been suggested that the risk of litigation could be higher now than ever before towards Board members (Black et al., 2005; Klausner et al., 2005) so that, in order to avoid litigation and its overarching effects, Audit Committee members would rather prefer to invest more to ensure auditing and reporting quality than suffer reputational damage and depletion in human capital.

This result is consistent with the findings in Goodwin-Stewart and Kent (2006) who found a strong positive relationship between audit fees and Audit Committee meeting frequency, but conflicts with Abbott et al. (2003b) who found no significant relationship between these variables. Collier and Gregory

(1996) using data from the period prior to Cadbury and Goddard and Masters (2000) are the only two UK studies that have examined this relationship and they also found a positive relationship between Audit Committee meeting frequency and audit fees. Although the current author found similar results, our finding is more robust because we used a measure that accounts for both audit and non-audit fees paid to the external auditor.

OWNERSHIP STRUCTURE AND EXTERNAL AUDITORS' FEES

H8 examines the relationship between ownership structure and external auditors' fees. Two variables were used to proxy for this in the model. The number of substantial investors owning more than 3 per cent of a company's ordinary shares (INVESTOR) and an indicator variable equal to 1 if management have a shareholding of up to 3 per cent in the company's ordinary shares (MGTOWNER) and 0 if otherwise. While INVESTOR showed a co-efficient of -0.059, a t-statistic of -1.31, MGTOWNER showed a co-efficient of -0.39, t-statistics of-1.74 indicating that it is statistically significant at 10 per cent.

A significant negative relationship between Managerial Ownership and external auditors' fees is consistent with previous findings such as Jensen and Meckling (1976). It has generally been documented that increase in Managerial Ownership reduces agency costs (McConnell and Servaes, 1990; Short and Keasey, 1999). Thus, management share ownership plays Corporate Governance mechanism and may in fact substitute for other form of control such as Audit Committee. A negative relationship between number of substantial outside investors and external auditors' fees shows that, presence of more substantial outside investors constrain external auditors' fees. This is because it is likely that such substantial investors would be able to monitor management action in ensuring auditing and reporting quality, thereby exerting a downward pressure on external auditors' fees. Therefore, to the extent that substantial investors are active in monitoring management action, this could translate into improvement in the client's control environment and may lead to a reduction in audit risk with one of the consequences being a reduction in audit fees. This result is similar to the findings in Mitra et al. (2007) who found a negative relationship between concentrated institutional ownership and audit fees. They explained that concentrated institutional investors are more effective in monitoring management action which may reduce audit risk and consequently reduce the audit fees. Mitra and Hossain (2007) found that in the presence of firm-specific control variables, and Board and Audit Committee governance variables, institutional stock ownership is negatively related to the ratio of non-audit services fees to total client fees. The author reports a negative association between ownership structure and total fees earned by the auditor from their client. Thus the author rejects the null hypothesis of no relationship between ownership structure and external auditors' fees and upholds the suggestion that the presence of substantial outside investors owning at least 3 per cent of the firms' share is negatively related to total fees paid to the external auditors. This indicates that the presence of substantial outside investors leads to a reduction in the total fees paid to the external auditors. This is a support for a form of substitution between the control mechanisms. This is an important finding as it can better inform our understanding of the control mechanisms. It may be important to think of a combination of control mechanism with a view to finding an optimal mix among them that can assure the achievements of Corporate Governance objectives.

PROFITABILITY, COMPLEXITY, FIRM SIZE AND EXTERNAL AUDITORS' FEES

H9, H10 and H11 examine the relationship between the control variables and external auditors' fees. Apart from H9 which showed a significant negative relationship between measures of firm profitability and external auditors' fees, all other control variables showed the researcher's anticipated sign and significance. For example, H10 tests the relationship between firm complexity (LNSUB) and external auditors' fees and showed a significant positive relationship with a co-efficient value of 0.277, a t-statistic of 2.06 and a p-value of 0.041 showing significance at the 5 per cent level. This finding indicates that the more risky the client the higher the total fee that would be earned by the auditor from such a risky client. This is because the auditor will evaluate the inherent risk of such clients to be high and this will increase the audit risk. This will require the auditor to undertake more substantive activities in order to gather sufficient audit evidence and thereby increase the fee. This may be the case with respect to non-audit services too.

With respect to H11, two variables (LNNOEMPLOY AND LNTOVER) were used as proxies for firm size and both showed a significant positive relationship with the external auditors' fee. LNNOEMPLOY showed a co-efficient value of 0.428, a t-statistic of 4.24 and a p-value of 0.000, while LNTOVER showed a co-efficient value of 0.363, a t-statistic of 2.65 and a p-value of 0.009 which indicate statistical significance at the 1 per cent level. These results indicate that it costs more to audit larger clients than smaller ones, just as it may cost more to provide non-audit services to larger clients compared to smaller clients, where size is measured with respect to the number of employees and total assets. In other words, the bigger the client, all things being equal, the higher the total fees earned from such a client.

H9 suggests that there are no relationships between a firm's profitability and external auditors' fees. The author found a statistically significant negative relationship between a firm's profitability and the external auditor's fee. Return on total assets was used to proxy for profitability and it was defined as the ratio of net income to total assets. The regression produced a co-efficient value of -0.023 and a t-statistic of -3.91, indicating significance at the 1 per cent level. A negative relationship between a measure of profitability and audit fees is explainable from the perspective of auditors' exposure to audit risk. Loss-making organizations potent going concern danger and may require more audit efforts in order to minimize audit risk and this may consequently lead to more fees being paid by such companies. This explanation may also be tenable in the case of non-audit services. Similar result was found by Reynolds et al. (2004).

These results are similar to findings documented by other studies including Mitra et al. (2007), Goddard and Masters (2000), O'Sullivan (1999), Collier and Gregory (1999) and Simunic (1984). Goddard and Masters (2000), O'Sullivan (1999) and Collier and Gregory (1999) are all UK studies and they all reported a significant positive relationship between measures of firm size, risk and complexity and fees paid to the external auditors. They explained that these factors continue to be the major determinants of external auditors' fees.

Generally, the results from the model are largely consistent with expectations from the literature and lend strong support to the proposition that there is an important relationship between Audit Committee activity and external auditors' fees. This importance has also been highlighted in a number of Corporate Governance provisions such as the Combined Code in the UK and the SOX in the US. This study has shown that the Audit Committee compliments the external auditors, evidenced by a positive relationship between Audit Committee activity and total fees earned by the auditors. The presence of the Audit Committee could therefore be argued to have enhanced the position of the external auditors, for the fact that the Audit Committee members are likely to encourage broader audit coverage. Increase coverage should reduce audit risk. This is because better coverage could improve the quantity and quality of audit evidence upon which audit opinions are formed. These have the tendency to reduce auditors' exposure to professional liability arising from wrong audit opinion. Thus although the common wisdom is that increase in the amount of economic bonding between the auditor and auditee are deemed to have the potential to compromise auditor independence, this study has found that the Audit Committees are willing to increase audit coverage notwithstanding the likelihood of a compromised auditor independence associated with increase in total fees paid to the auditor.

This result is particularly true of the situation in 2005/2006 when most of the listed companies in the UK would be complying with the convergence of reporting standards. Conversion from UK Generally Accepted Accounting Practice to International reporting standards would require additional audit and non-audit efforts with consequences being increase in total fees paid to auditors for both services.

Alternative Specifications of the Dependent Variable

TOTAL RELATIVE INCOME (TRI)

Using the total fee paid to the auditor as a measure of perception of auditor independence may be criticized for being tenuous. For example, it could be argued that a stronger measure would be to measure the total fee an auditor earns from a firm as a proportion of the auditors' total national fee. Thus the author explored alternative definitions of external auditors' fees (as a proxy for perceptions of independence). First the author uses the TRI of the auditor. This is defined as the total income paid to the auditor as a ratio of the auditor's total national income. Specifically in this study, TRI relates to the auditor's total income earned from the top 350 companies listed on the London Stock Exchange which is the main focus of this book.

To achieve this, the author collected information about audit and non-audit fees paid to their auditors by each of the 244 companies in the sample. From this the author then found the sum of the total fees paid to the auditors. He then calculated how much each of the five auditors auditing the 244 FTSE 350 companies earned from all their clients in the sample; this information is presented in Table 5.5 below. The next step was to express the total fees paid by each company in the sample as a ratio of the total fees earned by the auditing firm that audits each company. This is done for all the companies in the sample to find the TRI earned by each audit firm from a particular company in the sample.

Descriptive statistics of the data collected for this study showed that for the sample investigated, an average of 1.48 per cent of the auditor's total national fee is earned from one client. Average total audit fees paid by companies in the sample were between £1.6million for audit fee and £1.9 million for non-audit fees. 99 per cent of companies in the FTSE 100 are audited by the Big 4 audit firms with just one non-Big 4 audit firm (BDO). In the FTSE 350, around 97 per cent of companies are audited by the Big 4. One of the Big 4 (PricewaterhouseCoopers) has more than 35 per cent of the market share with over 110 out of the 314 companies in the FTSE 350 brackets. The only non-Big 4 audit firm audits seven out of a possible 314 companies in the FTSE 350.

Table 5.5 FTSE 350 by Auditors

Audit firm	Total UK fee (£m)	Total Income from FTSE 350 (£m)	FTSE 100 companies by auditor	FTSE 250 companies by auditor	FTSE 350 companies by auditor	Market share of Big 4 +1 (%)
Ernst & Young	945	181.8	16	35	51	16.2
KPMG	1281	228.7	21	47	68	21.7
PWC	1780	394.8	44	67	111	35.3
Deloitte & Touché	1550	180.6	18	58	76	24.2
BDO Stoy Hayward	275	6.9	1	6	7	2.3

The investigation was based on non-financial non-utility companies with all the required financial and governance information. The regression result is presented in Table 5.6. This is the fourth regression in this study. The dependent variable is the TRI for companies in the sample.

Regression Result and Discussions

CO-EFFICIENT OF DETERMINATION AND F-STATISTICS

The model produced a co-efficient of determination of 0.1932, indicating that the model explained 19.32 per cent of the variation in the TRI. The adjusted R^2 was 14.76 per cent which could mean that some of the variables were not really useful in explaining the variation in the dependent variable. The adjusted R^2

Table 5.6 Dependent variable: Total Relative Income

Variables	OLS	Std error	T-statistics	p-values
Constant	-12.080	3.401	-3.55	0.000***
BOSIZE	0.189	0.221	0.86	0.392
NONEXEC	0.270	0.318	0.85	0.396
BOARDMET	-0.251	0.114	-2.20	0.029**
AUSIZ	-0.148	0.346	-0.43	0.670
AUACT	0.578	0.211	2.75	0.007**
AUCHAT	-0.499	0.666	-0.75	0.454
AUEXP	0.071	0.583	0.12	0.903
INVESTOR	0.087	0.125	0.70	0.485
MGTOWNER	-0.322	0.626	-0.51	0.607
LNNOEMPLOY	-0.213	0.239	-0.89	0.375
LNSUB	0.051	0.249	0.21	0.837
LNTOVER	0.929	0.327	2.85	0.005**
ROC	0.001	3.401	0.03	0.975
R^2	0.1932			
Adj R^2	0.1476	F-statistics 4.24	0.000	
n= 244				

*, **,*** represent statistical significance at 10 per cent. 5 per cent and 1 per cent two-tailed.

shows the actual proportion of the variation in the dependent variables that is explained by the explanatory variables. Additional variables tend to lead to lower R^2 due to a loss of degree of freedom with every successive variable introduced into the model. The F-statistic is significantly different from zero with a value of 4.24. This shows that the model as a whole is significant in measuring the phenomenon under consideration.

TOTAL RELATIVE INCOME AND AUDIT COMMITTEE MEETING FREQUENCY

The result showed a significant positive relationship between the TRI and the measure of Audit Committee activity (meeting frequency). The results indicate that the more active the Audit Committee in a client's firm is, the more important the client is likely to be to the auditors in terms of TRI. This is because active Audit Committees buy more services from their auditors and this drives client importance. This reiterates earlier findings with total fees as the dependent variable and could be explained to mean that Audit Committee members seek audit and reporting quality and enhanced financial oversight functions and therefore buy more services from the external auditors. This could be because allowing for more audits and related services could enhance risk management and reduce the likelihood of litigation as a result of poor reporting and fraud. It also shows that firms with active Audit Committees buy more services from their auditors than firms with less active Audit Committees. However, it also implies that external auditors are more economically dependent on their clients with active Audit Committees than those with less active ones. This result is consistent with the findings reported by Stewart and Munro (2007). The value of the beta co-efficient is 0.58; the t-statistic and p-value are 2.75 and 0.007 respectively.

TOTAL RELATIVE INCOME AND BOARD MEETINGS

Board meeting maintains its negative and significant relationship with this alternative measure of perception of auditor independence. An increase in main Board meetings is associated with a decrease in TRI of the auditors. This is reflected in a co-efficient of -0.251 and a t-statistic of -2.20. Thus, while increased Audit Committee activity leads to more services being bought from the auditors, the main Board's activity does not enhance the purchase of services from the auditors. The explanation provided earlier regarding the fact that the Audit Committee rather than the main Board of directors has the primary remit for auditing and reporting quality in the organization and is charged with this oversight function would also explain this result.

TOTAL RELATIVE INCOME AND AUDITEE SIZE

In addition, the study also found that auditee size is positively related to the TRI. The larger the size of the firm the higher the proportion of the auditors' income from a particular client relative to the total income of the auditor from their entire client in the sample on which this study is based. The model found a significant positive relationship with the measure of economic bonding between the auditee and the auditor. It also shows that size is one of the main determinants of the value of fees earned by the auditor from their clients. The regression produced a high co-efficient of 0.929 and a t-statistic of 2.85 which shows statistical significance at 1 per cent.

Generally, the result from this regression is surprising, not only is the explanatory power of the model weaker, some of the variables that were significant in measuring total fees became insignificant. For instance, NONEXEC was no longer significant, same apply to ownership structure, control variables such as LNSUB, LNNOEMPLOY and ROC which measure firm complexity, size and profitability.

NATURAL LOGARITHMS OF AUDIT FEES AND NON-AUDIT FEES

To further show the relationship between auditors' fees and Corporate Governance features of firms, the author in this book redefined his dependent variables and used both natural logarithm of audit fees and non-audit fees. This is decoupling the total fees into their individual components and thus affords the examination of the effects of the Audit Committee on both components in order to appreciate the dynamics of each of the fees in the presence of governance and firm specific variables. This afforded the author the opportunity of understanding the behaviour of external auditors' fees and the sensitivity of his result to alternative definitions of economic bonding between the external auditors and their clients. Using total fees does not allow an in-depth appreciation of the individual effect of the explanatory variables on each of the fee variables. Examining individual fee variables against the explanatory variables has the tendency to improve our understanding of the impact of governance variables especially the Audit Committee on external auditors' fees. The results of these regressions are presented in Table 5.7 along with the related discussions. First the author used the natural log of non-audit fees and then natural log of audit fees.

The natural log of non-audit fee as the dependent variable is used here to test the sensitivity of the model to alternative definitions of the perception of auditors' independence. The author found that the model still has considerable power in explaining changes in non-audit fees as a result of the changes in the explanatory variables with an R^2 of 51 per cent. Audit committee meetings (AUACT) showed a positive and significance relationship with natural log of non-audit fees at 5 per cent with a p-value of 0.014 and a t-stat of 2.49. This result is surprising because the author would have expected that a negative relationship should exist between AUACT and non-audit fees given the fact that quite a number of governance code cautioned against auditors provision of non-audit services to their audit client. However, as pointed out earlier, this study focuses on the situation in 2005–2006 year end. This is the period when companies were complying with the conversion to International Accounting

Table 5.7 Natural Log of non-Audit fee and Audit fee as the dependent variable

Variable	Non-audit fee	t-stat	Audit fee	t-stat
Constant	0.128	0.15	1.170	1.99**
BOSIZE	0.075	1.34	-0.002	-0.05
NONEXEC	0.076	0.95	0.127	2.41**
BOARDMET	-0.056	-2.3**	-0.054	-3.12***
AUSIZ	-0.017	-0.21	0.099	1.93*
AUACT	0.125	2.49**	0.095	2.90***
AUCHAT	0.047	0.30	0.134	1.25
AUEXP	-0.009	-0.06	-0.077	-0.76
INVESTOR	-0.012	-0.38	-0.032	-1.60*
MGTOWNER	-0.207	-1.44	-0.125	-1.24
LNNOEMPLOY	0.188	2.85**	0.201	4.47***
LNSUB	0.134	1.64	0.155	2.53**
LNTOVER	0.250	2.85**	0.179	2.90***
ROC	-0.016	-3.45***	-0.009	4.15***
R^2	0.5157		0.6527	
Adj. R^2	0.4884		0.6332	
F-stat	25.49	0.000	33.40	0.000
N	244		244	

*, **,*** represent statistical significance at 10 per cent. 5 per cent and 1 per cent two-tailed.

Standards (IAS). This must have pushed up the volume of non-audit services bought during this period. The control variables showed the expected signs and were generally significant at the 1 per cent level. For example, the natural log of turnover (LNTOVER) and the natural log of number of employees (LNNOEMPLOY) were both used to proxy for auditee size and showed a significant positive relationship with the value of non-audit services bought from the auditors. The measure of auditee complexity (LNSUB) was positive but statistically insignificant. However, ROC, which is a measure of profitability and performance, showed a significant negative relationship with the level of non-audit services bought and indicates that apparently less profitable companies tend to buy more audit and related services

Also, Table 5.7 showed the regression result using the natural log of audit fee as a measure of the economic bonding between the auditor and their clients. The result of this regression is very similar to the outcome of the total fees regression. The model explained 65 per cent of the variation in the dependent variable. BOARDMET and AUACT are statistically significant at the 1 per cent level. BOARDMET maintained a consistent significant negative relationship with different definitions of perception of auditors' independence, which is proxied by the level of economic bonding between the auditor and their client.

AUSIZ showed a positive and statistically significance with audit fees. All the control variables showed the expected sign and are statistically significant. Interestingly, INVESTOR showed a negative and statistically significant relationship with natural log of audit fees at 10 per cent level. Confirming that substantial outside investors have a tendency to monitoring auditing and reporting activity of the firm such monitoring could improve the control environment and internal control of the firm thereby exerting a downward effect on the audit fees paid to the auditor.

RATIO OF NON-AUDIT TO AUDIT FEES

Some studies (Frankel et al., 2002; Abbott et al., 2003b) have used the ratios of audit to non-audit fees as a measure of auditor independence as well as the ratio of non-audit fees to total fees. These alternative definitions were considered and OLS regressions based on the use of these measures as the dependent variables were conducted. However, the results were surprising. Firstly, the explanatory power of the model became so low at 0.0404 and R^2 was -0.0136. The F-statistics was not significant. All the variables were no longer significant except BOARDSIZE and ROC both of which showed a positive and negative sign respectively and were both only significant at 10 per cent level. The result is presented in Table 5.8. The table also reports the regression using ratio of non-audit fee to total fees as a measure of perception of independence.

Section Summary

This section of the chapter examined the relationship between Corporate Governance proxy by Audit Committee and external auditors' independence,

Table 5.8 Regression with ratio of non-Audit to Audit fees and non-Audit fee to Total fees

	RN-A		RN-T	
Variable	**Coeff**	**t-stat**	**Coeff**	**t-stat**
Const	2.343	2.56	0.489	10.93***
NONEXEC	0.099	1.14	0.003	1.19
BOARDMET	-0.040	-0.83	-0.000	-0.59
INVESTOR	-0.008	-0.01	0.001	0.96
MGTOWNER	-0.106	-0.57	-0.012	-1.72*
AUEXP	0.097	0.51	-0.001	-0.18
AUSIZ	-0.245	-1.71*	-0.004	-1.07
AUACT	0.076	1.08	0.002	1.22
AUCHAT	0.032	0.18	-0.001	-0.22
LNNOEMPLOY	0.015	0.21	0.001	0.60
LNSUB	-0.164	-1.92*	-0.003	-1.16
LOSS	-3.60e-08	-1.41	-6.13e-11	-0.09
EXTRA	0.017	0.09	0.002	0.31
PENSION	-0.126	-0.23	0.010	0.35
ACQUI	0.126	0.40	0.005	0.56
ROC	0.000	0.00	-0.000	-1.33
R^2	0.0688		0.0842	

*, **,*** represent statistical significance at 10 per cent. 5 per cent and 1 per cent two-tailed.

proxy by its fees. The topics of auditor independence and the economic bonding of the auditor to their clients have enjoyed a considerable amount of attention in the academic literature over the last 35 years. Although independence in mind is not measurable, independence in appearance has been proxied by a number of variables of which the measure of the level of economic bonding between the auditor and the auditee has been used. Precisely, audit and non-audit fees have been used in previous studies. The author explored these measures creatively in the presence of governance and other control variables for a sample of UK listed companies. This particular investigation is unique in that these relationships have not been previously explored in the context of Corporate Governance in the UK except in the study by Collier and Gregory (1999). Other than this, the relationship has been assumed and not empirically established. The author was keen to examine the impact of governance mechanisms and especially that of the Audit Committee on perceptions of auditor independence.

The author found evidence that showed that when Audit Committees are active, they buy more services from their auditors for both audit and non-audit services. Furthermore, when economic bonding is measured by reference to client importance, the study also found that firms with active Audit Committees tend to be more important to the auditors than firms with less active Audit Committees. Surprisingly, the study did not find any significant relationship between the ratio of non-audit fees to audit fee and Audit Committee Activity. This shows that Audit Committee activity does not influence this measure of perception of auditor independence. Even when the ratio of non-audit fee to total fees was used as a measure of economic bonding between the auditor and their client, the relationship was found to be statistically insignificant. These findings show that these measures are not appropriate proxy for perception of auditors' economic bonding to their clients. This study has shown that increase in Audit Committee activity increases total fees and TRI of the auditors for listed companies in UK for the financial year 2005–2006. However, this was the year when listed companies were to start to report their performance in line with the IAS rather than the UK national reporting standard. This will necessarily lead to more auditing and non-auditing services being bought by the clients

All the measures showed a positive relationship between all the definitions of fees used in this study (total fees, total relative fees, audit fees, non-audit fees, and the ratio of non-audit fee to total fees) and frequency of committee meetings. The author interprets this to mean that the presence of the Audit Committee implied additional purchasing of services from the auditors. The author contends that this is explainable in the context of Audit Committee members being more vigilant and signalling a preference for a higher level of reporting and auditing quality. Furthermore, the author maintained that Audit Committee members have an interest in buying more services from the auditor primarily to ensure auditing and reporting quality in view of their enhanced remit, being charged with performing financial oversight functions on management. Further, the author reiterates concern over reputational damage and the effects on human capital as additional incentives for Audit Committees to buy additional services from the external auditors.

The study documents a consistent negative relationship between the variable measuring the main Board's meeting frequency and all definitions of perceived auditor independence except when the measure of audit fee was used. The author interpreted this finding to mean that the Board meeting focuses more on other areas of monitoring while delegating auditing and financial reporting oversight functions to the Audit Committee. Further, the author contends that the result supports previous studies in showing that more effective Boards reduce companies' operating agency costs which include the cost of monitoring and control.

The study has established that auditee size and complexity are important determinants of external auditors' fees. The larger the company and the more complex it is, the higher the fees paid to the auditor are likely to be and the higher the perception of a compromised independence. However this is not the case when the ratio of non-audit fee to audit fees was used as a measure of perception of auditor independence. Size and firm complexity were found to be negatively related to fee ratios. This is a surprising result and is not consistent with theoretical expectation that suggest that size and clients' complexity drives external auditors' fees. Even when ratio of non-audit fee to total fee was used as a measure of perception of economic bonding between auditor and their client, the negative relationship between size, complexity and external auditors' fees were consistent. These deserve further investigation. The issue of auditor independence has also been discussed around the threat to independence arising from the auditors' provision of non-audit services to their audit client. This has generated substantial debate and findings are inconclusive (Beattie and Fearnley, 2002). In the next chapter, the author examines the relationship between audit and non-audit fees in the presence of Audit Committee. This is with a view to understanding the interaction between these important variables. The author also contributes to the debate on whether there is a knowledge spillover between the services and how Audit Committee impact on this.

In the following section, the author presents the report of the third and final empirical investigation in the book. This focuses on the interplay between Audit committee, and audit and non-audit fees paid to the external auditors.

Audit Committee, Audit and Non-Audit Fees Paid to the External Auditors

Against the backdrop of the Corporate Governance guidelines that require the Audit Committee to predetermine the nature, type and value of non-audit services that can be purchased from the auditors and the concern that auditors use auditing services as a loss leader to gain more lucrative non-audit services, researchers have examined the relationship between audit and non-audit fees to see whether knowledge spillover actually takes place between audit and non-audit fees and in what direction (Lee and Mande, 2005; Whisenant et al., 2003; Antle et al., 2002). Positive relationships between the two have been interpreted to mean that knowledge spillover takes place from one to the other. If this is true then economies of scope benefits may accrue to the auditors as well as their clients for a number of reasons. The benefit to the auditors may arise in the sense that resources in terms of manpower could be better utilized. For the client, it might be economical and could lead to cost savings in terms of cost of contract negotiations to engage a new auditor compared to the incumbent auditor who would most probably have knowledge of the client's business and associated risks through the initial auditing engagement. Thus, knowledge and skills from auditing could be transferred to non-auditing contracts and that may enhance the auditing and reporting quality of the auditors to the benefit of their clients in terms of users' confidence and cost reductions for future audit and related services (Lee and Mande, 2005; Beattie and Fearnley, 2002).

However, previous studies have also raised concerns over endogeneity between the two services (Lee and Mande, 2005; Whisenant et al., 2003; Antle et al., 2002). A situation where the purchase of audit services from an auditor affects the purchase of non-audit services and vice versa. But apart from Lee and Mande (2005) no other study has examined how endogeneity issues between audit and non-audit fees are affected by Audit Committee activity. This is the focus of this section of the book.

Development of Hypotheses

Existing research in this area has been inconclusive (Beattie and Fearnley, 2002). While there are studies that have established a relationship between non-audit fees and investors' perceptions of auditor independence, audit fees and non-audit fees (Dopouch et al., 2003; Davies and Hollie, 2004), others have not found any significant relationship between the various factors and indeed have suggested that the provision of non-audit services to audit clients results in better understanding of client businesses and reduces audit risk. Lee and Mande (2005) found a positive relationship between audit and non-audit fees when estimated using a single equation model which implies that audit clients buy more non-audit services from their auditor and that more audit services purchased from the auditor may also lead to an increase in non-audit services supplied to the client, but found no significant relationship when their study was modelled using a simultaneous equation. Whisenant et al. (2003) have also documented positive relationships between audit and non-audit fees but noted that knowledge spillovers from audit to non-audit services depend on model specification and may result in different interpretations. It has been argued that single equation models of audit and non-audit fees are inadequate as they suffer from simultaneous equation bias (Whisenant et al., 2003). The implication here is that the estimates and test results are spurious.

The major concern of this part of the book is about methods and whether the established relationship between audit and non-audit fees is sustained under both single equation and simultaneous equation models of fees. This is important given the inconsistency and conflicting results in the literature. Thus, while the second main research question of this book addressed the relationship between external auditors' fees and Audit Committee activity, and has been undertaken on the assumption that audit and non-audit fees are not jointly determined. Furthermore, the researcher's estimates in the second main research question used each of the fees as the dependent variable. For example, when audit fee was the dependent variable, non-audit fees were not used as part of the explanatory variables and vice versa. One of the questions that this part of the book addressed is, what will happen to governance variables and other firm-specific control variables if one of the explanatory variables of each of the fee model has another fee variable? And how does Audit Committee activity impact on both audit and non-audit fees when they are estimated in a single equation model compared to when they are modelled endogenously? The following hypotheses are tested to examine these issues.

Single Equation Regression Result

AUDIT AND NON-AUDIT FEES

H12 examines the relationship between audit and non-audit fees in a single equation fee model. Table 5.9 presents the regression results for the single equation fee model. The explanatory variables in the audit fee model explained 82 per cent of the variation in audit fee. The variables of interest are the non-audit fee and the variable representing Audit Committee activity. The result shows a strong positive relationship between audit and non-audit fee with a co-efficient of 0.216 and a t-statistic of 6.11 indicating a significant positive relationship at the 1 per cent level. This implies that an increase in the audit fee could also be explained by auditors' provision of non-audit fees. The explanatory variables in the non-audit fee equation explained approximately

Table 5.9 Single equation regression results

	Audit fees		Non-audit fees	
Variables	**Co-effi**	**R.t-stat**	**Co-eff**	**R.t-stat**
Constant	-0.388	-0.28	-3.105	-1.49
LNAUDFEE			0.657	4.71***
LNNAUDFEE	0.216	6.11***		
AUACT	0.017	0.57	0.082	1.88*
BOSIZE	-0.013	-0.11	0.283	1.34
NONEXEC	0.007	0.00	4.710	1.46
BOARDMET	-0.013	-0.87	-0.229	-0.83
INVESTOR	-0.037	-2.31**	0.008	0.28
MGTOWNER	-0.018	-0.23	-0.151	-1.03
AUEXP	-0.004	-0.05	0.014	0.11
AUSIZ	0.119	2.72***	-0.107	-1.17
AUCHAT	0.130	1.59	0.083	0.66
LNNOEMPLOY	0.209	4.46***	0.082	0.97
LNASSET	0.199	3.63***	0.152	1.44
LNTOVER	-0.117	-1.55	-0.024	-0.16
LNDEBTOR	0.131	3.65***	0.036	-0.16
PENSION	0.561	2.52**	---	----
ACQUISI	----	----	0.061	0.31
ROA	0.002	0.87	-0.025	-0.52
LOSS	-0.172	-0.63	-0.427	-1.38
EXTRA	----	---	0.103	0.63
R^2	0.8243		0.6498	
ADJ R^2				
F-statistics	41.05	0.000	22.97	0.000
N	204		204	

*, **,*** represent statistical significance at 10 per cent. 5 per cent and 1 per cent two-tailed.

65 per cent of the variation in the non-audit fees. The result also showed a significant positive relationship between audit and non-audit fees with a co-efficient value of 0.657 and t-statistic of 4.71, indicating a statistically significant relationship.

These results are similar to the findings in Lee and Mande (2005), Antle et al. (2002) and Whisenant et al. (2003) in terms of finding a significant positive relationship between audit and non-audit fees in a single equation fee model. Thus the author rejects the null hypothesis and accepts the alternative hypothesis which states that there is a positive relationship between audit and non-audit fees. This basically suggests that there are economies of scope benefit that accrue by auditors providing non-audit services to their audit client and vice versa. This shows that knowledge spillover from non-audit services to auditing and from auditing services to non-auditing services is proved when modelled using single equation. Thus the null hypothesis is rejected in favour of the alternative hypotheses.

Although the variables of interest are the audit and non-audit fees, there a number of interesting and surprising results from these regressions. Firstly, while there is no significant positive relationship between audit fee and Audit Committee activity in the audit fee model, the non-audit fee model showed a significant positive relationship between non-audit fee and Audit Committee activity. This result is consistent with the perception that during this period, purchase of non-audit services by the client is likely to be higher due to conversion from national accounting standards to the IAS. Furthermore, both measures of ownership structure maintained consistent negative relationship with audit fees, with INVESTOR showing a strong and statistically significant relationship, while MGTOWNER is statistically insignificant although it maintained a negative sign. These suggest that ownership structures as measured above, and especially substantial outside shareholders, play active monitoring roles in firms which exert downward pressure on audit fees. In the non-audit fee model, both ownership structure measures were statistically insignificant, while INVESTOR turned positive, MGTOWNER maintained its negative sign.

Surprisingly, AUSIZ which measures the committee size, showed a strong positive relationship with audit fees at 1 per cent level. This indicates that the higher the size of the Audit Committees the more the demand for auditing and reporting coverage. All the firm specific control variables (LNNOEMPLOY, LNASSET, LNTOVER and LNDEBTOR) showed the expected positive relationship with audit fees and are all significant at 1 per cent level. Interestingly, our unique audit fee model variable PENSION, showed a positive relationship with audit fees at 5 per cent level. On the other hand, none of the other variables in the non-audit fees showed any statistically significant relationship with non-audit fees. This is rather surprising, not even the control variables were significant in explaining the variations in the non-audit fees. The non-audit fee regression result with a R^2 of 65 per cent but just two variables showing significance suggests that there could either be problem with multicollinearity or heteroscedasticity. The author conducted post-estimation diagnostics which showed high collinearity among a number of the variables. This shows that NONEXEC, BOARDSIZE are highly affected by multicollinearity. The author decided to remove these variables from the model (Maddala, 2001) and run another regression with non-audit fees as the dependent variable. Table 5.10 reports the rerun regression on non-audit fees. The result improves slightly with LNASSET showing significant positive relationship at 10 per cent level. Audit Committee activity also shows a stronger positive relationship with non-audit fees. This again may be due to possibly high volume of non-audit services companies would have bought for compliance and consultancy on the conversion to IAS.

SIMULTANEOUS EQUATION MODEL(SEM)

The author ran the simultaneous equation model with the predicted values of the fee variables. The result of the regression is presented in Table 5.11.

AUDIT AND NON-AUDIT FEES

The pseudo R^2 showed that the audit fee model explains 80 per cent of the variation while the non-audit fee model falls in its explanatory power from 65 per cent in the single equation model to 59 per cent. Both are still relatively reasonable results.

H13 examines the relationship between audit and non-audit fees in a simultaneous equation model. The variables of concern are the audit and non-audit fees. In the audit fee equation of the two equations, the result showed a strong positive relationship between audit and non-audit fees with a co-efficient of 1.021 and a t-statistic of 3.22 showing significance at the 1 per cent level. This shows that an increase in the provision of non-audit fees drives an increase in the audit fees. On the other hand, the non-audit fee model showed an insignificant positive relationship between audit and non-audit fees with a co-efficient of 5.275 and a t-statistics of 1.60. This is not statistically significant at conventional level of 10 per cent, 5 per cent or 1 per cent.

Table 5.10 Rerun of regression with non-Audit fee model

	Non-Audit fees	
Variables	Co-effi	R.t-stat
Constant	-1.225	-1.33
LNAUDFEE	0.717	5.91***
AUACT	0.104	2.17**
BOARDMET	-0.036	-1.25
INVESTOR	0.014	0.35
MGTOWNER	-0.153	-1.05
AUEXP	0.037	0.28
AUSIZ	-0.070	-0.86
AUCHAT	0.067	0.45
LNNOEMPLOY	0.077	0.95
LNASSET	0.160	1.72*
LNTOVER	-0.016	-0.08
LNDEBTOR	0.020	0.35
ACQUISI	0.091	0.49
ROA	-0.003	-0.84
LOSS	-0.000	-0.43
EXTRAORD	0.131	0.78
R^2	0.6441	
ADJ R^2	0.6136	
F-statistics	21.15	0.000
N	204	

*, **,*** represent statistical significance at 10 per cent. 5 per cent and 1 per cent two-tailed.

A positive relationship between non-audit fee and audit fee is consistent with findings in studies such as Davis et al. (1997), Ezzamel et al. (1996) and Bell et al. (2001) all of whom have found that non-audit fees significantly influence audit fees in a single equation model. A similar finding has also been documented by Antle et al. (2002) in a simultaneous equation model that also

Table 5.11 Result of the simultaneous equation fee model

	Audit fees		Non-audit fees	
Variables	Co-effi	R.t-stat	Co-eff	R.t-stat
Constant	2.747	1.64	0.319	0.28
LNAUDFEE_hat			5.275	1.60
LNNAUDFEE_hat	1.021	3.22***		
AUACT	-0.069	-1.58	-0.079	-0.63
BOSIZE	-0.281	-1.90*	0.077	1.14
NONEXEC	-4.572	-1.79*	-0.437	-1.26
BOARDMET	0.008	0.43	0.058	0.87
INVESTOR	-0.029	-1.65*	0.191	1.47
MGTOWNER	0.130	1.28	0.087	0.37
AUEXP	-0.018	-0.24	-0.442	-0.31
AUSIZ	0.161	3.22***	-0.509	-1.61
AUCHAT	-0.046	-0.43	-0.751	-1.27
LNNOEMPLOY	0.003	0.04	-1.096	-1.31
LNASSET	-0.082	-0.68	-1.079	-1.23
LNTOVER	-0.016	0.65	0.544	1.29
LNDEBTOR	0.008	0.15	-0.807	1.29
PENSION	0.561	2.88***		
ACQUISI			0.066	0.37
ROA	0.002	0.65	-0.001	-0.22
LOSS	0.384	1.25	1.007	0.93
EXTRAORD			0.294	1.77*
R^2	0.8040		0.5940	
ADJ R^2				
N	204		204	

*, **,*** represent statistical significance at 10 per cent. 5 per cent and 1 per cent two-tailed.

involved abnormal accruals; this was a UK study. This result conflicts with the findings in Whisenant et al. (2003) who found that non-audit services do not directly influence audit services when modelled jointly. In terms of whether auditing directly influences non-audit services, the author found that, contrary to Antle et al. (2004), the positive relationship between audit and non-audit services is statistically insignificant when modelled jointly.

This finding is consistent with Lee and Mande (2005), who found that the association between audit and non-audit fees only holds when the model is not modelled jointly. If the result is taken together, the author found that while knowledge spillover flows from non-audit to audit services, similar knowledge spillover is not statistically proved to flow from auditing to non-auditing services.

This result questions the claim that auditors use auditing as a loss leader. The result from this investigation show that non-audit services drive audit services rather than the auditor using audit services as bait to supply more lucrative non-audit services. This finding is consistent with perception that auditing services are a more stable source of income to the auditor and they would rather prefer a more stable and reliable source of income than rely on unpredictable sources of income like the non-audit services. These results also show that the claim that economies of scope result from an auditor providing non-audit services to its audit client is at best an inconclusive debate.

AUDIT FEE, NON-AUDIT FEE AND AUDIT COMMITTEE ACTIVITY

H14 and H15 examine the relationship between the fee variables and Audit Committee activity. The regression results in Table 5.11 support the null hypotheses in H14 and H15. These indicate that there are no significant statistical relationships between the fees and Audit Committee activity when modelled jointly. The regression results also show that Audit Committee activity is not statistically related to audit fee in the audit fee model with a co-efficient of 0.017 and a t-statistic of 0.57, but it shows a weakly significant positive relationship with non-audit fees with a co-efficient value of 0.082 and t-statistic of 1.88, significant at the 10 per cent level. Thus in terms of the sign of the relationship they both show the anticipated positive signs but are weak in terms of their statistical significance. This result is not consistent with the findings in Abbott et al. (2003a) who found a strong positive relationship between audit fees.

Summary

This chapter has examined the relationship between Audit Committee activity, auditor independence and between audit and non-audit fees. It makes an important contribution to the debate on whether or not auditors use auditing as a loss leader and whether or not knowledge spillover from one service to the other does or doesn't occur. The author has found that non-audit services directly affect auditing and not the other way round. This provides evidence that auditing is not used as a loss leader. Also the author finds that knowledge does spill from the services when the relationship is modelled in a single equation, but when endogeneity is controlled the relationship becomes inconsistent. The next chapter provides a summary, conclusions and some recommendations to the various stakeholders concerned with the issues addressed in the book, based on these findings.

6

Governance and Auditing – Theory, Practice, Policy and Research

Introduction

This chapter concludes the book by synthesizing what has become evident from the previous chapters, highlighting the major aspects of what has emerged and the extent to which all this has helped to achieve the author's objectives. The major findings of the author's research are discussed in the context of the immediate investigation, then in the context of a wider overview of the subjects touched upon. The theoretical implications of the findings are examined. Finally, the author provides a pathway for future research and presents some policy recommendations.

Research Objectives and Anticipated Outcomes

At the beginning of the book, the author set out to examine a number of issues related to the intersection between Corporate Governance and auditing. The objectives could be identified as:

- establish the type of relationship that currently exists between the Audit Committee as a tool of Corporate Governance and auditor independence;

- review the developments in the roles and responsibilities of the Audit Committee as a Corporate Governance mechanism;

- examine the determinants of Audit Committee activity and diligence;

- analyze the impact of an effective Audit Committee on auditor independence;
- establish the relationship between audit and non-audit fees;

The author also anticipated the following outcomes from the study:

- that the study would result in an enhanced understanding of the concept of Corporate Governance and auditor independence and the various ways in which it could be threatened, especially as it affects confidence in the market system in which the auditor plays a very crucial role;
- that the study would expound the importance of the Audit Committee as a Corporate Governance mechanism;
- that the study would enhance our understanding of the relationships between the Audit Committee and external auditors' fees and the perception of auditor independence;
- that the study would improve our understanding of the relationship between audit and non-audit fees.

In order to achieve the stated objectives and anticipated outcomes, the book's objectives were expressed in three main research questions as stated below:

- What are the determinants of Audit Committee activity?
- What is the relationship between the Audit Committee and perceptions of auditor independence?
- What is the relationship between audit and non-audit fees and Audit Committees?

These three main research questions formed the bases for three empirical studies in the book. These three fundamental questions were disaggregated into 15 testable null hypotheses. These hypotheses were based on agency theoretical assumptions and models.

Summary of Outcomes by Chapter

CHAPTER ONE

Here the author presented his research objectives, anticipated outcomes and the likely limitations of his study, as seen at the outset. The following paragraphs demonstrate how prescient or otherwise he was able to be.

CHAPTER TWO

In this chapter the author set the scene by providing a background and framework for the study. It helped locate a context for the study by reviewing the history and development of Corporate Governance in the UK. The important outcome of this chapter was the development of an integrated definition of Corporate Governance that encapsulates its system and process dimensions.

CHAPTER THREE

This chapter introduced the regulatory framework for auditing and Corporate Governance, but its main contribution was a thorough review of the key literature shedding light on what was an issue. This embraced auditing and Corporate Governance in the UK and elsewhere. The review focused on the two main areas of investigation: the Audit Committee and auditor independence. A thematic approach was adopted, whereby literature that addressed similar themes was grouped together. The review showed that there is a preponderance of US-based studies and a dearth of UK-based ones on the matters under investigation. One important outcome from this chapter is that it demonstrates where there were gaps in the existing stock of knowledge that the author might fill through his own investigation.

For instance, in terms of Audit Committee activities in the UK, the author realized that Collier and Gregory (1999), Spira (1998, 1999, 2002, 2003), Mangena and Pike (2005), Zaman and Collier (2005) and Turley and Zaman (2007) are the only major writers on research outcomes. So, in respect of Audit Committee activity and auditor independence, the author could only review a limited number of studies from the UK. This chapter recounts how the author conducted his appreciation of possible methods by which the research objectives might be achieved.

CHAPTER FOUR

This chapter focused on the theoretical underpinning for the study undertaken in the book and is where the author was able to provide a detailed explanation of the theoretical divides that drift into contention in the discourse on Corporate Governance issues. The relevance of the various theories was analyzed and the main outcome of the chapter was to identify Agency Theory as the most influential one in the debate and the one that went on to form the basis of the three empirical studies that were to follow.

CHAPTER FIVE

This chapter covered the three empirical studies that feature in the book. The first of these examined the determinants of Audit Committee activity and here the author justified the hypotheses to be tested, enumerated the methods and data used and discussed the findings from the regressions. The second empirical study examined the relationship between external auditors' fees and Audit Committee activity. Alternative measures of economic bonding between auditor and auditee were examined, regression results discussed and diagnostic tests reported. The third part of the chapter reported the findings of the investigation into the relationship between Audit Committee activity, audit and non-audit fees. Model specification issues were examined. Important results relating to knowledge spillover and the auditing process were reported. One significant consequence of the study undertaken was that the author needed to attend classes on statistical modelling and acquire skills to facilitate the use of new software such as STATA that would aid in the data analysis and interpretation stages of the research process.

Major Findings from the Study

The major findings of the study described in the empirical chapter of the book are summarized in the following paragraphs, with a focus on highlighting the implications of the author's discoveries for auditor independence.

DETERMINANTS OF AUDIT COMMITTEES' ACTIVITY

This study tested some of the assertions regarding the determinants of the activity or diligence of the Audit Committee in discharging its oversight functions. For example, some committees' reports and organizations (Combined Code, 2003; SOX, 2003; BRC, 1999; OECD, 2004; EU's Fifth directive, 2004; Treadway, 1987) have all suggested that Audit Committee activity or diligence is a function of the committee's independence, composition and structure, the presence of an expert on the committee and the definition of the terms of reference of the committee. Agency theorists have argued that firm complexities and size are important control variables in examining the determinants of Audit Committee activity.

AUDIT COMMITTEE ACTIVITY AND BOARD COMPOSITION

First, this study found evidence that shows that Audit Committee activity is directly related to the proportion of non-executive directors on the Board. The implication being that the more non-executive directors on the Board of directors, all things being equal, the more active the Audit Committee will be. The practical implication of this for Corporate Governance is that greater presence of independent non-executive directors on the Board may mean better protection of the interests of the shareholders, if the author assumes the monotonist's view, and of all stakeholders if the author assumes the pluralist's view. Although governance codes in the UK fall short of recommending the number of non-executive directors on the Board, the codes initially suggested that the Board should be balanced so that no single individual or group of related individuals is able to unduly influence the Board's decisions. This is so that the Board is able to discharge its oversight function in respect of monitoring, compliance with regulation and management control. Governance codes are now more categorical in suggesting that the Board should be comprised of more independent non-executive directors. This is because the greater presence of independent non-executive directors on the Board is expected to constrain conflicts of interest thereby reducing agency cost and preventing the exploitation of the shareholders.

This finding corroborates the various governance provisions that suggest that the Board of directors should be more independent of management and accountable. If these attributes are achieved it has the potential to increase confidence in the market system and could facilitate investing and financing activities in the economy. Improvements in investing and financing activities within an economy are an important prerequisite to sustained economic growth and development with its attendant effects on quality of life and well-being of the population.

Second, the study documents evidence that shows that increases in Board activity provides part of the explanation for the increase in Audit Committee activity. This finding reinforces the earlier mentioned result, that

Board independence improves Audit Committee activity. This is because an independent Board, all things being equal, is more likely to be active and it is thus more likely to enhance the activity of the Audit Committee. An active Audit Committee is more likely to ensure reporting quality. If reporting quality is improved, investors are more likely to have a clear picture of the performance of an enterprise and can therefore make much more informed economic decisions.

AUDIT COMMITTEE ACTIVITY AND OWNERSHIP STRUCTURE

Third, the study also documents evidence that is consistent with governance mechanisms substitution hypotheses. The study found a statistically significant negative relationship between the presence of managerial shareholdings of more than 3 per cent in the shares of a company and the level of activity of the Audit Committee at a 10 per cent level. This implies that the more active the Audit Committee is, the less important is the role of management shareholders in reducing agency costs of operation. It also indicates that managerial share ownership may substitute for the Audit Committee's governance activities. The studies also found that substantial outside investors are also likely to substitute for Corporate Governance roles played by the Audit Committee.

DEVELOPMENTS IN THE ROLES OF THE AUDIT COMMITTEE

Fourth, in terms of the activity of the Audit Committees, the study found that there have been significant changes in the content and scope of the responsibilities of the Audit Committee, from the traditional role of monitoring financial reporting to a more complex role of ensuring auditing and reporting quality, enhancing the firm's internal control procedures and risk management as well as assessing the scope of the work and independence of the external auditors. The study also found that the status of the Audit Committee has improved tremendously from a voluntary sub-committee which was set up to signify 'class', enjoy legitimacy and not really because of their intrinsic value nor because management really relied on them, to a more crucial and one of the most important mechanisms of Corporate Governances in organizations. Although the approach in the UK favours the comply-or-explain approach, the majority of listed companies now have Audit Committees and provide reports of their activities in their annual reports. This is not to suggest that all is well with the level of Audit Committee activities and disclosure in the UK, as there are still opportunities for improvement. Evidence of the increase in the scope and nature of the responsibilities of the Audit Committee was presented.

AUDIT COMMITTEES' ACTIVITY AND AUDITOR INDEPENDENCE

This part of the study was based on the conjecture that there are important relationships between Audit Committee activity and external auditor independence. This is because the Audit Committee is the only Board committee directly charged with ensuring auditing and reporting quality in the organization at Board level. The importance of this responsibility cannot be overemphasized especially in ensuring and sustaining market confidence. The importance of the need to sustain market confidence can be appreciated in the unfortunate scenario of Northern Rock where investors had to endure long queues and wait to withdraw their savings with dire consequences for investing and financing activities in the market simply because they feared the worst could happen to their savings and these actions directly relate to the loss of confidence in the ability of the management of the company to safely invest their funds and ensure returns. Lack of confidence in the market means that surplus funds in the investing end of the economic spectrum could not be channelled to the financing end of the spectrum. Investors become wary of the information and signals coming from the market and possibly fear the worst. One way of boosting confidence in the market system has been through certifications by the auditors. The auditor's report provides an opinion on the truth and fairness of the information in the financial statements about the performance and going concern situation of the auditee. This information is important for investment and financing decisions. The roles of the Audit Committee in respect of enhancing reporting quality have a direct impact on the issues of market confidence as well. The interactions between these two mechanisms with respect to ensuring reporting quality is therefore important for market confidence, sustainability of the free market system, economic growth and development. It is against these backgrounds that the following findings from the second empirical chapter of this book are reported.

BOARD STRUCTURE AND EXTERNAL AUDITORS' FEES

Fifth, the study found that independent Boards buy more services from their external auditors. This is unexpected. Independent Boards are expected to be more effective in monitoring and therefore this increased internal oversight should have a downward effect on external auditors' fees. However, this finding is interpreted to mean that the higher the proportion of independent non-executive directors on the Board, the higher the likelihood of buying more services from the external auditors for both audit and non-audit purposes. The implication of this finding is that independent Boards favour more audit and reporting coverage which, all things being equal, may improve auditor independence. Although an increase in the total fees paid to the auditor may indicate a higher level of economic bonding between the auditor and their client, to the extent that the auditor is highly dependent on the client by virtue of a substantial part of their income being earned from a client or group of related clients, then independence may be compromised. However, in order to ensure reporting quality an independent Board would want a better coverage and wider scope in respect of auditing and compliance functions from the auditor which should enhance reporting quality and ultimately improve market confidence in the corporate system.

The results from this study show that the average total relative income (TRI) from each client is just 1.48 per cent of the auditors' total income. This is a lot lower than the threshold of 10 per cent for listed companies and 15 per cent for other companies.

AUDIT COMMITTEE ACTIVITY AND EXTERNAL AUDITORS' FEES

Sixth, the study documents a surprisingly strong and consistently positive relationship between different measures of external auditors' fees and measures of Audit Committee activity. This indicates that increases in the activity of the Audit Committee, all things being equal, would lead to an increase in the total fees being paid to the external auditors for audit and non-audit services. This is counter intuitive. Agency cost theory suggests that introducing monitoring and control mechanisms should alleviate firms' exposure to agency costs. Especially in view of the fact that increases in measures of external auditors' fees have the tendency to give an impression of compromised auditor independence. The finding is consistent even when alternative measures of economic relationship with the auditor were used. However, this finding is consistent with the perception that Audit Committees favour auditing and reporting quality and coverage. Such coverage is reflected in a positive relationship between fees and Audit Committee activity. Interpreting the increase in the fees paid to the auditor to indicate increases for work performed by auditors for auditing and non-audit services supports the conjecture that the Audit Committee encourages additional purchases of auditing and non-auditing services from the external auditors.

Audit Committee members also have three incentives to buy more services from the auditors in order to ensure auditing and reporting quality. Firstly, human capital and the financial consequences of poor reporting quality could explain why Audit Committee members may favour the purchase of more services from the auditor, if such purchases are made to indicate auditing and reporting quality. Human capital effects suggest that members of the Audit Committees of firms with poor reporting records suffer depletion in their human capital worth. Secondly, reputational concerns could also explain why Audit Committee members will favour buying more services from the external auditors. Thirdly, litigation risk could also provide incentives for members of Audit Committees to buy more services from the external auditors so long as it protects them from the risk of litigation and it could also serve as evidence of their taking due care in the discharge of their responsibilities.

Seventh, the study found that control variables such as firm complexities and size continue to be key determinants of the level of economic bonding between the auditor and their auditee. However, firm complexity, measured by the natural log of number of subsidiaries, was not found to determine non-audit fees. Surprisingly, less profitable companies were found to be paying more to their auditors for both audit and non-auditing services. Furthermore, in line with the audit risk framework, firms with poor profitability performance seem to buy more audit and non-audit services from their external auditors. The increase in total fee may result from the additional audit work and analytical review and evidence gathering in order to reach a safe opinion on the firm's reports.

THE RELATIONSHIP BETWEEN AUDIT AND NON-AUDIT FEES AND AUDIT COMMITTEE ACTIVITY

This part of the study followed from the second research question. It addressed three main issues. First, what is the relationship between audit and non-audit fees? Secondly, how should we examine this relationship? And, thirdly, what is the effect of different modelling approaches on the relationship between the fees and Audit Committee activity? The importance of understanding the nature of the relationship between the fees is underscored by its impact on the perception of auditor independence. An increase in the proportion of non-audit fees to audit fees has the tendency to impair perceptions of independence, although there are conflicting views which posit that the provision of non-audit services to audit clients should enhance auditor independence since they may be able to deliver better services at a cheaper rate for their audit client due to knowledge spillover. The facts about knowledge spillover from one service to the other continue to be inconclusive. The view that auditing is used as a loss leader for more lucrative non-audit services is also unresolved and the interaction of these (audit and non-audit services) with Audit Committee activity has been under researched. All these were the focus of the third empirical study of the book.

RELATIONSHIP BETWEEN AUDIT AND NON-AUDIT FEES

Eighth, the study documents a stable and statistically significant positive relationship between audit fees and non-audit fees in a single equation fee model. This shows that the provision of audit services positively influences the provision of non-audit services to the same client. This indicates that clients who currently buy audit services from an external auditor are likely to buy their non-audit services from the same auditor. This may be because it is more economical for the client since they would not have to incur another round of contracting costs. It may also be economical to the auditor who may benefit from economies of scope. The economies may be in terms of resources management especially human resources.

Ninth, the study documents evidence of endogeniety between audit and non-audit fees. This shows that the findings in the single equation model suffer from simultaneous equation bias and the model results may be spurious. As a result, the relationship was examined with a simultaneous equation model.

Tenth, the study did not find evidence that auditors use auditing services as a loss leader for a more 'lucrative' non-audit service. This is because while a statistically significant positive relationship was maintained between audit and non-audit services, indicating that non-audit services directly influence audit services, an insignificant positive relationship was found between non-audit and audit services. This indicates that audit services do not directly influence non-audit services thus suggesting that although a positive relationship exists between non-audit and audit services this could be due to chance and therefore not reliable. However, the findings support the notion that providing non-audit services to a client could facilitate the provision of audit services to the same client and that knowledge spillover flows from non-audit services to audit services.

RELATIONSHIP BETWEEN AUDIT AND NON-AUDIT FEES AND AUDIT COMMITTEE ACTIVITY

Eleventh, the study documents evidence that show that the effects of Audit Committee activity are sensitive to model specifications. This is because Audit

Committee activity drives external auditors' fees when the model does not have fee variables as one of the explanatory variables, thereby showing a positive relationship. But when the independent variables include audit or non-audit fees, in either single or simultaneous equations, the positive relationship becomes negative. Surprisingly, all the control variables that would normally matter in determining audit and non-audit fees become insignificant.

Major Findings and Implications for Theory

In Chapter 4 the author enumerates the major theoretical underpinnings of the investigation. Agency Theory was found to be the dominant theoretical framework and this has been used widely in other studies. Basically, this section examines how well the theoretical underpinnings have been explained by the findings from the study. Here, the focus is between the independent non-executive directors, Audit Committee activities and auditor independence (proxied by external auditors' fees).

AGENCY THEORY VS. AUDIT COMMITTEE ACTIVITY, BOARD INDEPENDENCE AND AUDITOR INDEPENDENCE

Chapter 4 explains the main assumptions and implications of Agency Theory. In summary, firms reduce information asymmetry by instituting control and monitoring mechanisms within the organization. These control mechanisms, such as the Board of directors and Audit Committee of the Board, are supposed to reduce conflicts of interest as well between the shareholders and management by protecting the interests of the shareholders. These control mechanisms undertake decision control and supervisory roles in the organization. For instance, it is part of the responsibilities of the Audit Committee to review compliance with the internal control procedures in organizations, to review the risk management procedures in the firm and to review the independence of the external auditors. These are with the view that it should reduce the agency cost of operation incurred by the organization. Similar explanations can be proffered in respect of the independent non-executive directors.

Thus from an Agency Theoretical background, Audit Committees and independent Boards of directors should enhance internal monitoring and control of the firm and this should translate into reduced agency costs, including the costs of auditing and related services. Therefore, on the basis of the Agency Theoretical expectation an increase in Audit Committee activity as well as the presence of more independent non-executive directors on the Board should lead to a reduction in the total fees paid to the auditors for audit and non-audit services. This framework is presented in Figure 6.1.

However, findings from this investigation in respect of Corporate Governance and external auditors' fees do not confirm this theoretical framework. A positive relationship between Audit Committee activity, independent Boards and external auditors' fees appear more consistent with Stakeholder Theory. This is now explored below.

STAKEHOLDER THEORY VS. AUDIT COMMITTEE ACTIVITY, BOARD INDEPENDENCE AND AUDITOR INDEPENDENCE

The Stakeholder Theory was explained in Chapter 4. The theory suggests that the primary purpose of the firm is not the protection of the interests of the shareholders alone, but also the interests of all the stakeholders which include the shareholders. It was also shown in the section that firms need to optimize their performance by taking care of all their stakeholders. Thus to assume that the interest of the shareholders is the primary objective of the firm may

Figure 6.1 Agency theory, Corporate Governance and external Auditors' fees framework

be too simplistic, when the reality suggests that other stakeholders matter. A positive relationship between Audit Committee activity, Board independence and external auditors' fees found in this study may be an indication of the appreciation of the complexities involved in managing modern businesses. Therefore, in order to ensure reporting quality and discharge their oversight functions effectively, members of the Audit Committee and indeed the independent non-executive directors need to consider the interests of other stakeholders too. Thus the consideration would be beyond just agency cost reduction objectives, as Agency Theory may suggest, to a broader objective of transparent and responsible reporting that addresses the interests of all stakeholders. This includes the interests of the shareholders, society and members of the Audit Committees too. The framework below (Figure 6.2) explains how this result fits into Stakeholder Theory. The demand for reporting quality, transparency and accountability of the management to all stakeholders places additional pressures on the members of the Audit Committee and independent non-executive directors leading to demands for additional coverage and consequently increases in external auditors' fees. This seems to be a more realistic representation of the corporate environment in the post-Cadbury Report period.

Figure 6.2 Stakeholder theory, Corporate Governance and external Auditors' fees framework

Limitations and Implications for Future Studies

As with most empirical studies, this research is not perfect and has various limitations; therefore findings from the study should be used with caution to the extent of the following limitations.

First, the sample size in this study may be adjudged to be small, this is because the study is based on the FTSE 350 using the version that excludes investment companies. In addition companies in the financial and regulated sectors were removed as well as companies that did not meet the sample selection criteria. These left the author with just 245 companies for the first two investigations and 204 companies for the third empirical study. To this extent the results from the study may suffer from small sample bias. Future studies should use a larger sample and they may be able to deliver more robust and interesting results.

Second, the study used a number of proxy variables such as frequency of meetings as a measure of Audit Committee activity, external auditors' fees as a proxy for their economic bonding between them and their clients and a reflection of their independence. These are proxies and are not the actual measures of these phenomena. To this extent, they may contain bias and may therefore affect the findings. For instance, the proxy for Audit Committee activity has not taken care of the process dimension of the committee's activity. Equally, the proxy for economic bonding has not taken the magnitude of fees into consideration. Future research should design better proxies that can lead to improved understanding of these phenomena.

Third, this study is essentially a cross-sectional study that examines a phenomenon at a particular point in time. This may not give a complete picture of the phenomenon studied. For instance, the increase in non-audit fees relative to audit fees in 2005 may be temporary and not a continued occurrence. Thus a longitudinal study would have better captured the changes in the investigated phenomena over a longer period of time. In this light, future studies should be conducted that examine the relationship between the Audit Committee and the external auditor on a longitudinal basis. It will certainly be worthwhile to examine whether the increase in the non-audit relative to audit fees in 2005–2006 continues beyond 2008–2009 when the implementation of the conversion from national accounting standards to International Accounting Standards (IAS) for all listed companies would have been completed. Using a panel data approach can also capture other omitted variables that matter in the relationship between audit and non-audit fees as well as these relationships and Audit Committee activity.

Fourth, some of the variable definitions and specifications may be problematic. For instance, the use of a binary variable as a measure of whether a company has a pension scheme or not may not be a true reflection of the different types of pension scheme and their respective risks and complexity, which may have an impact on the outcomes of the study in the third empirical chapter. Future studies should improve on this measure and could therefore deliver more interesting outcomes.

Fifth, most of the governance data used in this investigation have been manually collected. Although the author took all necessary care to be accurate, he is, however, susceptible to human error in the process. Furthermore, some of the variables have been defined based on the researcher's decision and on previous studies. These may be sources of bias. A likely solution that future researchers may avail themselves of is the provision of Corporate Governance information by some private organizations such as Manifest and the International Shareholders Service (ISS). This should enable more accurate studies and more interesting results.

Sixth, the author tested for and documented the presence of endogeneity between audit and non-audit fees. But it is quite possible that other governance variables are also jointly determined with audit and non-audit fees. Future studies should consider this fact in their design and this should lead to improved findings and enhanced understanding of the relationship between these variables.

Seventh, the single equation fee model for non-audit fees produced surprising results in that, although the R^2 was high at 65 per cent, only two variables showed significance. The author checked and confirmed the presence of multicollinearity which was corrected by removing two variables that appeared to be highly affected. These were NONEXEC and BOARDSIZE. Although the results improved as a result of this modification, this may not have solved this problem completely. Future studies should be aware of this fact when designing studies that use similar models to the researcher's.

Contribution to Theory and Practice and Some Recommendations

The author conducted a detailed and comprehensive study on the Audit Committee and its interface with external auditors through an examination of the activity of the Audit Committee, its impact on external auditing, and the relationship with audit and non-audit fees. The research contributes to the literature in a number of ways including those enumerated below.

First, the author developed an integrated definition of Corporate Governance that incorporates both the system and process dimensions of the subject. He proposed that Corporate Governance should be perceived as an economic system that facilitates value creation, as a social system that enhances the sharing of values and enables interaction among individuals in the organization and as an ethical system that seeks to take care of the concerns of all stakeholders. Furthermore, the author also proposed that Corporate Governance should be seen as a process phenomenon that evolves over time (that is, an evolutionary process) and involves a communicative process as well as a control process so that corporate objectives can be achieved. This contribution should be helpful to academic and practitioners who often find it difficult to define Corporate Governance.

Second, the research detailed a chronological and historical development of Corporate Governance in the UK tracing it as far back as the 1970s. Analyzing the impact of politics, international treaties and the national economic situation on the evolution of Corporate Governance in the UK and how these have impacted on how we see Corporate Governance in the current corporate environments. This is important to academics and practitioners as it helps to put the discourse on Corporate Governance into an appropriate historical perspective and context.

Third, the author presented evidence that is consistent with the views that Corporate Governance mechanisms may substitute for one another. The negative relationship between Managerial Ownership and Audit Committee activity confirms this suggestion. Similarly, the negative relationship documented between substantial outside investors and Audit Committee activity further confirms this. This finding is important to regulators who may want to enhance the roles of institutional investors. Furthermore, the chapter also shows the lack of a relationship between the presence of financial experts and Audit Committee activity. This finding is not encouraging and may be indicative of the need for greater clarity on what counts as a financial expert. Regulators need to be more specific about this. They also need to be careful to avoid the Audit Committee and the main Board being dominated by financial experts so that this does not stifle the presence of non-financial experts who have business acumen and other skills that could be of immense benefit to businesses.

Fourth, the author documents a positive relationship between a number of measures of economic bonding between the auditor and their client and that Audit Committees appear to favour such increases. Despite the counter intuitive nature of this finding and its potential threat to the appearance of independence, the researcher's finding is consistent with a growing number of studies that have documented similar positive relationships between the Audit Committee and external auditors' fees. The analyses by the author show that this rise in 2005–2006 may be due to conversion by listed companies from national accounting standards to IAS. This finding is important to investors, academics and regulators, because it shows that Audit Committee members do have incentives to ensure reporting qualities through greater coverage by the external auditors. This may inevitably mean increased total fees being paid to the auditors. It is therefore important that the regulatory framework is flexible enough to accommodate contingencies.

Fifth, while other measures of economic bonding between auditors and their clients such as total fees, audit fees, non-audit fees and TRI show some interesting results, measures such as ratio of non-audit fee to audit fee, and ratio of non-audit fees to total fees do not show any meaningful results. While not doubting previous studies that have used these measures, it is important that such studies are re-examined for their specification, statistical power and perhaps the data used. When these two measures were used, they produced an R^2 that was less than 5 per cent with no significant relationship whatsoever.

Sixth, some of the findings challenged common wisdom in respect of Agency Theoretical expectations. For example, variables such as the log of number of employees, log of turnover, receivables plus stock as a function of total assets and so on which have been used to proxy for size and risk do not seem to matter when endogeneity was controlled for. This may indicate that the relationship between these variables and external auditors' fees is not as straightforward as it seems. This is an important message that could be useful to academics whose researches make use of some of these variables to consider alternative measures of size and risk as well as alternative model specifications. They could try polynomial specifications and market value could be used as a measure of size.

Seventh, the author found evidence consistent with knowledge spillover from both audit services and non-audit services. But he did not find any evidence that supports the proposition that auditors' use auditing as a loss leader for non-auditing services. The author also documents evidence that suggests that model specifications matter in the investigation of the relationship between audit and non-audit fees. These are important findings that will benefit businesses, academics, practitioners and regulators. Businesses may look at the synergistic advantages of knowledge spillover, while academics should be aware that when modelling the determinants of audit fees, they should not include non-audit fees as an explanatory variable because the result may become spurious and professional auditors should be aware that they need to consider the benefit of joint provision of services to their client in the light of the regulatory framework, that it may not be true that they use auditing as a loss leader and that there could be economies of scope benefits in providing both audit and non-audit services to clients. The same messages need to be appreciated by regulators in regulating joint provision of both auditing and non-audit services.

Finally, the general public and investors need to have a better understanding of the roles of the auditors in providing certification of the truth and fairness of the financial statements prepared by the management and that not all increases in the non-audit fees relative to audit fees compromise auditor independence. There could be genuine instances when clients would need to buy more non-audit services from their auditor. This is certainly the case with the conversion to IAS in 2005/2006.

Policy Implications and Challenges

The author's study and this book were designed to contribute both to academic knowledge and to the practitioner arena, so the book closes with suggestions for development of the regulatory and practitioner fields to take account of the author's findings and the recommendations to which they point. Firstly there are implications for company Board composition. Independence was found to be key to Corporate Governance, and this can only be achieved by a strong Board without undue dependence on a single directorial position. This has particular resonance in the current economic climate where companies are under pressure from shareholders to limit director compensation and so reduce the number of directors and/or to subsume the chair and CEO roles into one. This should be resisted by the regulators.

Regulatory processes should also recognize the changing role of Audit Committees which was identified in the research. This means that Audit Committee members require a greater understanding of their role, a greater level of expertise and an understanding of the nature of independence. This in turn requires a different approach to recruitment and training to incorporate better skill sets in the AC population, and consideration of the need for greater numbers of non-executive directors. This too is a challenge financially.

Awareness of these issues also needs to be promulgated by the regulators and the accounting profession if there is to be greater understanding of the importance of a strong Audit Committee, a strengthening of the independence of the auditor and of the financial implications of these components. Directors, accountants and the regulators of Corporate Governance need to ensure that all stakeholders understand that better governance involves diverse aspects of the organization and others who have a relationship with it. Shareholders, too, need to be aware that current and future business activity is mindful not only of their interest but also of the needs of a much wider range of stakeholders. Shareholders are likely always to be the primary consideration of management and auditors, but it may be envisaged that a broader responsibility to all stakeholders will become the norm.

It is for policy makers to ensure that Corporate Governance processes develop in line with what actually delivers effective governance in practice.

References

Abbott, L., Park, Y. and Parker, S. (2000), 'The Effects of Audit Committee Activity and Independence on Corporate Fraud', *Managerial Finance* 26(11), 55–67.

Abbott L.J., Parker S. and Peters G.F. (2004), 'Audit Committee Characteristics and Restatements', *Auditing: A Journal of Practice and Theory* 23(1), 69–68.

Abbott, L.J., Parker, S., Peters, G.F. and Raghunandan, K. (2003a), 'An Empirical Investigation of Audit Fees, Nonaudit Fees, and Audit Committees', *Contemporary Accounting Research*, 20(2), 215–234.

Abbott L.J., Parker, S., Peters, G.F. and Raghunandan, K. (2003b), 'Association between audit committee characteristics and audit fees', *Auditing: A journal of practice and theory* 22(2), 17–32.

Aboody, D. and Lev, B. (2000), 'Information Asymmetry, R&D, and Insider Gains', *Journal of Finance* 55(6), 2747–2766.

Admati, A.R., Pfleiderer, P. and Zechner, J. (1994), 'Large Shareholder Activism, Risk Sharing, and Financial Market Equilibrium', *Journal of Political Economy* 102(6), 1097–1130.

Agrawal, A. and Mandelker, G.N. (1990), 'Large Shareholders and the Monitoring of Managers: The Case of Antitakeover Charter Amendments', *Journal of Financial and Quantitative Analysis* 25(2), 143–161.

Anderson R.C., Mansi S.A. and Reeb D.M. (2003), 'Founding Family Ownership and the Agency Cost of Debt', *Journal of Financial Economics* 68(2), 263–285.

Antle, R., Gordon, E., Narayanmoorthy, G. and Zhou, L. (2002), 'The Joint Determination of Audit Fees, Non-Audit Fees, and Abnormal Accruals', Working Paper, Yale University.

Archambeault, D. and T. DeZoort (2001), 'Auditor Opinion Shopping and the Audit Committee: An Analysis of Suspicious Auditor Switches', International *Journal of Auditing* 5(1), 33–52.

Armour, J. and Skeel, D. (2007), 'Who Writes the Rules for Hostile Takeovers and Why? The Peculiar Divergence of US and UK Takeover Regulation', *Georgetown Law Journal* 95(6), 1727.

Ashbaugh, H., LaFond, R. and Mayhew, B. (2003), 'Do Non-Audit Services Compromise Auditor Independence? Further evidence', *The Accounting Review* 78(3), 611–639.

Auditing Practice Board (1995).

Auerbach, N.E. (1973), 'Audit Committee – New Corporate Institution', *Financial Executive*, September, 96–104.

Ayuso, S. and Argandona, A. (2007), 'Responsible Corporate Governance: Towards a Stakeholders Board of Directors?', Working Paper, University of Navarra 701.

Baltagi, B.H. (2001), *Econometric Analysis of Panel Data*, Chichester: Wiley.

Balsam, S., Bartov, E. and Marquardt, C. (2002), 'Accrual, Management, Investor Sophistication, and Equity Valuation: Evidence from 10Q Fillings', *Journal of Accounting Research* 40(4), 987–1012.

Barnhart, S.W. and Rosenstein, S. (1998), 'Board Composition, Managerial Ownership, and Firm Performance: An Empirical Analysis', *The Financial Review* 33(4), 1–36.

Bartlett S.A. and Chandler R.A. (1997), 'The Corporate Report and the Private Shareholder: Lee and Tweedie Twenty Years On', *British Accounting Review* 29(3), 245–261.

Basioudis, G.I. (2007), 'Auditor's Engagement Risk and Audit Fees: The Role of Audit Firm Alumni', *The Journal of Business Finance and Accounting* 34(9–10), 1393–1422.

Baysinger, B. and Butler, H. (1985), 'Corporate Governance and the Board of Directors: Performance Effects of Changes in Board Composition', *Journal of Law, Economics, and Organizations* 1(1), 101–124.

BBC News (1998), Fat Cats under Threat, British Broadcasting Corporation online (internet). Available at www.news.bbc.co.uk/1/hi/business/51265.stm [Accessed on 23/03/09].

Beasley, M.S. (1996), 'An Empirical Analysis of the Relation between the Board of Director Composition and Financial Statement Fraud', *Accounting Review* 71(4), 443–465.

Beattie, V. and Fearnley, S. (2002) 'Auditor Independence and Non-Audit Services: A Literature Review', Institute of Chartered Accountants in England and Wales, London.

Beattie, V., Fearnley, S. and Brandt, R. (2001), *Behind Closed Doors: What Company Audit is Really About.* Basingstoke, UK and New York, NY: Palgrave.

Beattie, V., Goodacre, A., Pratt, K. and Stevenson, J. (2001), 'The Determinants of Audit Fees- Evidence from the Voluntary Sector', *Accounting and Business Research*, 31(4), 243–274.

Bebchuk, L.A. and Cohen, A. (2005), 'The Costs of Entrenched boards', *Journal of Financial Economics* 78(2005), 409–433.

Bebchuk, L. and Fried, J. (2004), *Pay without Performance: The Unfulfilled Promise of Executive Compensation.* Cambridge, MA: Harvard University Press.

Bedard, J., Chtourou, S.M. and Courteau, L. (2004), 'The Effect of Audit Committee Expertise, Independence, and Activity on Aggressive Earnings Management', *Auditing: A Journal of Practice & Theory* 23(2), 13–35.

Berle, A. A., Jr. (1931), 'Corporate Powers as Powers in Trust,' *Harvard Law Review* 44, 1049–1074.

Berle A.A and Means, M.C. (1932), *The Modern Corporation and Private Property.* New York, NY: Harcourt, Brace & World (1968).

Berry, R.H. and Waring, A. (1995), 'A User Perspective on "Making Corporate Reports Valuable"', *British Accounting Review* 27(2), 139–152.

Bird, R.B. and Smith, E.A. (2005), Costly signaling and cooperative behavior. In: Gintis, H., Bowles, S., Boyd, R. and Fehr, E. (eds) *Moral Sentiments and Material Interests: On the Foundations of Cooperation in Economic Life*, pp 115-148. MIT Press: Cambridge.

Birkett, L. (1986), 'The Recent History of Corporate Audit Committees', *Accounting Historians Journal* 13(2), 109–124.

Black, B.S. (1990), 'Shareholders Passivity Re-examined', *Michigan Law Review*, 89, 520–608.

Black, B., Cheffins, B. and Klausner, M. (2005), 'Why Directors' Damages May Harm Investors', *Financial Times* (January 20).

Blue Ribbon Committee on Improving the Effectiveness of Corporate Audit Committee (BRC) (1999), Report and Recommendations of the Blue Ribbon Committee on Improving the Effectiveness of Corporate Audit Committees. New York, NY: New York Stock Exchange and National Association of Securities Dealers.

Boyle, A.J. (1978), 'Company Law and the Non-executive Directors – The USA and Britain Compared', *International and Comparative Law Quarterly*, 27(3), 487–509.

Bradley, M., Schipani, C.A., Sundaram, A.K. and Walsh, J.P. (1999), 'The Purposes and Accountability of the Corporation in Contemporary Society: Corporate Governance at a Crossroads', *Law Contemporary Problems* 62(3), 9–86.

Bradbury, M.E.(1990), 'The Incentive for Voluntary Audit Committee Formation', *Journal of Accounting and Public Policy* 9(1), 19–36

Branco, M.C. and Rodrigues, L.L. (2006), 'Corporate Social Responsibility and Resource Based Perspectives', *Journal of Business Ethics* 69(2), 111–132.

Branco, M. C., and Rodrigues, L. L. (2007), 'Positioning stakeholder theory within the debate on corporate social responsibility', *EJBO Electronic Journal of Business Ethics and Organization Studies*, 12(1), 5–15.

Brandon, D.M., Crabtree, A.D. and Maher, J.J. (2004), 'Non-Audit Fees, Auditor Independence, and Bond Ratings', *Auditing: A Journal of Practice & Theory* 23(2), 91–105.

Brenner, S.N., and Cochran, P. (1991), *The Stakeholder Theory of the Firm: Implications for Business and Society Theory and Research*. A paper presented at the annual meeting of the international association for business and society Sundance, Utah, US.

Brickley, J., Lease, R. and Smith, C. (1988), 'Ownership Structure and Voting on Antitakeover Amendments', *Journal of Financial Economics* 20(1-2), 267–291.

Bryman, A. and Bell, E (2003), *Business Research Methods*. Oxford: Oxford University Press.

Bryman, A. and Bell, E (2007), *Business Research Methods*, 2nd ed. Oxford: Oxford University Press.

Buchholtz A.K. and Ribbens. B. (1994), 'The Role of the CEO in Takeover Resistance: Effects of CEO Incentives and Individual Characteristics', *Academy of Management Journal* 37(3), 554–579.

Buck, T., Bruce, A., Main, B. and Udueni, H. (2003), 'Long Term Incentive Plans, Executive Pay and UK Company Performance', *Journal of Management Studies* 40(7), 1709–1727.

Bu-Peow Ng, T. and Tan, H. (2003), 'Effect of Authoritative Guidance Availability and Audit Committee Effectiveness on Auditors' Judgements in an Auditor-Client NMegotiation context', *Accounting Review* 78(3), 801–818.

Cadbury, Sir Adrian (1992), *Report of the Committee on the Financial Aspects of Corporate Governance*. London: Gee & Co. Ltd.

Cadbury, Sir Adrian (2000), Global Corporate Governance Forum, World Bank. Available at www.emeraldplanet.asia.com/corporate-governance-html [Accessed on 26/03/2009].

Cameron, K.S. (1986), 'A Study of Organisational Effectiveness and Its Predictors', *Management Science* 32(1), 87–112.

Canyon, M. and Peck, S. (1998), 'Board Control, Remuneration Committees, and Top Management Compensation', *Academy of Management Journal* 41(2), 146–157.

Canyon, M. and Schwalbach, J. (2000a), Corporate governance, executive pay and performance in Europe. In: Carpenter, J.N. and Yermack, D.L. (eds) *Executive Compensation and Shareholder Value*, pp 13–33. Boston: Kluwer Academic Publishers.

Carcello, J. V. and Neal, T.L. (2000), 'Audit Committee Composition and Auditor Reporting', *The Accounting Review* 75(4), 453–467.

Carcello J.V., Hermanson, D.R. and Neal T.L. (2002) 'Disclosures in audit committee charters and reports', *Accounting Horizon* 16(4), 291–304.

Carcello, J.V. and Neal, T.L. (2003), 'Audit committee characteristics and auditor dismissals following new going concern reports', *The Accounting Review* 78(1), 95–117.

Carey, J. and Doherty, W. (1966), *Ethical Standards of the Accounting Profession*. New York, NY: AICPA.

Carr, A.Z. (1968), 'Is Business Bluffing Ethical?', *Harvard Business Review* 46(1), 143–153.

Chandler, A. (1990), *Scale and Scope. The Dynamics of Industrial Capitalism*. Cambridge MA: Harvard University Press.

Charkman, J. (1994), *Keeping Good Company; A Study of Corporate Governance in Five Countries*. Oxford, UK: Clarendon Press.

Cheffins, B.R. (2001), 'History and the Global Corporate Governance Revolution: The UK Perspective', *Business History* 43(4), 87–118.

Clarke, T. (1998), 'The Contribution of Non-Executive Directors to the Effectiveness of Corporate Governance', *Career Development International* 3(3), 118–124.

Coase, R.H. (1937), 'The Nature of the Firm', *Economica* 4(16), 386–405 and 13–16.

Coffee, J.C. Jnr (1991), 'Liquidity Versus Control: The Institutional Investor as Corporate Monitor, *Columbia Law Review* 91(6), 1277–1368.

Collier, P. (1993), 'Audit Committees in Major UK Companies', *Managerial Auditing Journal*, 8(3), 25–31.

Collier, P. and Gregory, A. (1996), 'Audit Committee Effectiveness and the Audit Fee', *The European Accounting Review* 5(2), 177–198.

Collier, P. and Gregory, A. (1999), 'Audit Committee Activity and Agency Costs', *Journal of Accounting & Public Policy* 18(4-5), 311–332.

Collier, P. and Zaman, M. (2005), 'Convergence in European Corporate Governance: The Audit Committee Concept', *Corporate Governance*, 13(6), 753–768.

Combined Code (2003), *The Combined Code on Corporate Governance*. London: Financial Reporting Council.

Committee on the Financial Aspects of Corporate Governance (1992), *Report with Code of Best Practice* [Cadbury Report]. London, UK: Gee Publishing.

Consultative Committee of Accountancy Bodies (1977), *Audit Committee: Their Roles in UK Companies*. London, UK: CCAB.

Cotter, J., Shivdasani, A. and Zenner, M. (1997), 'Do Independent Directors Enhance Target Shareholder Wealth During Tender Offers?', *Journal of Financial Economics* 43(2), 195–218.

Cotter, J. and Silvester, M. (2003), 'Board and Monitoring Committee Independence', *Abacus* 39(2), 211–232.

Coughlan, A.T. and Schmidt, R.M. (1985), 'Executive Compensation, Management Turnover, and Firm Performance: An Empirical Investigation', *Journal of Accounting and Economics* 7(1-3), 43–66.

Craswell, A., Stokes, D.J. and Laughton, J. (2002), 'Auditor Independence and Fee Dependence', *Journal of Accounting and Economics* 33(2), 253–275.

Crowther, D. and Martinez, E.O. (2007), 'No Principal, No Principles and Nothing in Reserve: Shell and the Failure of Agency Theory', *Social Responsibility Journal* 3(4), 4–14.

Crowther, D. and Rayman-Bacchus, L. (eds) (2004), *Perspectives on Corporate Social Responsibility*. London, UK: Ashgate Publishing.

Curran, J. and Blackburn, R. (2001), *Researching the Small Enterprise*. London, UK: Sage.

Cuthbertson, K. and Nitzsche, D. (2004), *Investments: Spot and Derivative Markets*. Chichester: Wiley.

Dahya, J., McConnell, J.J. and Travlos, G.N. (2002), 'The Cadbury Committee, Corporate Performance and Top Management Turnover', *Journal of Finance* 57(1), 461–483.

Danielsen, B.R., Van Nees, R. and Warr, R.S. (2007), 'Auditor Fees, Market Microstructure, and Firm Transparency', *Journal of Business Finance and Accounting* 34(1–2), 202–221.

Davey, J. and Laurance, B. (2008), M & S Under Fire: How the City Turned Against Stuart Rose, *Times* online (internet), 16 March. Available at: http://business.timesonline.co.uk/tol/business/industry_sectors/retailing article355858 [Accessed on 26/03/09].

Davidson III, W.N., Xie, B. and Weihong, X. (2004), 'Market Reaction to Voluntary Announcements of Audit Committee Appointments: The Effect of Financial Expertise', *Journal of Accounting and Public Policy* 23(4), 279–293.

Davis, S.M. and Hollie, D.Y. (2004), 'An Experimental Investigation of Non-Audit Service Fees and Investors' Perception of Auditor Independence: Post-ENRON Era', A Paper presented at the British Accounting Association Auditing Special Interest Group held at Aston Business School between 11–12 March 2005.

Davis, J.H., Schoorman, F.D. and Donaldson, L. (1997), 'Toward a Stewardship Theory of Management', *Academy of Management Review* 22(1), 20–47.

Day, J.F.S. (1986), 'The Use of Annual Reports by UK Investment Analysts', *Accounting and Business Research* 16(64), 295–307.

DeAngelo, L.E. (1981), 'Auditor Size and Audit Quality', *Journal of Accounting and Economics* 3(August), 183–199.

Dechow, P.M., Sloan, R.G. and Sweeney, A.P. (1996), 'Causes and Consequences of Earnings Manipulation: An Analysis of Firms Subject to Enforcement Actions by the SEC', *Contemporary Accounting Research* 13(1), 1–36.

Dedman, E. (2003), 'Executive Turnover in UK Firms: the Impact of Cadbury', *Accounting and Business Research* 33(1), 33–50.

Dedman, E. (2004), 'Discussion of Reactions of the London Stock Exchange to Company Trading Statement Announcements', *Journal of Business Finance and Accounting* 31(1–2), 37–47.

DeFond, M.L. and Jiambalvo, J. (1991), 'Incidence and Circumstance of Accounting Errors', *The Accounting Review* 66(3), 643–655

DeFond, M., K. Raghunandan, and K.R. Subramanyam (2002), 'Do Non-Audit Service Fees Impair Auditor Independence? Evidence from Going Concern Auditor Opinions', *Journal of Accounting Research* 40(4), 1247–1274.

Denis, D.J. and Denis, D.K. (1995), 'Performance Changes Following Top Management Dismissals', *Journal of Finance* 50(4), 1029–1058.

Denis, D., Denis, D. and Sarin, A. (1997), 'Agency Problems, Equity Ownership, and Corporate Diversification', *The Journal of Finance* 52(1), 135–160.

Denis, D., Denis, D. and Yost, K., (2002), 'Global Diversification, Industrial Diversification, and Firm Value', *Journal of Finance* 57(5), 1951–1979.

Dey, A. (2008), 'Corporate Governance and Agency Conflict', *Journal of Accounting Research* 46(5), 1143–1181.

DeZoort, F.T. (1997), 'An Investigation of Audit Committee Oversight Responsibilities', *Abacus* 33(2), 208–227.

DeZoort, F.T., Hermanson, D.R. and Houston, R.W. (2003), 'Audit Committee Member Support for Proposed Audit Adjustments: A Source Credibility Perspective', *Auditing* 22(2), 176–199.

DeZoort, F.T. and Salterio, S. (2001), 'The Effect of Corporate Governance Experience and Financial Reporting and Audit Knowledge on Audit Committee Members' Judgements', *Auditing: A Journal of Practice & Theory* 20(2), 31–47.

Dickerson, A.P., Gibson, H.D. and Tsakalotos, E. (1998), 'Takeover Risk and Dividend Strategy: A Study of UK Firms', *Journal of Industrial Economics* 46(3), 281–300.

DiMaggio, P.J. and Powell, W.W. (1983), 'The Iron Cage Revisited: Institutional Isomorphism and Collective Rationality in Organizational Fields', *American Sociological Review* 48(2), 147–160.

Dodd, E. M. Jr. (1932), 'For Whom Are Corporate Managers Trustees?' *Harvard Law Review* 45, 1145–1163.

Donaldson, L. and Davis, J.H. (1991), 'Stewardship Theory or Agency Theory: CEO governance and shareholder returns', *Australian Journal of Management* 16(1), 49–65.

Donaldson, L. and Davis, J.H. (1993), 'The Need for Theoretical Coherence and Intellectual Rigour in Corporate Governance Research: Reply to Critics of Donaldson and Davis', *Australian Journal of Management* 18(2), 213–225.

Donaldson, T. and Preston, L. (1995), 'The Stakeholder Theory of the Corporation: Concepts, Evidence and Implications', *Academy of Management Review* 20(1), 65–91.

Dopuch, N., King, R.R. and Schwartz, R. (2001), 'An Experimental Investigation of Retention and Rotation Requirements', *Journal of Accounting Research* 39(1), 93–117.

Dopuch, N. and Simunic, D. (1980), The nature of competition in the auditing profession. In: Buckley, J.W. and Weston, J.F. (eds) *Regulation and the Accounting Profession*, pp. 77–94. New York, NY: Lifetime Learning.

Earl, M.J. (ed.) (1983), *Perspectives on Management*. Oxford, UK: Oxford University Press.

Eichenseher, J. and Shields, D. (1985), 'Corporate Director Liability and Monitoring Preferences', *Journal of Accounting and Public Policy* 4(1), 13–31.

Eisenhardt, K.M. (1985), 'Control: Organizational and Economic Approaches', *Management Science* 31(2), 134–149.

Elkington, J. (2004), Enter the triple bottom line. In: Henriques, A. and Richardson, J. (eds) *The Triple Bottom Line – Does It All Add Up?*, pp. 1–16. London, UK: Earthscan.

El-Gazzar, S.M. (1998), 'Pre-disclosure Information and Institutional Ownership: A Cross-sectional Examination of Market Revaluations During Earnings Announcement Periods', *Accounting Review* 73, 119–129.

Elliot, B. and Elliot, J. (2005), *Financial Accounting and Reporting*, 9th ed. Harlow: Pearson.

Emby, C. and Davidson, R.A. (1997), 'The Effect of Power Factors on Auditor Independence'. Paper presented at the 1997 International Symposium on Audit Research in Singapore.

Ezzamel, M., Gwilliam, D.R. and Holland, K.M. (1996), 'Some Empirical Evidence from Publicly Quoted Companies on the Relationship between the Pricing of Audit and Non-Audit Services', *Accounting and Business Research* 27(1), 3–16.

Faccio, M. and Lasfer, M.A. (2000), 'Do Occupational Pension Funds Monitor Companies in Which They Hold Large Stakes?' *Journal of Corporate Finance* 6(1), 71–110.

Falk, H., Lynn, B., Mestelman, S. and Shehata, M. (1999), 'Auditor Independence, Self-interested Behaviour and Ethics: Some Experimental Evidence', *Journal of Accounting and Public Policy* 18(4-5), 395–428.

Fama, E.F. (1980), 'Agency Problems and the Theory of the Firm', *The Journal of Political Economy* 88(2), 288–307.

Fama, E. and Jensen, M. (1983), 'Separation of Ownership and Control', *Journal of Law and Economics* 26, 301–325.

Farinha, J. (2003), 'Corporate Governance: A Review of the Literature', *Research Centre on Industrial, Labour and Managerial Economics*, University of Porto, Portugal.

Farmer, T.A., Rittenberg, L.E. and Trompeter, G.M. (1987). 'An Investigation of the Impact of Economic and Organizational Factors on Auditor Independence', *Auditing: A Journal of Practice & Theory* 7(Fall), 1–14.

Fearnley, S., Hines, T., McBride, K. and Brandt, R. (2002), 'The Impact of The Financial Reporting Review Panel on Aspects of The Independence of Auditors and Their Attitude to Compliance in the UK', *British Accounting Review* 34(2), 109–139.

Ferguson, M., Seow, G. and Young, D. (2004), 'Non-audit Services and Earnings Management: UK Evidence', *Contemporary Accounting Research* 21(4), 813–841.

Firth, M., Fung, P. and Rui, O.M. (2002), 'Ownership, Governance Mechanisms, and Agency Costs in Chinese firms', working paper, The Hong Kong Polytechnic University, Hong Kong.

Fleischhauer, K.A. (2007), 'A Review of Human Capital Theory: Microeconomics, University of St. Gallen, Department of Economics Discussion Paper No. 2007-01. Available at SSRN: http://ssrn.com/abstract=957993 [Accessed on 25/03/2009].

Flint, D. (1988), *Philosophy and Principles of Auditing: An Introduction.* London: Macmillan Education Ltd.

Frankel, R., Johnson, M. and Nelson, K. (2002), 'The Relation between Auditors' Fees for Non-audit Services and Earnings Management', *The Accounting Review* 77, 71–105.

Franks, J. and Mayer, C. (1996), 'Hostile Takeovers and the Correction of Managerial Failure', *Journal of Financial Economics* 40(1), 163–181.

Franks, J., Mayer, C. and Renneboog, L. (2001), 'Who Disciplines the Management of Poorly Performing Companies?', *Journal of Financial Intermediation* 10, 209–248.

Fraser, I. and Pong, C. (2009), 'The Future of the External Audit Function', *Managerial Auditing Journal* 24(2), 104–113.

Freeman, R.E. (1998), A stakeholder theory of the modern corporation. In: Pincus, L.B. (ed.), *Perspectives in Business Ethics*, McGraw-Hill, Singapore, pp. 171–181.

Freeman, R.E. (1984), *Strategic Management: A Stakeholder Approach.* Boston: Pitman.

Freeman, R.E., A.C. Wicks, B. Parmar (2004), 'Stakeholder Theory and "The Corporate Objective Revisited"', *Organisational Science* 15(3), 364–369.

French, J. and Raven, B.H. (1959), The bases of social power. In: Cartwright, D. (ed.) *Studies in Social Power*, pp. 150–167. Ann Arbor, MI: Institute for Social Research.

Friedman, M. (1957). *A Theory of the Consumption Function*. Princeton, NJ: Princeton University Press.

Garvey, G.T. and Hanka, G. (1999), 'Capital Structure and Corporate Control: The Effect of Antitakeover Statutes on Firm Leverage', *Journal of Finance* 54(2), 519–546.

Gaver, J.J. and Gaver, K.M. (1993), 'Additional Evidence on the Association between the Investment Opportunity Set and Corporate Financing, Dividend, and Compensation Policies', *Journal of Accounting and Economics* 16(January/April/July), 127–160.

Gawthrop, L.C. (1970), *The Administrative Process and Democratic Theory*. Boston, MA: Houghton Mifflin.

Gebhardt, W., C. Lee, and B. Swaminathan (2001), 'Towards an Implied Cost of Capital', *Journal of Accounting Research* 39, 135–176.

Gendron, Y. and Bedard, J. (2006), 'On the Constitution of Audit Committee effectiveness', *Journal of Accounting, Organisations and Society* 31(3), 211–239.

Gilson, S. (1989), 'Management Turnover and Financial Distress', *Journal of Financial Economics* 25(2), 241–262.

Goddard, A. and Masters, C. (2000), 'Audit Committee, Cadbury Code and Audit Fees; An Empirical Analysis of UK Companies, *Managerial Auditing Journal* 15(7), 355–371.

Goldman, A. and Barlev, B. (1974), 'The Auditor-Firm Conflict of Interest: Its Implications for Independence', *The Accounting Review* October, 707–718.

Gomez-Mejia, L.R. and Wiseman, R.M. (2007), 'Does Agency Theory Have Universal Relevance? A Reply to Lubatkin, Lane, Collin, and Very', *Journal of Organizational Behaviour* 28, 81–88.

Goodwin-Stewart, J. and Kent, P. (2006), 'Relationship Between External Audit Fees, Audit Committee Characteristics and Internal Audit', *Accounting and Finance* 46(3), 387–404.

Gray, I. and Manson, S. (2005), *The Audit Process: Principles, Practice and Cases*, 3rd ed. London, UK: Thomson.

Greenbury, Sir Richard (1995), *Directors' Remuneration*. London, UK: Gee & Co. Ltd.

Hampel, Sir Ronnie (1998), *Committee on Corporate Governance: Final Report*. London, UK: Gee & Co. Ltd.

Harris, M. and Raviv, A. (1991), 'The Theory of Capital Structure,' *Journal of Finance* 46(1), 297–355.

Heckman J.J. (1979), 'Sample Selection Bias as a Specification Error', *Econometrica* 47(1), 153–161.

Hermalin, B.E. and Weisbach, M.S. (1988), 'The Determinants of Board Composition', *The Rand Journal of Financial Economics* 19(4), 589–606.

Hickson, C.R. and Turner, J.D. (2005), 'The Genesis of Corporate Governance: Nineteenth-Century Irish Joint-Stock Banks', *Business History* 47(2), 174–189.

Higgs, D. (2003), *Review of the Role and Effectiveness of Non-Executive Directors*. London: Department for Trade and Industry.

Hoitash, U., Hoitash, R. and Bedard, J.C. (2009), 'Corporate Governance and Internal Control over Financial Reporting: A Comparison of Regulatory Regimes', *The Accounting Review*, May 2009.

International Federation of Accountants Code of Ethics. Available at http://www.ifac.org/sites/default/files/meetings/files/0803. Pdf. {accessed on 24 August 2009}

Jarrell, G. and Poulsen, A. (1987), 'Shark Repellants and Stock Prices: The Effects of Antitakeover Amendments Since 1980', *Journal of Financial Economics* 19, 127–168.

Jensen, M.C. (1986), 'Agency Costs of Free Cash Flow, Corporate Finance and Takeovers', *American Economic Review* 76, 323–339.

Jensen, M. (2001) 'Value Maximisation, Stakeholder Theory and the Objective Function', *European Financial Management* 7(3), 297–317.

Jensen, M.C. and Meckling, W.H. (1976), 'The Theory of the Firm: Managerial Behaviour, Agency Costs and Ownership Structure', *Journal of Financial Economics* 3(4), 305–360.

Johnson, G. and Scholes, K. (2002), *Exploring Corporate Strategy*, 6th ed. Harlow: Prentice Hall, Pearson.

Johnstone, K.M., Sutton, M.H. and Warfield, T.D (2001), 'Antecedents and Consequences of Independence Risk: Framework for Analysis', *Accounting Horizons* 15(1), 1–18.

Jones, J. (1991), 'Earnings Management During Import Relief Investigations', *Journal of Accounting Research* 29(2), 193–228.

Jones, T.M. and Wicks, A.C. (1999), 'Convergent Stakeholder Theory', *Academy of Management Review* 24(2), 206–221.

Judge, W. and Zeithaml, C. (1992), 'An Empirical Comparison Between the Board's Strategic Role in Non-profit Hospitals and in For-profit Industrial Firms', *Health Services Research* 27(1), 47–64.

Kalbers, L.P. and Fogarty, T.J. (1993), 'Audit Committee Effectiveness: An Empirical Investigation of the Contribution of Power', *Auditing: A Journal of Practice & Theory* 12(1), 24–49.

Kalbers, L. and Fogarty, T. (1996), *A Comparative Assessment of Organizational and Economic Explanations of Corporate Control: An Investigation of Audit Committee Oversight*. Cleveland, OH: American Accounting Association (AAA).

Kane, G.D. and Velury, U. (2004), 'The Role of Institutional Ownership in the Market for Auditing Services: An Empirical Investigation', *Journal of Business Research* 57(9), 976–983.

Kaplan, S. (1989), 'The Effects of Management Buyouts on Operating Performance and Value', *Journal of Financial Economics* 24(2), 217–254.

Kaplan, S. and Reishus, D. (1990), 'Outside Directorships and Corporate Performance' *Journal of Financial Economics* 27(2), 389–410.

Kaplan, S. and Ruback, R. (1995), 'The Valuation of Cash Flow Forecasts: An Empirical Analysis', *Journal of Finance* 50(4), 1059–1093.

Karamanou, I and Vafeas, N. (2005), 'The Association between Corporate Boards, Audit Committees, and Management Earnings Forecasts: An Empirical Analysis', *Journal of Accounting Research* 43(3), 453–486.

Karpoff, J., Malatesta, P. and Walking, R. (1996), 'Corporate Governance and Shareholder Initiatives: Empirical Evidence', *Journal of Financial Economics* 42(3), 365–395.

Keasey, K. and Wright, M. (1993), 'Issues in Corporate Accountability and Governance', *Accounting and Business Research*, 23(91A), 291–303.

Kennedy, V. and Limmack, R. (1996), 'Takeover Activity, CEO Turnover, and the Market for Corporate Control', *Journal of Business Finance and Accounting* 23(2), 267–293.

Key, S. (1999), 'Toward a New Theory of the Firm: A Critique of Stakeholder Theory', *Management Decision* 37(4), 317–328.

Klausner M., Munger, C., Munger, N., Black, B. and Cheffins B. (2005), 'Outside Directors' Liability: Have WorldCom and Enron Changed the Rules?', *Discovery* (Winter), 36–39.

Klein, A. (2002), 'Audit Committee, Board of Director Characteristics and Earning Management', *Journal of Accounting and Economics* 33(3), 375–400.

Klien, A. (1998), 'Firm Performance and Board Committee Structure', *Journal of Law and Economics*, 41(1), 275–303.

Knapp, M. (1985), 'Audit Conflict: An Empirical Study of the Perceived Ability of Auditors to Resist Management Pressure', *The Accounting Review*, LX(2), 202–211.

Knapp, M.C. (1987), 'An Empirical Study of Audit Committee Support for Auditor Involved in Technical Disputes with Client Management', *The Accounting Review* 62(3), 578–588.

Knapp, M.C. (1991), 'Factors that Audit Committee Members Use as Surrogate for Audit Quality', *Auditing: A Journal of Practice & Theory* 10(Spring), 32–35.

Kochan, T.A. and Rubinstein, S.A. (2000), 'Toward a Stakeholder Theory. Stakeholder Theory of the Firm: The Saturn partnership', *Organization Science* 11(4), 367–386.

Kohlberg, L. (1969), Stages and sequences: The cognitive development approach to socialisation. In: D. Goslin (ed.) *Handbook of Socialisation Theory and Research*. pp. 348–480. Chicago, IL: Rand McNally.

Konstantinos, S., Susanne E. and Martin, W. (2004), 'UK Executive Compensation Practices: New Economy versus Old Economy', *Journal of Management Accounting Research* 16(1), 57–92.

Kosnik R.D. (1987), 'Greenmail: A Study of Board Performance in Corporate Governance', *Administrative Science Quarterly* 32(2), 163–185.

Lane, P.J., Cannella Jr., A.A. and Lubatkin, M.H. (1998), 'Agency Problems as Antecedents to Unrelated Mergers and Diversification: Amihud and Lev Reconsidered', *Strategic Management Journal* 19(6), 555–578.

La Porta, R., Lopez-de-Silanes, F., Shleifer, A. and Vishny, R. (2002), 'Investor Protection and Corporate Valuation', *Journal of Finance* 57(3), 1147–1170.

Lee, T.A. (1986), *Company Auditing*, 3rd ed. London: Chapman & Hall.

Lee, H.Y. and Mande, V. (2005), 'The Relationship of Audit Committee Characteristics with Endogenously Determined Audit and Non-Audit Fees', *Quarterly Journal of Business & Economics*, 44(3 and 4), 93–112.

Lee, H.Y., Mande, V. and Ortman, R. (2004), 'The Effect of Audit Committee and Board of Director Independence on Auditor Resignation', *Auditing: A Journal of Practice & Theory* 23(1), 131–146.

Lennox, C.S. (1999), 'The Accuracy and Incremental Information Content of Audit Reports in Predicting Bankruptcy', *Journal of Business Finance & Accounting* 26(5/6), 757–778.

Livingstone, D.W. (1997), 'The Limit of Human Capital Theory: Expanding Knowledge, Informal Learning and Underemployment', *Policy Options* (July), 9–13.

Maddala, G.S. (2001), *Introduction to Econometrics*, 3rd edn. Chichester: John Wiley & Sons, Limited.

Magill, M.H. and Previts, G.J. (1991), *CPA Professional Responsibilities: An Introduction*. Cincinnati, OH: Southwestern Publishing Company.

Mallin, C.A. (2004), *Corporate Governance*. Oxford, UK: Oxford University Press.

Mangena, M. and Tauringana, V. (2008), 'Audit Committees and Voluntary External Auditor Involvement in UK Interim Reporting', *International Journal of Auditing* 12(1), 4–63.

Mangena, M. and Pike, R. (2005), 'The Effect of Audit Committee Shareholding, Financial Expertise and Size on Interim Financial Disclosures', *Accounting and Business Research* 35(4), 327–349.

Marcoux, A.M. (2003), 'A Fiduciary Argument Against Stakeholder Theory', *Business Ethics Quarterly* 13(1), 1–24.

Mathiesen, H. (2002), *Managerial Ownership and Financial Performance*, PhD Thesis, Copenhagen Business School, Denmark.

Mautz, R.K. and Neumann, F.L. (1970), *Corporate Audit Committees: Policies and Practices*. Cleveland, OH: Ernst &Ernst.

Mautz, R.K. and Neumann, F.L. (1977), *Corporate Audit Committee: Policies and Practices*. New York, NY: Ernst & Ernst.

Mautz, R.K. and Sharaf, H.A. (1961), *The Philosophy of Auditing*. Sarasota, FL: American Accounting Association.

Maw, N., Lord Lane of Horsell, and Craig-Cooper, M. (1994), *Maw on Corporate Governance*, ed. by Alsbury, A. London, UK: Dartmouth Publishing.

McMullen, D.A. (1996), 'Audit Committee Performance: An Investigation of the Consequences Associated with Audit Committees', *Auditing: A Journal of Practice & Theory* 15(1), 87–103.

McConnell, J. and Servaes, H. (1990), 'Additional Evidence on Equity Ownership and Corporate Value', *Journal of Financial Economics* 27(2), 595–612.

McMeeking, K.P. (2001) 'An Empirical Analysis of Initial Audit and Non-audit Service Fees', Working Paper, University of Exeter.

Megginson, W.L. (1997) *Corporate Finance Theory*. Reading, MA: Addison-Wesley.

Mehran, H., Nogler, G.E. and Schwartz, K.B. (1998), 'CEO Incentive Plans and Corporate Liquidation Policy', *Journal of Financial Economics* 50(3), 319–349.

Menon, K. and Williams, J.D. (1994), 'The Use of Audit Committees for Monitoring', *Journal of Accounting and Public Policy* 13, 121–139.

Mitchell, R.K., Agle, B.R. and Wood, D.J. (1997), 'Toward a Theory of Stakeholder Identification and Salience: Defining the Principle of Who and What Really Counts', *The Academy of Management Review* 22(4), 853–886.

Mitra, S. and Hossain, M. (2007), 'Ownership Composition and Non-audit Service Fees', *Journal of Business Research* 60, 348–356.

Mitra, S., Hossain, M. and Deis, D. (2007), 'The Empirical Relationship between Ownership Characteristics and Audit Fees', *Review of Quantitative Finance and Accounting* 28(3), 257–285.

Moerland, P. (1995), 'Alternative Disciplinary Mechanisms in Different Corporate Systems', *Journal of Economic Behaviour and Organization* 26, 17–34.

Moir, L. (2001), 'What do we mean by corporate social responsibility?', *Corporate Governance*, 1(2), 6–22

Monk, R.A.G. (2001), *The New Global Investors*. Oxford: Capstone Publishing

Monks, R.A.G. and Minow, N. (1995), *Corporate Governance*. Cambridge, MA: Blackwell Publishers.

Morck, R. (2006), 'Corporations', Harvard Institute of Economic Research, Discussion Paper Number 2101. Available at http://post.economics.harvard.edu/hier/2006papers list.html [Accessed on 20/3/2009].

Morck, R. and Steier, L. (2005). The global history of corporate governance: An introduction. In: R. Morck(Ed.), *The History of Corporate Governance Around The World: Family Business Groups to Professional Advisors* (pp. 1–64). Chicago: University of Chicago Press.

Morck, R., Shleifer, A. and Vishny, R. (1988), 'Management Ownership and Market Valuation: An Empirical Analysis', *Journal of Financial Economics* 20(1–2), 293–315.

Murphy, K.J. and Zimmerman, J.L. (1993). 'Financial Performance Surrounding CEO Turnover', *Journal of Accounting and Economics* 16(1-3), 273–315.

Myers, S, (1977), 'Determinants of Corporate Borrowing', *Journal of Financial Economics* 5(November), 147–176.

Ndofor, H.A. and Levitas, E. (2004), 'Signalling the Strategic Value of Knowledge', *Journal of Management* 30(5), 685–702.

Nelson, R.R., and Winter, S.G. (1982), *An Evolutionary Theory of Economic Change.* Cambridge, MA: Harvard University Press.

Nichols, D.R. and Price, K.H (1976), 'The Auditor-firm Conflict: An Analysis Using Concepts of Exchange Theory', *The Accounting Review* 51(2) 335–346.

Nuttall, R. (1999), 'Take-Over Likelihood Models for UK Quoted Companies', Nuffield College Working Paper, Oxford University.

Oakland, J. (1998), *British Civilisation: An Introduction*, 4th edn. London: Routledge.

OECD (Organisation for Economic Co-operation and Development) (1999) *Principles of Corporate Governance.* Paris, France: OECD.

Organisation for Economic Co-operation and Development (OECD) (2004), *OECD Principles of Corporate Governance.* Paris, France: OECD.

O'Sullivan, N. (1999), 'Board Characteristics and Audit Pricing Post-Cadbury: A Research Note', *The European Accounting Review* 8(2), 253–263.

O'Sullivan, N., and Diacon, S.R. (1999). 'Internal and External Governance Mechanisms: Evidence from the UK Insurance Industry', *Corporate Governance: An International Review* 7(4), 363–373.

O'Sullivan, N. (2000), 'The Impact of Board Composition and Ownership on Audit Quality; Evidence From Large UK Companies', *The British Accounting Review* 32(4), 397–414.

Page, M, and Spira, L.F. (2005), 'Ethical Codes, Independence and the Conservation of Ambiguity', *Business Ethics: A European Review* 14(3), 301–316.

Parkinson, C. and Dobbins, R. (1993), 'Returns to Shareholders in Successfully Defended Takeover Bids: UK Evidence, 1975–1984', *Journal of Business Finance and Accounting* 20(4), 501–520.

Palmrose, Z.V. (1999), *Studies in Accounting Research 33: Empirical Research in Auditor Litigation: Considerations and Data.* Sarasota, Florida: The American Accounting Association.

Peasenell, K.V., Pope, P.F. and Young, S. (2005), 'Board Monitoring and Earnings Management: Do Outside Directors Influence Abnormal Accruals', *Journal of Business Finance & Accounting* 32(7/8), 1311–1346.

Perri, T.J. (2002), 'Signaling Versus Contingent Contracts With Costly Turnover', *Journal of Economic Behaviour & Organisation* 48(4), 365–374.

Pfeffer, J. (1981), *Power in Organizations*. Boston: Pitman.

Phillips, R.A. (1997), 'Stakeholder Theory and a Principle of Fairness', *Business Ethics Quarterly* 7(1), 51–66.

Pincus,K., Rusbarsky, M., and Wong, J. (1989), 'Voluntary Formation of Corporate Audit Committee Among NASDAQ Firms', *Journal of Accounting and Public Policy* 8, 239–265.

Ponemon, L.A. and Gabhart, D.R.L. (1990), 'Auditor Independence Judgements: A Cognitive–Development Model and Experimental Evidence', *Contemporary Accounting Research*, 7(1), 227–251.

Porter, M.E. (1980), *Competitive Strategy*. New York, NY: Free Press.

Porter, B., Simon, J. and Hatherly, D. (2003), *Principles of External Auditing*, 3rd edn. Chichester: Wiley.

Pound, J. (1988), 'Proxy Contests and the Efficiency of Shareholder Oversight,' *Journal of Financial Economics* 20(January-March), 237–265.

Power, M. (1997), *The Audit Society: Rituals of Verification*. Oxford: Oxford University Press.

Pratt, J.W. and Zeckhauser, R.J. (1985), Principals and agents: An overview. In: Pratt, J.W. and Zeckhauser, R.J. (eds) *Principals and Agents: The Structure of Business*. Boston, MA: Harvard Business School Press, pp. 1–35.

Raghunandan, K. and Rama, D.V. (2003), 'Audit Committee Composition and Shareholder Actions: Evidence from Voting on Auditor Ratification', *Auditing: A Journal of Practice & Theory* 22(2), 253–263.

Raghunandan, K., Read, W.J. and Rama, D.V. (2001), 'Audit Committee Composition, "Grey Directors", and Interaction with Internal Auditing', *Accounting Horizons* 15(2), 104–118.

Rainsbury, E., Bradbury, M. and Cahan, S. (2008), 'Firm Characteristics and Audit Committees Complying with "Best Practice" Membership Guidelines', *Accounting and Business Research* 38(5), 393–408.

Raven, B.H. (1974), The comparative analysis of power and power preferences. In: J. Tedeschi, *Perspective on Social Power*, pp 172–198. Chicago, IL: Aldine.

Reed, M. (1985), *Redirection in Organisational Analysis*. London: Tavistock.

Renneboog, L. and Trojanowski, G. (2005). Control Structures and Payout Policy. European Corporate Governance Institute. Finance Working Paper No 80/2005, Social Science Research. Available athttp://papers.ssrn.com/sol3/papers.cfm?-abstract_id=707421 [accessed on 21/3/2009].

Rest, J. (1979). *Development in Judging Moral Issues*. Minnesota: University of Minnesota.

Reynolds, K.J., Deis Jr., D.R. and Francis, J.R. (2004), 'Professional Services Fees and Auditor Objectivity', *Auditing: A Journal of Practice and Theory* 23(1), 29–52.

Rezaee, Z. (2009), *Corporate Governance and Ethics*. Danvers, MA: John Wiley & Sons, Inc.

Rezaee, Z., Kingsley, O.O. and Minmier, G. (2003), 'Improving Corporate Governance: The Role of Audit Committee Disclosures', *Managerial Auditing Journal* 18(6/7), 530–537.

Riahi-Belkaoui, A. (2000), *Acounting Theory*, 4th edn. London: London Business Press.

Riahi-Belkaoui, A. (2004), 'Corporate Reputation, Internalization and the Market Valuation of Multinational Firms', *Scientific Journal of Administrative Development* 2, 93–111.

Riley, J.G., (1975), 'Competitive Signalling', *Journal of Economic Theory* 10(2), 174–186.

Rodger, P. and Hotten, R. (1995), Power Storm Shakes Greenbury, The Independent online (internet), 17 July. Available at: http://www.independent.co.uk/news/business/power-storm-shakes-greenbury-150187 [Accessed on 23/03/09].

Roe, M. (2002), 'Corporate Law's Limits', *The Journal of Legal Studies* 31(2), 233-271I.

Riddell, P. (1993), *The Thatcher Era*. Oxford: Blackwell.

Roe, M. J. (1994), *Strong Managers, Weak Owners: The Political Roots of American Corporate Finance*. Princeton, NJ: Princeton University Press.

Rosenstein, S. and Wyatt, J. (1990), 'Outside Directors, Board Independence and Shareholder Wealth', *Journal of Financial Economics* 26(2), 175–191.

Ruddock, C., Taylor, S. and Taylor, S. (2006), 'Non Audit Services and Earnings Conservatism: Is Auditor Independence Impaired?', *Contemporary Accounting Research* 23(13), 701–746.

Safieddine, A. and Titman, S. (1999), 'Leverage and Corporate Performance: Evidence from Unsuccessful Takeovers', *The Journal of Finance* 54(2), 547–580.

Sarbanes-Oxley Act (2002), US Legislature.

Saunders, M., Lewis, P. and Thornhill, A. (2007), *Research Methods for Business Students*, 3rd edn. Harlow: Prentice Hall, Pearson.

Scarborough, D.P., Rama, D.V. and Raghunandan, K. (1998), 'Audit Committee Composition and Interaction with Internal Auditing: Canadian Evidence', *Accounting Horizon* 12(1), 51-62

Shivdasani, A. (1993), 'Board Composition, Ownership Structure, and Hostile Takeover', *Journal of Accounting and Economics* 16(1-3), 167–298.

Shleifer, A. and Vishny, R.W. (1986), 'Large Shareholders and Corporate Control', *Journal of Political Economy* 94(3), 461–488.

Shleifer, A. and Vishny, R.W. (1989), 'Management Entrenchment: The Case of Manager-specific Investments', *Journal of Financial Economics* 25(1), 123–139.

Shleifer, A. and Vishny, R.W. (1997), 'A Survey of Corporate Governance', *The Journal of Finance* LII(2), 737–783.

Shockley, R.A. (1981), 'Perceptions of Auditors' Independence: An Empirical Analysis', *The Accounting Review* 56(4),785–800.

Short, H. and Keasey, K. (1999). 'Managerial Ownership and the Performance of Firm: Evidence from the UK', *Journal of Corporate Finance* 5(1), 79–101.

Simunic, D. (1980), 'The Pricing of Audit Services: Theory and Evidence', *Journal of Accounting Research* 18(1) 161–190.

Simunic, D.A. (1984) 'Auditing, Consulting, and Auditor Independence', *Journal of Accounting Research* 22(2), 679–702.

Smith, A. (1990), 'Corporate Ownership Structure and Performance: The Case of Management Buyouts', *Journal of Financial Economics* 2, 143–164

Smith, Sir Robert (2003), *Audit Committees Combined Code Guidance*. London, UK: Financial Reporting Council.

Smith, A. (1838), *The Wealth of Nations*. London, UK: Ward Lock.

Solomon, A. and Solomon, J.F. (1999), 'Empirical Evidence of Long-termism and Shareholder Activism in UK Unit Trusts', *Corporate Governance: An International Review* 7(3), 288–300.

Sommer, A.A. Jr. (1991), 'Auditing Audit Committee: An Educational Opportunity for Auditors', *Accounting Horizons* 5(2), 91–93.

Song, J., and Windram, B. (2004), 'Benchmarking Audit Committee Effectiveness in Financial Reporting', *International Journal of Auditing* 8, 195–205.

Spence, M. (1973), 'Job Market Signaling', *The Quarterly Journal of Economics* 87(3), 355–374.

Spence, M. (1974), *Market Signaling: Informational Transfer in Hiring and Related Screening Processes*. Cambridge, MA: Harvard University Press.

Spira, L.F. (1998), 'An Evolutionary Perspective on the Audit Committee Effectiveness', *Corporate Governance: An International Review* 6(1), 29–38.

Spira, L.F. (1998), 'Creative Accounting', *Critical Perspectives on Accounting* 9(3), 376.

Spira L.F. (2002), *Audit Committee Performing Corporate Governance*. Boston, MA: Kluwer Academic Publishers.

Spira, L.F (2003), 'Audit Committees: Begging the Question?' *Corporate Governance: An International Review* 11(3), 180–188.

Spira, L.F. and Bender, R. (2004), 'Compare and Contrast: Perspectives on Board Committees', *Corporate Governance* 12(4), 489-499.

Spira, L.F. and Page, M. (2005), 'Ethical Codes, Independence and the Conservation of Ambiguity', *Business Ethics: A European Review* 14(3), 301–316.

Steier, L and Morck, R (2005), 'The Global History of Corporate Governance: An Introduction', NBER Working Paper No. W11062. Available at SSRN: http://ssrn.com/abstract=652361 [Accessed on 21/3/2009].

Stewart, J.D. and Munro, L.A. (2007), 'The Impact of Audit Committee Existence and Audit Committee Meeting Frequency on the External Audit: Perceptions of Australian auditors', *International Journal of Auditing* 11(1), 51–69.

Stone, M. and Rasp. J. (1991), 'Tradeoffs in the Choice between Logit and OLS for Accounting Choice Studies', *The Accounting Review* 66(1), 170–187.

Stulz, R. (1988), 'Managerial Control of Voting Rights: Financing Policies and the Market for Corporate Control', *Journal of Financial Economics* 20(January-March), 25–54.

Stulz, R.M. (1990), 'Managerial Discretion and Optimal Financing Policies', *Journal of Financial Economics* 26(1), 3–27.

Sudarsanam, S., Holl, P. and Salami, A. (1996), 'Shareholder Wealth Gains in Mergers: Effect of Synergy and Ownership Structure', *Journal of Business Finance and Accounting* 23(5-6), 673–698.

Teoh, S.H., Welch, I. and Wong, T. (1998), 'Earnings Management and the Long Run Market Performance of Initial Public Offer', *Journal of Finance* 53(6), 1935–1974.

Tipuric, D., Hruska, D. And Aleksic, A. (2007), 'Corporate Governance and Ownership Concentration in Croatia', *The Business Review* 7(1), 207-211.

Tjosvold, D. (1989), 'Interdependence and Power Between Managers and Employees: A Study of the Leader Relationship', *Journal of Management* 15(1), 49–62.

Tomkins, C. and McKnight, P.J. (2002), 'CEO Stock Options and Shareholder Return: Empirical Evidence from the UK(November 1, 2002)'. University of Bath Working Paper. Available at SSRN: http://ssrn.com/abstract=350820 or DOI: 10.2139/ssrn.350820 [Accessed on 23/03/09].

Tosi, H.L., Werner, S., Katz, J. and Gomez-Mejia, L.R. (2000), 'How Much Does Performance Matter? A Meta-analysis of CEO Pay Studies', *Journal of Management* 26(2), 301–339.

Tsui, J., Jaggi, B. and Gul, F. (2001), 'CEO Domination, Discretionary Accruals and Audit Fees', *Journal of Accounting, Auditing and Finance* 16(3), 189–207.

Treadway, J.C. (1987), *Report of the National Commission on Fraudulent Financial Reporting*. Washington, DC: National Commission on Fraudulent Financial Reporting.

Tricker, R.I (1984) *Corporate Governance: Practices, Procedures, and Power in British Companies and Their Boards of Directors*. Aldershot, Hants and Brookfield, Vt: Gower Publishing Company.

Tricker, B. (2000), 'Corporate Governance – The Subject Whose Time Has Come', *Corporate Governance: An International Review* 8(4), 286–296.

Turley, S. and Zaman, M. (2007), 'Audit Committee Effectiveness: Informal Processes and Behavioural Effects', *Accounting, Auditing & Accountability Journal* 20(5), 765–788.

Turner Review (2009) *The Turner Review: A Regulatory Response to the Global Banking Crisis*. London, UK: The Financial Services Authority.

Ullmann, A.A. (1985), 'Data in Search of a Theory: A Critical Examination of the Relationships among Social Performance, Social Disclosure, and Economic Performance of U.S. Firms', *Academy of Management Review* 10(3), 540–557.

Vafeas, N. (1999), 'Board Meeting Frequency and Firm Performance', *Journal of Financial Economics* 53(1), 113–142.

Vafeas, N. and E. Theodorou. (1998), 'The Relationship between Board Structure and Firm Performance in the UK', *The British Accounting Review* 30(4), 383–407.

Van der Laan Smith, J., Adhikari, A. and Tondkar, R.H. (2005), 'Exploring Differences in Social Disclosures Internationally: A Stakeholder Perspective', *Journal of Accounting & Public Policy* 24, 124–151.

Van Slyke, M. (2006), 'Agents or Stewards: Using Theory to Understand the Government-Nonprofit Social Service Contracting Relationship', *Journal of Public Administration Research and Theory* 17(2), 157–187.

Vargas Sánchez A (2004). Development of corporate governance systems: Agency theory versus stewardship theory in welsh agrarian cooperative societies. Paper presented at the 4th Annual Conference of EURAM (European Academy of Management). St. Andrews (Scotland): 5-8 May.

Venkatachalam, R.S.M. (1998), 'The Role of Institutional Investors in Corporate Governance: An Empirical Investigation', Working Paper, University of Washington.

Verma, R. and Verma, P. (2006), 'Noise Trading and Stock Market Volatility', *Journal of Multinational Financial Management* 17(3), 231–243.

Verschoor, C.C. (1990), 'Miniscribe: A New Example of Audit Committee Ineffectiveness', *Internal Auditing (US)* 5(4),13–19.

Verschoor, C.C. (2002), 'Reflections on the Audit Committee's Role', *Internal Auditor* 59(2), 26-35.

Vicknair, D., Hickman, K. and Carnes, K.C. (1993), 'A Note on Audit Committee Independence: Evidence from the NYSE on "Grey" Area Directors', *Accounting Horizons* 7(1), 53–57.

Walker Review (2009), *A Review of Corporate Governance in the UK Banks and Other Financial Industry Entities*. London, UK: The Walker Review Secretariat.

Walsh, J.P. and Seward, J.K. (1990), 'On the Efficiency of Internal and External Corporate Control Mechanisms', *Academy of Management Review* 15(3), 421–458.

Weisbach, M.S. (1988), 'Outside Directors and CEO Turnover', *Journal of Financial Economics* 20(January-March), 432–460.

Weir, C., Laing, D. and McKnight, P.J. (2002). 'Internal and External Governance Mechanisms: Their Impact on the Performance of Large UK Public Firms', *Journal of Business Finance &Accounting* 29(5-6), 579–611.

Whisenant, S., Sankaraguruswamy, S. and Raghunandan, K. (2003), 'Evidence on the Joint Determination of Audit and Non-audit fees', *Journal of Accounting Research* 41(4), 721–742.

Windram, B. and Song, J. (2004), 'Non-executive Directors and the Changing Nature of Audit Committees: Evidence from UK Audit Committee Chairmen', *Corporate Ownership & Control* 1(3), 108–115.

Windsor, C.A. and N.M. Ashkanasy. (1995). 'The Effect of Client Management Bargaining Power, Moral Reasoning Development, and Belief in a Just World on Auditor Independence', *Accounting, Organizations and Society* 20(7/8), 701-720.

Windsor, C. and Warming-Rasmussen, B. (2009), 'The Rise of Regulatory Capitalism and the Decline of Auditor Independence: A Critical and Experimental Examination of Auditors' Conflicts of Interests', *Critical Perspectives on Accounting* 20, 267–288.

Wolnizer, P.W., (1995), 'Are Audit Committees Red Herrings?', *Abacus* 31(1), 45-66.

Woodlock, P. (2006), 'Building an Effective Audit Committee', *Journal of Corporate Accounting & Finance* 17(4), 51–56.

Wooldridge, J.M. (2000), *Introductory Econometrics: A Modern Approach*. Boston: South-Western College Publishing.

Xie, B., Davidson III, W.N. and DaDalt, P.J. (2003), 'Earning Management and Corporate Governance: The Role of the Board and the Audit Committee', *Journal of Corporate Finance* 9(3), 295–316.

Yadong, L. (2004), 'Corporate Governance and Accountability in Multinational Enterprises: Concepts and Agenda', *Journal of International Management* 2(1), 1–18.

Yang, J.S. and Krishnan, J. (2005), 'Audit Committees and Quarterly Earnings Management', *International Journal of Auditing* 9(3), 201–219.

Yermack, D. (1996), 'Higher Market Valuation for Firms with a Small Board of Directors', *Journal of Financial Economics* 40, 185–211.

Zaman, M. and Collier, P. (2005), 'Convergence in European Corporate Governance: The Audit Committee concept', *Corporate Governance: An International Review* 13(6), 753–768.

Further Reading

Agle, B.R., Donaldson, T., Freeman, R.E., Jensen, M.C., Mitchell, R.K. and Wood, D.J. (2007), 'Dialogue: Towards Superior Stakeholder Theory', Dialogue at the National Meeting of the Academy of Management, held in Philadelphia, USA.

Agrawal, A. and Charles, R.K. (1996), 'Firm Performance and Mechanism to Control Agency Problems between Managers and Shareholders', *Journal of Financial and Quantitative Analysis* 31(3), 377–397.

Anderson, R. and Bizjak, J. (2002), 'An Empirical Examination of the Role of the CEO and the Compensation Committee in Structuring Executive Pay,' Working Paper, American University.

Ashkanasy, N.M. and Windsor, C.A. (1997), 'Personal and Organisational Factors Affecting Auditor Independence: Empirical Evidence and Directions for Future Research', *Research on Accounting Ethics*, 3, 35–48

Bloomfield, R. (2008), 'Discussion of Annual Report Readability, Current Earnings, and Earnings Persistence', *Journal of Accounting and Economics* 45(2-3), 221–247.

Bouwman, M. J., Frishkoff, P.A., and Frishkoff, P. (1987), 'How do Financial Analysts Make Decisions? A Process Model of the Investment Screening Decision', *Accounting, Organizations and Society*, 12(1), 1–29.

Bullock Committee (1977), *Industrial Democracy: Report of the Committee of Enquiry*, Cmnd, 6706, London: HMSO.

Byrd, E.G. (1977), 'The Benefits of Audit Committee – a Practitioner's Viewpoint', *The Accountant* 24 March, 47–49.

Campbell, N. (1990), 'Holding Audit Committees Accountable', *Canadian Business Law Journal* 16, 134–159.

Chang, L.S. and Most, K.S. (1985), *The Perceived Usefulness of Financial Statements for Investors Decisions*. Miami, FL: Florida International University Press.

Charlton, M.A. (1976), 'Audit Committee – the First Step towards Resolving Auditors' Problems', *Accountants Weekly* 29 October, 12–14.

Chou, W.L. and Lee, D.S. (2003), 'Co-integration Analysis of Audit Pricing Model: A Panel Unit Root Test Approach', *Journal of Business Finance and Accounting* 30(7-8), 1141–1164.

Clifford, P. and R., Evans. (1997), 'Non-Executive Directors: A Question of Independence', *Corporate Governance: An International Review* 5(4), 224-231.

Cohen, J.R. and Hanno, D.M. (2000), 'Auditors' Consideration of Corporate Governance and Management Control Philosophy in Preplanning and Planning Judgements', *Auditing: A Journal of Practice and Theory* 19(2), 133–146.

Combined Code (1998), *Combined Code, Principles of Corporate Governance*. London: Gee & Co. Ltd.

DeAngelo, H. and Rice, E. M. (1983). 'Antitakeover Charter Amendments and Stockholder Wealth', *Journal of Financial Economics* 11(1-4), 329–359.

Dechow, P. and Sloan, R. (1991), 'Executive Incentives and the Horizon Problem: An Empirical Investigation', *Journal of Accounting & Economics* 14(1), 51–89.

Dechow, P.M., Sloan, R.G. and Sweeney, A.P. (1995), 'Detecting Earnings Management', *The Accounting Review* 70(2), 193–225.

Deli, D.N. and Gillan, S.L. (2000), 'On the Demand for Independent and Active Audit Committees', *Journal of Corporate Finance* **6**(2), 427–445.

DeZoort, F.T., Hermanson, D.R., Archambeault, D.S. and Reed, S.A., (2002), 'Audit Committee Effectiveness: A Synthesis of the Empirical Audit Committee Literature', *Journal of Accounting Literature* 21, 38–74.

Fan, J. and Wong, T. (2005), 'Do External Auditors Perform a Corporate Governance Role in Emerging Markets? Evidence from East Asia', *Journal of Accounting Research* 43(1), 35–72.

Geiger, M.A. and Rama, D.V. (2003), 'Audit Fees, Non-audit Fees, and Auditor Reporting on Stressed Companies', *Auditing: A Journal of Practice & Theory* 22(2), 53–69.

Geiger, M. and Raghunandan, K. (2002), 'Auditor Tenure and Audit Reporting Failures', *Auditing: A Journal of Practice and Theory* 21(1), 67–78.

Gray, R., Kouhy, R. and Lavers, S. (1995), 'Corporate Social and Environmental Reporting, A Review of the Literature and a Longitudinal Study of UK Disclosure', *Journal of Accounting, Auditing and Accountability* 8(2), 47–77.

Goergen, M., Renneboog, L. and Roe, M. (2008), 'Contractual Corporate Governance', *Journal of Corporate Finance* 14(3), 166–182.

Gough, C.B. (1978), 'How to Establish an Audit Committee', *The Accountant* 23 November, 707.

Greene, W.H. (2003), *Econometric Analysis*, 5th ed. Upper Saddle River: Prentice Hall, pp. 285, 291, 293, 304.

Gujarati, D. (1992), *Essential of Econometrics*, 2nd ed. Singapore: McGraw-Hill.

Gujarati, D. (2006), *Essential of Econometrics*,3rd ed. New York: McGraw-Hill.

Han, K.C. and David, Y.S. (1998), 'The Effect of Ownership Structure on Firm Performance: Additional Evidence' *Review of Financial Economics*, 7(2), 143–155.

Harvey, K.D and Shrieves, R.E (2001), 'Executive Compensation Structure and Corporate Governance Choices', *Journal of Financial Research* 24(4), 495–512.

Heil, O. and Robertson, T.S. (1991), 'Toward a Theory of Competitive Marketing Signalling: a Research Agenda', *Strategic Management Journal* 12(6), 403–418.

Holland, L. and Boon Foo, Y. (2003), 'Differences in Environmental Reporting Practices in the UK and the US: The Legal and Regulatory Context', *The British Accounting Review* 35(1), 1–18.

Hooghiemstra, R. (2000), 'Corporate Communication and Impression Management – New Perspectives Why Companies Engage in Corporate Social Reporting', *Journal of Business Ethics* 27(1/2), 55–68.

Hsiao, C. (2002), *Analysis of Panel Data,* 2nd ed. Cambridge: Cambridge University Press.

Jager, P. (2008), 'Panel Data Techniques and Accounting Research', *Mediatari Accounting Research* 16(2), 53–68.

Jansson, E. (2005), 'The Stakeholder Model: The Influence of the Ownership and Governance Structures', *Journal of Business Ethics* 56(1), 1–13.

Jiraporn, P., Kim, Y.S., Davidson, W.N. and Singh, M. (2005), 'Corporate Governance, Shareholder Rights and Firm Diversification: An Empirical Analysis', *Journal of Banking & Finance* 30(3), 947–963.

Keasey, K., Thompson, S. and Wright, M. (1997), *Corporate Governance: Economic, Management and Financial issues*. London: Oxford University Press.

Keenan, J. (2004), 'Corporate Governance in UK/USA Boardrooms' *Corporate Governance: An International Review* 12(2), 172–176.

La Porta, R., Lopez-de-Silanes, F., Shleifer, A. and Vishny, R. (2000), 'Investor Protection and Corporate Governance', *Journal of Financial Economics* 58(1-2), 3–27.

Lebar, M.A. (1982), 'A General Semantics Analysis of Selected Sections of the 10-k, the Annual Report to Shareholders, and the Financial Press Release', *The Accounting Review* 57, 176–189.

Lee, T. and Tweedie, D. (1975), 'Accounting Information: An Investigation of Private Shareholder Usage', *Accounting and Business Research* 21, 280–291.

Littlejohn, S.W. (1983), *Theories of Human Communication,* 2nd edn. Belmont, CA: Wadsworth Publishing Company.

Mathiesen, H. (2002), Available at: www.encycogov.com [Accessed on 20/3/2009).

Mattessich, R. (1964), *Accounting and Analytical Methods: Measurement and Projection of Income and Wealth in the Micro and Macro-Economy.* Homewood, IL: Richard D. Irwin, Inc.

Mayners' Report (2001), *Myners Report on Institutional Investment.* London: HM Treasury.

Murphy, K.J. (1985), 'Corporate Performance and Managerial Remuneration: An Empirical Analysis', *Journal of Accounting and Economics* 7(1-3), 11–42.

Organisation for Economic Co-operation and Development (OECD) (1999), 'Corporate Governance: The Way Ahead', Publication in the context of the 1999 Ministerial meeting.

Riahi-Belkaoui, A. (1980), 'The Interprofessional Linguistic Communication of Accounting Concepts: An Experiment in Socialinguistics', *Journal of Accounting Research* 18(2), 362–374.

Ridley, J. (1976), 'Audit Committees', *The Accountant* 9 December, 686.

Robson, C. (2002), *Real World Research*, 2nd edn. Oxford: Blackwell.

Remenyi, D., Williams, B., Money, A. and Swartz, E. (1998), *Doing Research in Business and Management*. London: Sage Publications.

Reinstein, A. and Weirich, T.R. (1996), 'Testing for Bias in the Audit Committee', *Managerial Auditing Journal* 11(2), 28–35.

Rhys-Williams, Sir Brandon (1976), The Case for Audit Committees; Accountancy Age, London, 1976 [Bill to amend the law relating to the directors of companies, 1977].

Schroeder, M.S., Solomon, I. and Vickrey, D. (1986), 'Audit Quality: The Perceptions of Audit-Committee Chairpersons and Audit Partners', *Auditing: A Journal of Practice & Theory* 5(2), 88–94.

Sengupta, P. (1998), 'Corporate Disclosure Quality and the Cost of Debt', *Accounting Review* 73, 459–474.

Seward, K. and Walsh, J.P. (1990), 'On the Efficiency of Internal and External Corporate Control Mechanisms', The *Academy of Management Review* 15(3), 421–458.

Smith, C. Jr. and Watts, R.L. (1992). 'The Investment Opportunity Set and Corporate Financing, Dividend, and Compensation Policies', *Journal of Financial Economics* 32(3), 263–292.

Stanton, P. and Stanton, J. (2002), 'Corporate Annual Report: Research Perspectives Used', *Journal of Accounting, Auditing and Accountability* 15(4), 478–500.

Sykes, A. (1994), Proposals for a reformed system of corporate governance to achieve internationally competitive long-term performance. In: Dimsdale, N. and Prevezer, M. (eds) *Capital Markets and Corporate Governance 111*, Oxford: Clarendon Press.

Tafara, E. and Peterson, R.J. (2007), 'A Blueprint for Cross-Border Access to U.S. Investors: A New International Framework', *Harvard International Law Journal* 48(1), 31–67.

Tashakkori, A. and Teddlie, C. (2003). The past and future of mixed methods research: From data triangulation to mixed model designs. In: Tashakkori, A. and Teddlie, C. (eds) *Handbook of Mixed Methods in Social and Behavioral Research*, 671–702. Thousand Oaks, CA: Sage.

Tauringana, V. and Chong, G. (2004), 'Neutrality of Narrative Discussion in Annual Reports of UK Listed Companies', *Journal of Applied Accounting Research* 7(1), 74–107.

Teoh, H.Y. and Lim, C.C. (1996), 'An Empirical Study of the Effect of Audit Committees, Disclosure of Non-audit Fees, and Other Issues on Audit Independence: Malaysian Evidence', *Journal of International Accounting, Auditing & Taxation* 5(2), 231–248.

Tuckman, B.W. (1965), 'Developmental Sequence in Small Groups', *Psychological Bulletin* 63, 384–399. The article was reprinted in *Group Facilitation: A Research and Applications Journal* 3(Spring), 2001.

Turnbull, N. (1999), *Internal Control: Guidance for Directors on the Combined Code*. London: Institute of Chartered Accountant in England and Wales.

Tricker, R.I. (1978), *The Independent Director – A Study of the Non-executive Director and of the Audit Committee*. London: Tolley with Deloitte, Haskins and Sells.

Tylecote, A. and Ramirez, P. (2006), 'Corporate Governance and Innovation: The UK Compared with the US and "Insider' economies", *Research Policy* 35(1), 160–180.

Vanasco, R.R. (1994), 'The Audit Committee: An International Perspective', *Managerial Auditing Journal* 9(8), 18–42.

Van der Laan Smith, J., Adhikari, A., & Tondkar, R.H. (2005). 'Exploring Differences in Social Disclosures Internationally: A Stakeholder Perspective', *Journal of Accounting and Public Policy* 24, 123-151

Van Hoek, A. (1988), 'Audit Committees and the Internal Auditor', Proceedings of the 2nd European Conference of the Institute of Internal Auditors, Brussels.

Wilmshurst, T.D. and Frost, G.R. (2000), 'Corporate Environmental Reporting. A Test of Legitimacy Theory', *Accounting, Auditing & Accountability Journal* 13(1), 10–26.

Wooldridge, J.M. (2002), *Econometric Analysis of Cross-Section and Panel Data*. Cambridge, MA: MIT Press.

Wooldridge, J.M. (2009), *Introductory Econometrics: A Modern Approach*, 4th edn. Boston: South-Western College Publishing.

Zaman, M. (2001), 'Turnbull – Generating Undue Expectations of the Corporate Governance Role of Audit Committees', *Managerial Auditing Journal* 16(5), 5–9.

Zhang, Y., Zhou, J. and Zhou, N. (2007), 'Audit Committee Quality, Auditor Independence and Internal Control Weaknesses', *Journal of Accounting and Public Policy* 26(3), 300–327.

Index

FSC
www.fsc.org
MIX
Papier | Fördert
gute Waldnutzung
FSC® C083411

Kolibri 360 GmbH
Ferdinand-Jühlke-Straße 7
99095 Erfurt, Deutschland
produktsicherheit@kolibri360.de